THE GLOBAL FINANCIAL
SYSTEM 1750–2000

GLOBALITIES

Series editor: Jeremy Black

GLOBALITIES is a series which reinterprets world history in a concise yet thoughtful way, looking at major issues over large time-spans and political spaces; such issues can be political, ecological, scientific, technological or intellectual. Rather than adopting a narrow chronological or geographical approach, books in the series are conceptual in focus yet present an array of historical data to justify their arguments. They often involve a multi-disciplinary approach, juxtaposing different subject-areas such as economics and religion or literature and politics.

In the same series

Why Wars Happen
Jeremy Black

A History of Language
Steven Roger Fischer

The Nemesis of Power
Harald Kleinschmidt

Geopolitics and Globalization in the Twentieth Century
Brian W. Blouet

Monarchies 1000–2000
W. M. Spellman

A History of Writing
Steven Roger Fischer

The Global Financial System 1750–2000

LARRY ALLEN

REAKTION BOOKS

For Terry

Published by Reaktion Books Ltd
79 Farringdon Road, London EC1M 3JU, UK

www.reaktionbooks.co.uk

First published 2001

Printed and bound in Great Britain by
Cromwell Press, Trowbridge, Wiltshire

British Library Cataloguing in Publication Data
Allen, Larry
    The global financial system 1750 – 2000. –
    (Globalities)
    1. international finance 2. Financial institutions
    I. Title
    332'.042

ISBN 1 86189 109 1

Contents

Preface

This book strives to bring together all the threads of financial development that played a role in creating the globally integrated financial system of today. It is a history book, tracing the development of the world financial system since 1750 and when necessary reaching further into the murky recesses of economic history, searching for the seeds that grew into the current global system.

Historians have long adjusted to the idea that economic events rival political events in historical importance, that the passage from hunting to tillage (Agricultural Revolution) and the passage from domestic industry to the factory system (Industrial Revolution) rank on a level with the French Revolution or the American Revolution. Great political events are often the product of economic factors.

Financial markets put a premium on knowledge of the future. Expectations of the future and a passion to decipher it can engender a contempt for the past, for historical knowledge regarded as as dead and useless to market participants as the snake's dead skin is to the snake that has just shed it. Constantly teased by a modestly illusive future, players in financial markets are too busy to look back, their minds a battleground for hopes and fears that feed on partial knowledge, too focused for rational thought. The powerful emotions that recurring fluctuations induce in experienced market participants suggests that more perspective is needed in the understanding of financial markets, the type of perspective not supplied from the vast statistical and time series studies of existing financial markets, but a perspective akin to the wisdom that comes from the study of history in a wide sweep. The historical sweep brings to light an obstinate force of organic growth more powerful than social and political institutions, one that continues to drive innovation and evolution in the global financial system.

In the not too distant past, evolution of the global financial system required governments to abandon a gold standard hallowed by time, considered the mark of financial probity, in favour of an inconvertible paper standard, previously the symptom of unsound public finance. More recently governments have given up trade barriers, and formed trading blocs of political rivals, decisions as difficult as giving up the gold standard. Current problems of the global financial system call for hard choices to be made, choices between regulation and deregulation, between fixed and flexible exchange rates, between trade restrictions and free trade, between competition and cooperation and between capitalism and socialism. As evolution of the global financial system accelerates, governments may have to adapt even faster, facing issues equally difficult, having less time to settle them. A historical knowledge of the global financial system will remind us these dramatic adaptations are not new.

The research for this book was done at the Mary and John Gray Library on the Lamar University campus in Beaumont, Texas. I am grateful to the librarians who assisted me and to my students at Lamar University whose questions remind me that mastering a subject is a lifelong process.

Introduction

Let us imagine that the global financial system's history is a dome of many-coloured glass, presenting to insiders a different view from each angle of observation. As we observe the historical dome from different angles the financial system graduates from landed wealth to financial wealth, from family businesses to corporations, from debtor's prison to limited liability, from mercantilism to *laissez-faire*, from free banking to central banking, from a gold standard to a paper standard, from government initiative to private initiative, from national enterprises to multinational enterprises, and from isolation to globalization. Since the global financial system is an interdependent system, the first question before us is where to start, which angles offer observers the deepest insights into the global financial system, which bring into focus those components whose evolution can be traced over a significant span of time, and whose role in the global financial system have helped pave the way for growth in its size and interdependence.

We will begin with the corporation, trying to find the secret impetus to bigness in these irrepressible business organizations. Multinational corporations are not a late development in the corporate form of business organization, but rank among the first corporations organized. The ability of individuals to quietly buy into part ownership of a corporation, or sell out a partial ownership, without the permission of other owners (stockholders), enabled bold corporations to amass larger amounts of capital, and assemble groups of owners from wider geographical areas. By limiting potential loss to the amount of initial investment, these corporations reduced the risk to owners (stockholders), reducing the rate of profits required to attract capital. These corporations became a conduit for capital surplus nations to invest in remote areas of the globe (remote to Western Europeans at least), where risks were high because knowledge of local conditions was poor.

Next the growth of the corporate form of business organization cleverly enrolled the exuberant forces of speculation in the service of global expansion. Because corporations from the outset marched to the beat of foreign trade, stockholders had imperfect and limited knowledge of economic conditions governing the profits of individual companies. Stockholders in corporations floated on a thin film of confidence, rapidly rising or sinking with the next day's inflow of partial and fragmentary information. By the end of the twentieth century the globe is brightly dotted with animated financial markets sensitive to financial inflows and outflows emanating from a global reservoir of capital, reinvigorating parts of the world once thought moribund.

A financial system is a framework that facilitates financial transactions, and these transactions require an accepted form of money, something that can serve as a medium of exchange, a unit of account, a store of wealth, and a standard of deferred payment. The swelling ranks of corporations, propelled by speculative fever, searching the globe for markets and raw materials, brought the added momentum needed for the development of a global financial system, but for it to freely run its course a world monetary system was necessary. Trade itself can function, awkwardly, on the basis of barter, and credit agreements can be individually negotiated under a barter system if political entities exist that can enforce contracts. The rub to a barter system is the investment of time in finding opportunities for transactions, since each transaction requires a coincidence of wants between the parties to it. An acceptable form of money multiplies the rate of exchange for goods and services, and the number of viable creditor–debtor relationships. A global monetary system facilitated transactions between economies as diverse as the colony of Virginia, where tobacco functioned as money, and the province of Canada, where beaver skins served as money.

Gradually the diverse economies of the world take hesitant steps toward developing a monetary system capable of facilitating trade on a global scale. Money-smart English investors asked

Parliament for the banishment of paper money in busy American colonies, not wanting to extend loans to colonists if these loans could be repaid in the depreciated paper money of colonial governments. In the late nineteenth century budding Russia reverently adopted the gold standard, wanting to become more attractive to foreign investors. In the eyes of anxious investors in England and Germany, only the stiff-necked gold standard could secure the safety of investments in Russia, Japan, and other capital-short countries, assuring that profits earned in these places were transferable back to England or Germany, and that investments could be liquidated and returned to the country of origin without loss from currency depreciation.

The gold standard triumphantly advanced to the forefront of monetary metals as the volume of trade expanded and stretched over wider distances, putting a premium on forms of money that carry the maximum value per unit of weight, reducing the burden of transport. As gold edged out silver as the reigning monetary metal, countries without either of these metals began daring experiments with paper money, a form of circulating money that maximized value per unit of weight. Sweden, warmly rich in copper deposits, boldly issued copper notes, redeemable in copper. In seventeenth-century Sweden copper coins circulated as money but were too heavy for convenient transportation in transactions involving large sums of money. Lighter copper notes redeemable in copper lightened Sweden's burden of coinage transportation, but evolved into an inconvertible paper money system, a stage of development that all paper money systems eventually reach. Sweden experienced currency debauchery and political chaos before turning up its nose at copper and paper and establishing a silver standard in 1776. This paper money drama was played out again and again in the Old and the New World. Central banks progressed in managing paper money without monetary licentiousness, without maintaining convertibility of paper money into a precious metal, and without causing inflation or deflation. The stately rise of reigning world currencies, such as the US dollar, and the intelligent development of foreign exchange markets for currencies, removed an immeasurable impediment to the easy flow of goods, services and capital between societies endlessly different in culture, political organization and geographical location. Finally, in the latter half of the twentieth century, an overworked world monetary system impatiently shrugged off the last vestiges of a gold standard, coldly putting the world's economies at the mercy of newly fledged inconvertible paper systems, counting solely on sound central banks to manage money stocks, disciplined by freely fluctuating exchange rates between top-ranking currencies.

The growth in international banking began in Italy, where gold coinage, after disappearing from Europe during the Middle Ages, returned in the thirteenth century. The monetary system of the Mediterranean, rooted in gold and silver, afforded the kind of protection to creditors necessary for the multiplication of creditor–debtor relationships crossing national boundaries. With the flowering of trade between Europe and the Far East, coupled with the mining of precious metals in the New World, precious metals poured into Europe, and international banking blossomed. The Fugger family of bankers, enthroned on a mining empire of silver and copper deposits, patiently developed methods for raising the monumental sums of capital needed to finance wars between France and Spain. Then came the rise of baronial banking houses in Europe and America, the Rothschilds, Barings and Morgans, merchant princes applying the same methods to finance private ventures during the Industrial Revolution. The Rothschilds helped finance England's heroic struggle against Napoleon (1800–15), and the strategic purchase of the controlling interest in the Suez Canal Company (1866). In the New World Barings helped the United States finance the Louisiana Purchase (1803). In the classic years of the gold standard (1875 to 1914) the Rothschilds, Barings, Morgans and other merchant bankers quietly wielded vast political and financial power, proudly financing railroads and canals around the globe, often allowing European governments to use access to credit as a political lever, 'to jingle the purse instead of rattling the sabre'. In the twentieth century Switzerland became a top-ranking world gold market and a centre of international banking. By the end of the twentieth century vast banking corporations in Japan and Europe ranked among the largest banks worldwide, operating branches in every quarter of the globe, holding deposits and making loans in several currencies. The growth of digital communications enabled even small rural banks to participate in international banking.

The moneyed paths followed by financial capital lead to an old question: whether imperialistic governments obediently followed the paths of tender-footed financial capital to other parts of the world, or whether capital followed the groping influence of imperialistic governments. Poor but self-respecting countries proudly discouraged an influx of foreign capital, fearing that shiny foreign investments would attract a dark and bitter foreign influence to local governments. In the name of protecting foreign investments owned by domestic corporations, controlling economic superpowers such as the United States heavy-handedly involved itself in the politics of foreign countries. The paths of colonialism and regional clashes between capitalism and communism helped channel the flow of capital from capital-exporting countries. Towards the end of the twentieth century we see many countries quietly lifting restrictions on capital flows, and foreign investment moving upwards to heights not seen since the end of the nineteenth.

With a suitable monetary system, communication and transportation systems that can overcome distance, and financial markets and institutions that can finance trade and move capital, the remaining barriers to unrestricted global trade are legal restrictions intended to give a nurturing advantage to domestic products and to immunize domestic economies from contagions in the global economy. The idea of free trade took root in Great Britain, a relatively small country geographically but often a rival of larger countries of the European continent. England, intoxicated with the Industrial Revolution, manufactured products far in excess of domestic needs, and its unequalled shipping capabilities enabled it to trade worldwide. English economists explained the superiority of free trade policies for maximizing living standards in individual countries and worldwide. Germany, France, the United States and others unfurled the banner of trade restrictions to protect their own domestic manufacturing from foreign competition. Eventually even Great Britain forsook the side of free trade and joined the fray as the world's major trading partners embroiled themselves in a vicious trade war during the 1930s, sparked by the unthinking enactment of the Smoot–Hawley Tariff in the United States. Post World War II the United States joined the side of free trade, successfully urging a reduction of trade barriers worldwide. The rise of regional trading blocs, such as the European Union and the North American Free Trade Agreement, provides for free trade in individual regions.

Lastly we cover the development of the global financial system, beginning in the late 1970s with a capitalism revolution in Great Britain and the United States which swept through the global economy, emphasizing privatization, deregulated markets, freedom to import and export and unrestricted capital flows between countries. Just when the introduction of flexible exchange rates added a speculative touch to foreign investment and trade, legal and political barriers to foreign trade and capital flows came crumbling down, and innovations in communication and information systems gave investors opportunities in virtually any quarter of the globe. Foreign trade, investment and speculation experienced a burst of growth amid a worldwide wave of fresh confidence in market institutions. In 1997–8 the old nemesis of capitalism reappeared when financial crises in several countries rocked the global financial system, raising new questions and old fears about its stability. The postmortem on these financial crises is ongoing at the beginning of the twenty-first century.

ONE

The Coming of the Corporation

The world's financial centres, New York to Hong Kong, boast stock markets whose stirring rallies and jittery retreats are measured by arithmetic indices, the most readily available means of taking the temperature and pulse of the global financial system. These stock markets owe their noisy existence to the triumphant rise of the corporate form of business organization, whose exuberant growth largely coincided with the strident growth in world trade following the swashbuckling age of discovery and the reorientation of world trade from the Mediterranean to the Atlantic.

Corporations are creatures of the law, legal entities that in the eyes of the law have many of the privileges of individual persons, including the acquisition of resources, and the production and marketing of goods and services. Money can be borrowed in the name of the corporation, which itself can be a lender, and before the courts a corporation can sue or be sued just as a person. As a legal entity a corporation may enjoy a life of unlimited duration, well beyond the lifespan of its original founders.

This special status as a separate legal entity confers upon the corporation an immeasurable advantage over other forms of business organization, an advantage referred to as 'limited liability' because of the limited liability of the owners (stockholders) for the debts of the corporation. In contrast to business partnerships, which render each individual partner personally and equally liable for all debts incurred by a failed business venture, an individual stockholder cannot be sued for the debts of a corporation, limiting the investor's maximum loss to the value of stock invested.

Furthermore, under the corporate form individual business partners can sell their shares of stock without permission of other partners, and anyone can buy shares of stock put up for sale without the permission of existing business partners, or stockowners. Before the advent of the corporation personal relationships among business partners stood paramount, and joint business ventures were often kept within a circle of family members who could be trusted because of bonds of kinship. With personal relationships left aside as a factor in business ownership, capital could be amassed from around the globe to finance business ventures, encouraging the quiet flow of capital across political boundaries.

The various evolutionary threads of corporate development do not necessarily stem from a single root, but the primal seed of the corporate business organization may have lain embedded in the double-entry method of bookkeeping, which records all business transactions within the logical framework of a formula that equates total business assets with total business liabilities plus owner's equity. The sale of goods reduces assets invested in inventories but increases assets invested in cash, adding an equal amount to assets and owner's equity if the transaction is profitable. The payment of debt reduces assets invested in cash, but reduces business liabilities by an equal amount, leaving untouched the equality between assets on one side, and liabilities and owner's equity on the other. The credit for formally introducing this system belongs to a friend of Leonardo da Vinci, Luca Pacioli, a mathematics professor at the University of Pavia who inserted a chapter on double-entry bookkeeping in a arithmetic textbook, *Summa Di Arithmetica, Geometria, Proportioni È Proportionalita*.

With double-entry bookkeeping the business organization buds as an impersonal abstract concept independent of an individual owner. The throbbing life of a business lies recorded in a sober ledger of transactions that maintains a balance in an accounting equation, and shows the impersonal impact of each transaction upon owner's equity. The transparent logic of double-entry bookkeeping cranks out with stern precision a measure of profits independent of the judgement of a particular business owner, and changes in business ownership have no necessary impact on the life of the business as recorded in the ledger.

Independent of the growth in the business organization as an abstract concept emerged the practice of governments legally recognizing various towns and communities as legal entities with a permanent existence independent of current membership, and of possible unlimited duration. Monasteries and churches may have unwittingly furnished the first models of corporate charters. Members of governing boards shielded from responsibility for communal debts, a practice that gave birth to the concept of limited liability, governed these incorporated communities. As accepted by English courts in the fifteenth century, the principle of limited liability set limits on how much an alderman of the Liverpool Corporation owed if the city fell into debt or bankruptcy.

Transferable stock shares probably evolved from the early Italian public banks that began as organizations of the government's creditors. In the twelfth century the Republic of Venice politely forced citizens to make loans to the government, and kept a ledger of the amount the government owed each citizen. The government paid interest on the debt, the principal became security for bank money that took the form of bookkeeping entries, and this bank money changed hands by bookkeeping adjustments to the accounts of each citizen. In the fourteenth century the city of Genoa, faced with war with Venice, borrowed funds from citizens. In 1407 the holders of the government's promissory notes organized themselves into a bank, the Casa di San Georgio, or House of St George. This bank functioned as a full bank of deposit, accepting deposits of coins, and issuing bookkeeping bank money that circulated as a medium of exchange. The organization of this bank specifically involved ownership of shares of stock, and these shares of stock circulated as money, the shares exchanging hands through bookkeeping entries at the bank before a notary.

Within less than a century of Columbus's discovery of the New World, the English began the practice of granting corporate charters with transferable stock shares and limited liability to business organizations devoted to exploiting the new commercial opportunities opened for Europe during the age of discovery. The first colonial empires, however, made no use of incorporated business organizations. After Vasco da Gama rounded the Cape of Good Hope in 1497, Portugal opened up direct oceanic trade with the Indies, bypassing Muslim overland traders and Venice, and reorienting East–West trade from the Mediterranean to the Atlantic seaboard. By 1509 European trade with India passed through the hands of Portugal, by 1512 Portugal monopolized trade with the Moluccas or Spice Islands, and by 1540 Portugal directly imported Chinese and Japanese goods to Europe. In the New World Brazil fell within the Portuguese trading sphere. The Portuguese crown never chartered private enterprises to conduct trade with the Indies, unlike the English who chartered the English East India Company, the Dutch (the Dutch East India Company) or the French (French East India Company). The Portuguese colonial empire operated along the lines of what is called 'monarchial capitalism' or 'royal mercantilism'. The Portuguese crown opened up trade with the Indies and trade was conducted on government-owned ships. Captains of royal ships received a salary from the Portuguese crown, and the vast bulk of the merchandise on each ship belonged to the king of Portugal. A small portion of the cargo space was allotted to the captain to trade goods on his own account, the only private entrepreneur in the process. The East India trade was a jealously guarded royal monopoly, the king of Portugal owning the ships and bearing the risks.

Spain began its imperial career on the Portuguese model, but found itself facing an entirely different challenge in the New World where a boundless supply of natural resources awaited exploitation. Finding government initiative inadequate, Spain soon opened up the New World to private initiatives, but the trade remained highly regulated by the Spanish crown. Not until the eighteenth century did Spain charter private joint-stock companies, comparable to the English East India Company, to trade with the New World.

In the last half of the sixteenth century England saw a burst of joint-stock company formation from which we can trace the history of the modern corporation. The immediate forebears of the English joint-stock company were what Adam Smith called regulated companies. These were essentially guilds of merchants, sanctioned by the crown, and given a royal monopoly on trade with certain areas of the world. The regulated company chartered ships and allocated cargo space to each member, but members maintained separate capital stock and failed or succeeded individually.

In 1554 the English crown chartered the Russia Company, one of the earliest joint-stock companies with the purpose of organizing and monopolizing English trade with a foreign market. The East India Company, most famous of the English joint-stock companies, first received a royal charter from Elizabeth I to act as a regulated company with a monopoly on trade with India, but in 1612 was reorganized as a joint-stock company. The charters necessary to form these companies required royal approval and Acts of Parliament, involving considerable expense and available only to those with political connections. To maintain their charters, the companies remained closely allied to governments, making loans to them and counting on their help to reduce the risks of overseas operations. These companies were financed with transferable shares, and the stockholders enjoyed the protection of limited liability, no small consideration in a time when debtors' prison awaited the owners of bankrupt businesses.

The East India Company began by organizing joint-stocks for each separate voyage, but by 1642 the company had organized a permanent capitalization to finance what today would be called a multinational corporation. The company maintained a military presence and operated factories in foreign countries, and organized an international management structure complete with executives stationed around the world. Stockholders owning stocks above a threshold value were members of a General Court, which elected a governor, deputy governor and 24 members of a powerful Court of Directors. The strategic management of the company rested in the hands of these elected officials. In European ports the company purchased silver fresh from the New World, traded the silver for cotton textiles in India, traded the textiles for spices in Indonesia, and either returned directly to Europe with spices, or traded them for silk, sugar, coffee and tea in China and Japan before returning to Europe. The company's stock paid dividends, 6 per cent at first, gradually raised to 10 per cent at the height of prosperity. Profitability began to decline in the late eighteenth century as the company began to lose privileges, including its commercial monopoly in 1813, and it ceased to exist in 1873.

The close relationship between the early joint-stock companies and home governments is more clearly seen in the case of the Dutch East India Company, formed in 1602, two years after the English East India Company. The States General, the Dutch Republic's institution of representative government, chartered the company, became its largest stockholder, and a seventeen-member directorate of the company was chosen from the membership of the States General. Ordinary stockholders had no direct voice in the selection of directors who were elected by local political groups and officials of smaller companies merged into the Dutch East India Company. A Governor General wielded substantial authority within broad guidelines set out by the directors, and all administrative officials swore fealty to the Dutch government. The Governor General ruled an empire of Java and its surrounding islands as the head of a sovereign government that could strike treaties, fight wars, erect forts and appoint and dismiss regional governors. In its heyday the company monopolized the East Indian spice trade, and paid a 22 per cent return to its stockholders. To maintain the prices of clove and nutmeg, the company ordered the wholesale destruction of clove and nutmeg trees, only sparing the trees on the island of Amboyna and the Banda group, reducing production to one-fourth of the pre-Dutch level. The company was as much a sea power and political entity as it was a trading company. By the end of the eighteenth century corruption and debt had caught up with it, and in 1799 the Dutch government assumed its debts, and took control of its possessions.

In 1621 the Dutch West India Company was formed along the same lines as the Dutch East India Company. The company was intended to compete with Spain and Portugal in the New World but was never as successful as the Dutch East India Company, and the Dutch government took the company over in 1791.

The French East India Company was formed in 1664, the brainchild of Jean Baptiste Colbert, the famous finance minister under Louis XIV. The company was organized as a joint-stock company but was never sufficiently capitalized, despite the fact that its formation gave the world one of the first nationwide stock-selling campaigns. Louis XIV raised the articles of the company to the level of law, apparently including the third article which read: 'the shares of individuals were not to be seized by the king, even if they belonged to the subject of a nation at war with France.' The French East India Company remained dependent upon the French government, and vanished during the French Revolution of 1789.

The seventeenth century saw steady growth in the joint-stock form of business organization. Markets developed for trading the transferable shares of stock and by 1698 London could boast its own stock market. A major setback to the joint-stock model came in the aftermath of a major speculative mania that gripped the London stock market in 1720: the South Sea Bubble, named after the South Sea Company whose plan to exchange South Sea stock for government obligations helped spark the mania. The government endorsed the plan as a means of reducing interest payments on government debt. By then many joint-stock companies had been formed without a charter granted by Parliament or the crown, and a craze developed for investing in stock. The crash came when Spain acted to dampen the South Sea Company's trade with the New World.

The South Sea Bubble led Parliament to enact legislation intended to tame the excesses of speculation but which also retarded the growth of the corporate form of business organization in England until the nineteenth century. The Bubble Act of 1720 specifically forbade companies to organize as corporations without a charter approved by Parliament, and also made it more difficult to obtain these charters. For over a century it held back the growth of the corporate form in England, favouring instead partnerships and family-based business organizations that could not meet the capital needs of the Industrial Revolution. The Act was rescinded in 1825.

France experienced an even worse speculative fiasco in 1720, the Mississippi Bubble, more of a monetary debacle than the South Sea Bubble, but it nevertheless brought stricter supervision of markets for joint-stock shares in France.

An important step in the development of the corporate form of business came with the Napoleonic Code of Commerce, which provided for the organization of a corporation without special acts of government granted on a case-by-case basis. The process was generalized for groups meeting certain conditions, but the process involved strict regulations that continued to hamper the growth of corporations in France. The Napoleonic Code provided for the organization of corporations either with or without stockholder protection of limited liability. Belgium, Holland, Switzerland, Italy, Spain, Prussia and the Hanse cities adopted the principles of company law set forth in the Code. In the 1820s and 1830s both France and Belgium saw a boom in joint-stock company formation arising from a rash of canal building.

Following the American Revolution, the state legislatures in the United States followed the English practice of granting charters of incorporation on a case-by-case basis. Various groups complained that businesses gaining charters to organize as corporations were receiving special privileges owing to political connections, sometimes to bribery. Connecticut led the American states toward the liberalization of company laws with the adoption in 1837 of an act that established a routine and mechanical process for chartering corporations. Applicants for a corporate charter needed only to file certain information with a state office, dispensing with the need to lobby the legislatures or wait for legislative action to approve the charter. Connecticut's precedent was infectious in other state legislatures and the United States became fertile ground for the corporate form of business organization, leaving behind Britain, France and the rest of Europe. Britain would only catch up in 1856, and in 1867 France would substantially streamline the process for establishing corporations with limited liability. In Germany joint-stock companies were rare before 1850.

Despite the walls thrown up by the Bubble Act, Britain experienced another burst of joint-stock company formation during a canal mania in the last half of the eighteenth century. Between 1758 and 1803 over 165 acts came before Parliament for the construction of canals. The boom reached mania pitch after the interest rate paid by British Consols dropped precipitously following the War of American Independence. Parliament enacted 81 acts involving canals and navigation between 1791 and 1794. Joint-stock shares were mainly issued in large denominations, often in the £200 range and rarely below £50.

The advantages offered by the corporate form of business organization enticed many large-scale businesses to officially organize as partnerships while unofficially functioning as corporations without charters from Parliament. The ownership of these businesses was spread among large numbers of partners unacquainted with each other and uninvolved in the management of the company. These unincorporated partnerships exploited a provision in partnership law requiring that lawsuits directed against a partnership name each partner individually, a requirement that could not be met if the names of some partners were secret, or some partners could not be reached. By concealing the identity of silent partners and including partners resident outside the country, partners were protected from lawsuits against the partnership, effectively conferring on individual partners the same protection of limited liability enjoyed by the stockholders of officially incorporated joint-stock companies. Meanwhile, however, legal entanglements mounted as existing partners sold to new partners and some partners regarded themselves as creditors to the partnership rather than stockholders. Given these complications, the law was poorly equipped to adjudicate disputes. Investors were also afforded little protection from fraudulent moneymaking schemes.

The British Parliament repealed the Bubble Act in 1825, partly because of the proliferation of companies organized as corporations without approval of Parliament. The new legislation still required an act of Parliament to obtain a corporate charter, but it lifted restrictions on the use of the joint-stock form of business organization and made corporate charters easier to obtain. After 1824 the number of corporate charters with parliamentary approval grew at a faster rate. In 1834 and 1837 Parliament took further steps to encourage the corporate form of business organization, making it possible for companies to receive from the Board of Trade the legal identity needed to sue or be sued, and to confer upon partners the protection of limited liability. The Board of Trade, however, acted cautiously in clothing individual companies with the status of a separate legal entity. Fraud continued to be a problem with joint-stock companies without official incorporation, and in 1844 Parliament took action that gave companies firm standing as separate legal entities capable of suing and being sued, but stopped short of endowing stockholders with the protection of limited liability. The Joint-stock Companies Registration, Incorporation and Regulation Act allowed a group of persons to incorporate by a simple registration procedure showing proof of a minimum paid-up capital and a filing of prospectuses. This act also required companies to file semi-annual, audited balance sheets with the Board of Trade.

In 1856 the British Parliament removed the last major legal obstacle to the growth of corporations with limited liability. Under the Joint-stock Companies Act of 1856 seven or more persons, simply by meeting standardized rules and filing a memorandum of association, could form a corporation enjoying limited liability, significantly streamlining the process of forming a limited liability company. With this act the British Parliament abandoned its caution towards sanctioning limited liability companies, and the following decade saw a multiplication of new incorporations.

The act required investors to file a memorandum of association with a Board of Trade stating the name and purpose of the company and whether the investors enjoyed the protection of limited liability. The newly formed corporation had a choice between proposing its own set of rules, or adopting a standard set of rules set forth by the act. The standard rules provided that stockholders receive a balance sheet at an annual stockholder meeting and that accountants appointed by the Board of Trade could inspect a company's books at the request of one-fifth of the stockholders in number and in value.

The railways were the first industrial companies to adopt the corporate form of business organization on a broad scale. Of the eleven stocks listed in the first Dow Jones average in 1884, nine were railway companies. Railways were ideal for the corporate form of business organization from both the companies' and the stockholders' points of view. Highly capital intensive, the railway industry needed to amass capital in amounts exceeding what a handful of investors could furnish, and the protection of limited liability enabled the railway to attract capital from as many investors as possible. From the investor's perspective, railway business took place in open spaces where investors could inspect the quality of equipment and number of customers from casual observation, and deterioration in service or maintenance of equipment as well as loss of business or new competition were readily apparent. Railways usually enjoyed some degree of government support, perhaps a publicly sanctioned monopoly, which increased their credibility in the eyes of investors.

As the corporate form of business organization grew in the nineteenth century the close connection between the state and the corporation, such as existed between the East India Company and the British government, began to disappear. The sheer growth in numbers of corporations, coupled with the rise of *laissez-faire* ideas, reduced the government's interest and involvement in the affairs of individual companies, a contrast to the first mercantile joint-stock companies which were viewed as extensions of the state.

In the second half of the nineteenth century a new force began to play a role in the development of corporations as the world economy entered the phase of finance capitalism, which concentrated economic power in the hands of large investment banks. Investment banking houses such as the Rothschilds, successful in marketing government securities and raising loans for governments, put their talents to work marketing corporate stocks. These bankers purchased large blocks of stocks in newly formed companies, and sold these shares to the public as the companies began to report profits.

The trend towards finance capitalism became evident in 1852 when Napoleon III's French government established the Société Génerale de Crédit Mobilier, the first joint-stock bank in France, created for the purpose of raising capital to meet the long-term financing needs of railways and heavy industry. The Crédit Mobilier held customer deposits, sold bonds and sold shares of its own stock to raise capital. Its deposits were large and from large businesses. It invested its capital in purchase of corporate stocks and bonds, which it sometimes resold to the public. By controlling access to long-term financing and holding large blocks of stocks in competing companies, the Crédit Mobilier possessed the power, which it exercised, to promote cooperation instead of competition among rival companies. The Crédit Mobilier was heavily involved in financing railways in France, Spain, Austria, North Italy, Russia and Switzerland. It furnished the model for the big commercial banks of Central Europe that combined deposit banking with investment in corporate stock and provision of long-term financing for large businesses. The close association between banks and industry became the cornerstone of finance capitalism, a phase of capitalism that reached its full flowering in the late nineteenth century, particularly in Germany.

In the United States one individual personified finance capitalism: John Pierpont Morgan, a private merchant banker. Private merchant bankers were not subject to the regulations of government-chartered corporate bankers. While merchant bankers like Morgan held deposits for a few large business clients, they emphasized the transference of funds necessary for the conduct of international trade and marketing issues of government bonds and corporate stock. As a condition for purchasing stock or bonds from a corporation, Morgan required that his associates be placed on the board of directors, mainly to protect the interest of the financiers. Out of this practice grew a web of interlocking directorates that placed enormous power in Morgan's hands, which he used to restrict competition among his clients and reduce the risks on his investments. An individual serving on the boards of two or more corporations is in a position to encourage cooperation and reciprocity and discourage competition. Morgan also used his power to consolidate railways and manufacturing firms. One of his greatest accomplishments was the consolidation of several steel firms into United States Steel, which became the largest corporation in the world.

In 1912 a congressional committee investigating the 'money trusts' found that Morgan had positioned one or more of his associates on the boards of 32 corporations.[1] Morgan himself was on the rosters of boards of directors or voting trustees for the New York Central Railroad; the New York, New Haven, and Hartford Railroad; the Southern Railway Company; the Philadelphia and Reading Railroad; the International Mercantile Marine Company; Adams Express; International Harvester; General Electric and Western Union. In addition numerous banks either belonged to Morgan or fell under his control. By

1920 Morgan and Company had placed 167 representatives on boards, creating a network of 2,450 interlocking directorates, stretching its control over about one-quarter of the total corporate assets in the United States.[2] The Clayton Act of 1914 prohibited a person from serving on the boards of two competing organizations, but it did not prevent a company executive from serving on the board of a competing company. As late as 1968 a study for the United States government reported that 49 commercial banks were involved in interlocking directorates that spanned over 286 of the 500 largest corporations.[3]

Germany felt the force of finance capitalism more thoroughly than any other country. While banking in England and Italy grew out of a need to finance international trade, in Germany it evolved to meet the financing needs of large-scale industrial enterprises. While Germany had been slow to accept the corporate form, it began to develop in the 1870s. In 1843 Prussia had made legal provision for the establishment of joint-stock companies, subject to individual government approval for each company. Between 1870 and 1872 Germany enacted a series of laws that allowed the formation of corporations by compliance with standardized criteria, no longer requiring individual government approval.[4] In June 1870 a mere 410 incorporated businesses existed in Prussia, a number that increased more than five-fold by the end of 1874. Between 1870 and 1872 Germany saw the formation of 107 incorporated banks alone. Many of these banks failed in the financial crisis of 1873, which may have been a factor in Germany's wholehearted embrace of finance capitalism at the expense of *laissez-faire*.

In today's parlance the German banks combined deposit banking with investment banking, accepting customers' deposits and investing them, with bank capital, in shares of corporate stock, a practice banned in the United States in the 1930s. Customers opening deposit accounts at German banks also consented to purchase all corporate stock investments through the bank, usually with the condition that the bank act as proxy for the shareholder at stockholder meetings. While the purchaser held ownership of the stock and rights to dividends, the voting rights of stockholders fell into the hands of the banks. These banks purchased blocks of new stock issues, and sold them to individual investors. They also made long-term loans to major industrial enterprises, and often reserved the right to convert loans into stock shares and debentures, which could be sold to other investors.

Holding blocks of stock and the stock proxies of bank customers, German banks wielded vast power over industrial enterprises dependent on the banks for short-term and long-term capital, demanding wide representation on directorates and supervisory boards and enjoying ready access to what is now called insider information. After the financial crisis of 1873 precipitated a wave of bankruptcies among banks and other businesses, German banks used their power to encourage industries to form cartels: agreements among a group of firms to monopolize an industry, cooperatively restricting production and supply to raise prices to monopoly levels, dividing markets into different sectors monopolized by individual firms, and undertaking various cooperative initiatives to create a national or even international monopoly. Cartels were seen as a cure for the cutthroat competition that drove prices down in the midst of industrial depression, rendering companies unable to repay debts to banks.

The trend towards the cartelization of industry accelerated after 1879 when the German government abandoned a philosophy of free trade and significantly raised trade barriers against imported goods. Under the protection of a high tariff wall, German cartels could raise domestic prices well above world market levels, creating a fertile environment for exploiting the market power of cartels. The largest cartels controlled the coal, iron and steel industries. The degree of control that cartels exercised over individual firms varied in different industries. 'Produktion' cartels allocated to each firm a share of the industry output, and assigned individual firms to monopolize specific regional markets. The most advanced cartels, called 'syndicates', operated an industry-wide selling office that processed the sales of individual cartel members, and pooled industry profits for distribution to individual firms. Some syndicates organized production for a particular product from the raw material stage of production to the retail sale, controlling prices at each stage. Cartels tended to set prices sufficiently high to cover the cost of uncompetitive firms, but clearly unprofitable plants were shut down in favour of more efficient facilities. The German government continued to encourage the formation of cartels until the end of World War II.

After the Meiji Restoration in 1868, a form of finance capitalism developed that continues to exert a strong influence on the organization of corporate business in Japan. Comparable to holding companies, giant financial combines, *zaibatzu*, rose up, becoming the dominant factor in the industrial organization for the advanced capitalist sector of Japan. *Zaibatsu* translates into English as 'money-clique' and the *zaibatzu* were family-owned holding companies, holding corporate securities of businesses in a wide range of industries, organized under one family to maintain cooperation among companies with potentially diverging interests. Besides maintaining a pre-eminent role for family ownership and control in era of giant industrial corporations, the *zaibatzu* created a form of industrial organization bearing a strong kinship with finance capitalism. On the roster of subsidiaries owned by each *zaibatzu* a bank furnishing capital to the whole enterprise could invariably be found. At the apex of the *zaibatsu* stood a family partnership owning all the capital in a holding company that controlled a group of subsidiaries, appointing directors and managers.

During World War I the *zaibatzu* grew rapidly, and by the 1930s virtually every sector of the Japanese economy felt the influence, and often the domination, of four *zaibatzu* – Mitsui, Mitsubishi, Sumitomo and Yasuda. Mitsui, the largest, belonged to eleven families sharing a common ancestry with the firm's founder. Within Mitsui were six flagship components, Mitsui Bank, Mitsui Bussan, Mitsui Mining, Mitsui Trust, Toshin Warehouse and Mitsui Life Insurance, and each of these controlled numerous subsidiaries. Mitsui Bussan owned or controlled subsidiaries in flour milling, rayon, cotton merchanting, engineering, electrical apparatus, condensed milk, marine and fire insurance, and oil refining, and each of these companies had subsidiaries, creating a pyramid organization.

During the 1930s *zaibatzu* controlled four of the six leading banks in Japan, and the Japanese public, investing primarily in fixed-interest bank deposits rather than corporate securities, kept 70 per cent of its deposits with *zaibatzu* trust companies. *Zaibatzu* used access to credit as leverage over small companies, extracting concessions and special consideration for *zaibatzu* products. After World War II, occupation authorities formed the Holding Company Liquidation Commission for the express purpose of liquidating the *zaibatzu*, putting an end to family ownership and dissolving the largest holding companies.

Despite anti-monopoly legislation, monopoly practices and cartelization remained an important characteristic of Japanese corporations in the post-World War II era. Trade associations replaced *zaibatzu* as instruments for promoting economic cooperation at the expense of competition. Japanese corporations, usually affiliated to a bank, have remained highly dependent on bank financing. Japan's economic difficulties of the 1990s brought to light the difficulties created when banks begin to think they cannot afford to let certain corporate customers fail.

In the United States, trusts, mergers and holding companies achieved much the same purpose as cartels in Germany and *zaibatzu* in Japan. In 1879 the Standard Oil Company organized itself as a trust, the first industrial trust in the United States. Under a trust stockholders of member corporations handed over the right to control individual corporations to a group of trustees responsible for controlling all member corporations. Stockholders surrendered stock certificates in particular corporations and received in return trust certificates, entitling each stockholder to a share of the earnings of the trust proportional to the share of the total value of the trust contributed by the stockholder. Holders of trust certificates elected a board of trustees that oversaw the management of all the member corporations, comparable to a board of directors for an individual corporation. Traded like shares of stock, 1899 saw more trades in trust certificates than in stock shares. The board of trustees made sure that the member corporations cooperated rather than competed with each other, effectively fixing industry prices and controlling industry output, even shutting down some facilities. The 'trust' inspired the antitrust laws in the United States, beginning with the Sherman Antitrust Act of 1890, which banned price fixing and marketing agreements.

The Sherman Act struck directly at trusts, but a new form of centralized control emerged, achieving the same results. Mergers were still legal under the Sherman Act. In 1889 corporations chartered in New Jersey won the right to purchase and hold the stock of other corporations and to pay for the stock with issues of their own stock. In 1893 New Jersey further amended its corporation law to enable New Jersey corporations to purchase corporations chartered out of state and assume all rights of ownership. In 1892 the trustees of the Standard Oil trust, then composed of twenty member corporations, voted to dissolve the trust, and reorganized as Standard Oil of New Jersey, a single corporation owning the stock in the twenty member corporations of the Standard Oil trust.

The action of the Standard Oil trustees marked the beginning of the first wave of mergers in US history. Depression struck the United States in 1893, and corporations sought refuge in industrial combines that could fix prices without violating the Sherman Act. Between 1898 and 1902 the United States saw over 2,600 mergers, and the number of industrial combinations with capitalization equal to or exceeding $1 billion increased from 10 to 300 by 1900, notwithstanding the enforcement of the Sherman Act. Industries most affected by the turn-of-the-century merger wave were petroleum, iron and steel, copper, sugar, lead and salt. The US census of 1900 reported that 0.5 per cent of the nation's manufacturing establishments owned 15 per cent of the industrial capital and employed 8 per cent of the industrial output.

Companies such as Standard Oil of New Jersey were called holding companies, because they owned (held) a controlling interest in several corporations. They are also sometimes called parent corporations, and corporations whose stock is held by a parent company are called subsidiaries. A subsidiary is wholly owned when the parent corporation owns 100 per cent of its stock, but a parent corporation can own substantially less than 50 per cent of the stock of a subsidiary and still have controlling interest. Holding companies issue their own stock to purchase controlling interest in the stock of other corporations.

One of the most famous holding companies in history was American Telephone and Telegraph (AT&T), a vast corporation that monopolized the telecommunications industry in the United

States until the mid 1980s. For many years the federal government allowed AT&T to function as a monopoly subject to substantial government regulation, including of prices. Regional telephone companies such as Southwestern Bell were wholly owned subsidiaries of AT&T, which also owned Western Electric, the equipment-producing arm of the telecommunications giant. Wholly owned subsidiaries monopolized long-distance service, the manufacture of telecommunication equipment and much of the local phone service. In 1984 the US Justice Department settled an antitrust action against AT&T which forced it to spin-off the local Bell operating companies.

Holding companies in the United States remain legal as long as the effect is not to restrain competition. Today a holding company may own large stock investments in two non-competing corporations without violating antitrust laws, one reason why holding companies are common. In the 1990s more than 90 per cent of bank deposits in the United States were held by large bank holding companies such as Citicorp or Chase Bank. Large banks organized themselves as holding companies, creating wholly owned subsidiaries to sidestep federal and state laws against branch banking. Public utilities operating in several states with different utility regulations also found it convenient to organize separate, stand alone subsidiaries in each state as a means of separating entities subject to different regulations. By organizing into holding companies, public utilities can avoid questions about how regulations in one state affect customers, service and profitability in another state.

Even where the effect of holding companies is not to lessen competition, there remains the potential for difficulty. The stock market boom of the 1920s sparked another wave of mergers and holding company formation. Electrical utility and other industries built pyramids of holding companies that concentrated vast power in the hands of a small group of investors, but at the risk of extreme financial leverage. The system was complicated but worked as follows: a subsidiary at the base of the pyramid owning $100 million in assets was financed 50 per cent by debt and 50 per cent by stock. All the stock of the company at the base of the pyramid was owned by a holding company in the first tier of the pyramid, giving the holding company control over $100 million in assets with only a $50 million investment. The first-tier holding company was also financed 50 per cent by debt and 50 per cent by stock, allowing its stockholders to control $100 million in assets with only $25 million of their own money. The $25 million in stock of the first-tier holding company could be held by a second-tier holding company also financed 50 per cent by debt and 50 per cent by stock, enabling the second-tier holding company stockholders to control $100 million in assets with only a $12.5 million investment of their own assets, the remaining $87.5 million financed by debt holders with no voice in the management of the corporation. The heavy dependence upon debt financing left these holding company pyramids vulnerable to the deflation of the 1930s, since interest on indebtedness, unlike stock dividends, must be paid regardless of the level of profits (or losses). The failure of pyramid companies accelerated a downward spiral of business failures during the 1930s, bringing to light an Achilles heel in the US corporate structure.

The second decade of the twentieth century saw important legal developments in the United States that significantly redirected the evolution of the modern corporation. In 1914 Congress enacted the Clayton Act, partly to close loopholes in the Sherman Act, which had tried to prevent monopolies. The Clayton Act specifically forbade one corporation to purchase the stock of another if the effect was to lessen competition. The intention of the Act was to ban what are called horizontal mergers, that is, mergers of firms in the same industry, competing in the same markets. But even the Clayton Act had a loophole: the US Supreme Court ruled in 1926 that the Act did not prohibit a corporation from purchasing the assets of a competing corporation, only the stock. Nevertheless the Clayton Act discouraged horizontal mergers, and vertical mergers (mergers of firms engaged in different production stages of the same product) were often found by the courts to lessen competition, and were therefore illegal under the antitrust laws.

In 1918 Congress adopted the Webb-Pomerene Act enabling American firms to cooperate in export markets and form cooperative export associations without violating antitrust laws. Congress justified this action because governments in countries such as Germany and England encouraged domestic firms to organize cartels in export markets, so allowing American firms to compete by the same rules should promote competition in world markets. In 1919 Congress passed the Edge Act allowing federally chartered corporations to engage in foreign banking or foreign investment banking.

These legislative changes acted to spur two important developments in the evolution of the corporation, developments that allowed corporations to grow in power and size without infringing upon competition in US markets. Coupled with the edge that American business gained over European business during World War I, the Webb-Pomerene Act and the Edge Act encouraged the rapid growth of multinational corporations in the United States. Multinational corporations operate production and marketing facilities worldwide, inside the sovereign boundaries of numerous governments, forming strategies in the light of global trends and opportunities.

By the turn of the century multinational corporations headquartered in the United States were already active, particularly in Latin America. At that time the United Fruit Company was aggressively monopolizing the banana industry and ruthlessly exploiting labour in Central America. This company already had a long history of meddling in the affairs of these countries when it became famous in 1954 for enlisting the support of the US government in overthrowing a hostile government in Guatemala. The turn of the century also saw Eastman Kodak, General Electric and Standard Oil begin to look beyond national boundaries for markets and resources. In the 1920s the American industries that had received the greatest boost from World War I, the automobile, chemical, petroleum and machine tool industries, took on an international stature. The expansion of Germany during the 1930s, and the worldwide depression, stifled the growth of multinational enterprises in the United States, but following World War II the expansion continued at a heady pace. The 1960s saw multinational corporations headquartered in the United States more than double the book value of foreign investments. By 1974 the United States was headquarters for 24 of the largest 50 multinational corporations in the world.[5] By 1998, despite the rapid growth of

Japanese multinationals, the United States remained headquarters for nineteen of the largest 50 multinational corporations.[6] Of the five largest multinationals in 1999, two were American, General Motors and Ford Motor Company; two Japanese, Mitsui & Co. Ltd and Mitsubishi Corporation; and one European, Dutch Royal/Shell Group.

In the early 1970s it was already obvious that multinational corporations in terms of output exceeded the gross national product of numerous small countries. Exxon, the largest multinational corporation in 1974, with total sales of $42.1 billion, exceeded in size the gross national product of Belgium, Denmark or almost any Latin American country. Thirteen down the list was International Business Machines, with sales of $13 billion, comparable in value to the gross national product of Austria. Industries figuring prominently in the ranks of multinational corporations were automobiles, machinery, tools, chemicals, oil, drugs, electrical equipment, electronics and high technology.

International banking has a history as long or longer than multinational corporations but as multinationals transcended national boundaries in search of markets and resources, large banks aggressively followed, often forming consortia with other banks from different countries to make international loans. By 1997 six of the ten largest banks in the world were headquartered in Japan, the remaining four in Europe.

The Clayton Act of 1914 had banned horizontal mergers that lessened competition. It left corporations free to form mergers of firms in unrelated or only distantly related businesses, called conglomerate mergers; the resulting corporations are called conglomerates. Conglomerates began to grow rapidly in the 1950s after the Celler-Kefauver Act of 1950 closed remaining loopholes in the Clayton Act. The Clayton Act banned one corporation from purchasing the stock of another corporation when the effect was to lessen competition, but did not prohibit one corporation from purchasing the physical assets of another with the effect of lessening competition. Amidst more stringent antitrust legislation, conglomerate mergers remained perfectly legal and 88 per cent of all mergers fell into the conglomerate category by 1970. The conglomerate movement seemed to have no industry favourites, manifesting itself in manufacturing, banking, insurance, retail trade and service industries.

The first corporation to catapult itself into the ranks of giant corporations by pursuing a strategy of conglomerate mergers was International Telephone and Telegraph (ITT). ITT was a rather modest telecommunications company before World War II, providing telephone, telegraph, cable and wireless communication services, mainly in the Caribbean area. The company entered upon a course of expansion in the 1950s, adding the manufacture of telecommunication and defence-related equipment to its product lines. By the 1960s it was clear that conglomerate mergers were the least likely to provoke a challenge from the Justice Department. ITT threw itself energetically into conglomerate diversification, acquiring firms in remote and unrelated industries including, but not limited to, automobile rental (Avis); hotels and inns (Sheraton); consumer finance and insurance (Aetna Finance Co.); baking (Continental Baking); fire and casualty insurance (Hartford Fire Insurance) and residential construction (Levitt & Sons). Eventually ITT swallowed up more than a hundred domestic and foreign firms, leading the conglomerate movement in number of acquisitions, and reducing the share of revenue generated by its utility operations to 4 per cent of total company revenue.

By the late 1960s the growth of conglomerates had kindled concern about the vast economic and political power wielded by giant corporations. ITT set a well-publicized example of rapid growth through mergers, and in 1969 the Justice Department filed an antitrust suit against ITT to test the applicability of existing antitrust laws in regulating conglomerates.[7] The Justice Department saw a tendency towards concentration of control of manufacturing assets in ITT's strategy of broad diversification through conglomerate mergers, and emphasized the possibilities for impairment of competition because of reciprocity agreements between ITT subsidiaries. The Justice Department's suit targeted three acquisitions: the Grinnell Corporation, a manufacturer of sprinklers and power plant piping; Canteen Corporation, a vending machine manufacturer; and Hartford Fire and Casualty. Before the case reached the Supreme Court

ITT and the Justice Department reached a settlement, which required that ITT divest itself of several acquisitions.

Currently companies in the United States acquiring another company submit the acquisition to the Justice Department for prior approval. If this is given, the Department agrees not to bring a suit to block the merger or to force the acquiring company to divest itself of the new acquisition. The Justice Department rarely contests conglomerate mergers.

American antitrust laws favoured multinational and conglomerate corporations as the preferred corporate model for unlimited growth, and the rapid growth of international trade provided the fertile ground for theses forms to realize their potential. Most European governments continued to tolerate monopolistic business mergers and collusion until the end of World War II. The British Parliament enacted its first antitrust legislation in 1948 with the passage of the Restrictive Trade Practices Act, and strengthened the legislation with the Restrictive Trade Practices Act of 1956. In 1946, after occupation authorities liquidated the Japanese *zaibatzu*, the new Japanese government enacted the Anti-Monopoly Law, but that was later repealed. Japan now has an anti-monopoly law but it is not considered effective or strongly enforced. In 1957 Germany outlawed domestic cartels, but continued to allow domestic companies to form cartels in foreign markets.

Concern about the vast power wielded by giant multinational and conglomerate corporations mounted in the decades following World War II. The fact that giant corporations seemed the first to raise prices in a spiral of inflation suggested in itself a dangerous aspect to their size. President Kennedy publicly rebuked steel corporations, drawing a sharp contrast in the attitude of giant steel companies, who had announced a steel price increase, and other Americans making great sacrifices. In 1973 ITT, which had already drawn the ire of the Justice Department over antitrust issues, assisted in the overthrow of President Salvador Allende, the democratically elected President of Chile.[8] ITT used its influence to prod the US government and the Central Intelligence Agency into assisting the military coup that ended in the murder of President Allende, and the establishment of a military dictatorship mainly remembered for its ruthless murder of thousands of Chilean citizens. The public saw something sinister in multinational corporations shopping around for countries with lax environmental laws, poorly paid workers and no unions.

Anger over the exercise of brute power may have inspired much of the criticism of giant corporations, but cannot account for the diversity of criticism, often founded in closely reasoned arguments. Apologists for the giants usually fall back on the superior efficiency of large-scale production over small-scale, and the ability of large corporations to finance expensive research and development. Critics claim that giant corporations have become too large for intelligent management; that innovative and imaginative leadership exerted at the apex of the corporate pyramid becomes diffused or lost before reaching the base; and that giant corporations, like dinosaurs, are too inflexible to adjust to their environment. A former General Motors executive compared GM's Chevrolet division to a monster which could have its tail twisted at one end without anything happening at the other end for months.[9]

Critics not willing to assign these giant corporations to the ignominious oblivion of inert giants cite other evil social, economic and cultural effects. While conglomerates may use their vast resources to finance research and development, they may also deploy vast resources to manage demand for product lines, paying for advertising and television programmes that condition the public's wants, and creating needs in the minds of consumers which they would never have developed on their own. While resources are channelled into the production of electric toothbrushes, striped toothpaste and automobiles with electric trunk lids, no one is putting equal resources into the promotion of highway construction or programmes for juvenile delinquents. Critics see the management and leadership of corporations furnished by a managerial and technical elite that has thoroughly wrested control from stockholders and pursues its own goals, sometimes at the expense of stockholder welfare.

The trend towards ever enlarging corporations may have crested in the last two decades of the twentieth century. In 1975 about 19 per cent of all US employees held jobs with *Fortune* 500 and *Forbes* 400 companies. By the mid 1990s this number had fallen to 9 per cent. A new generation of smaller corporations inspired by entrepreneurial leadership put once invincible giants such as International Business Machines on the defensive. Smaller companies seemed better able to keep pace with rapidly changing technologies than giant corporations laden with administrative managers and executives substituting salesmanship for leadership.

The same rapid technological advances that favour small companies over large may have helped put multinational enterprises from around the world on the same footing as multinationals headquartered in the United States. In 1960 US multinationals ranked first in ownership of foreign investment, owning 47.1 per cent of the world's total foreign investment, while British multinationals ranked second at 18.3 per cent. By 1985 the share of US multinationals had dropped to 35.1 per cent, and of British to 14.7 per cent. Japanese multinationals, which had accounted for only 0.7 per cent of foreign investment in 1960, had increased their share to 11.7 per cent by 1985, and German multinationals increased their share from 1.2 per cent to 8.4 per cent over the same period.[10] Between 1960 and 1985 Swiss multinationals increased their share of world foreign investment from 3.4 per cent to 6.4 per cent, and multinationals from less developed countries collectively increased their share from 1 per cent to 2.7 per cent. Among the world's 50 largest manufacturing corporations can found companies headquartered in the smaller European countries, such as the Netherlands, and multinationals are springing up in the newly industrialized parts of the world.

TWO

The Making of Financial Markets

The global financial system has woven the earth over with an infinite web of subtle forces, currents and tensions. The fundamental unit in this web is the market, an economic crossroads intelligently harmonizing the wishes of groping buyers and sellers, maintaining a precarious balance between the hidden forces of supply and demand. In a commodity market for wheat, buyers and sellers trade in contracts to deliver wheat either on the spot, or at some date six months or a year ahead. Similar markets exist for individuals and corporations impatiently holding excess demands for and supplies of financial assets, such as money, bonds, stocks, etc. Households save out of current income, building up stores of wealth for financial security or to maintain themselves during retirement years. Businesses need to finance far-flung enterprises, requiring the construction of sprawling production complexes, warehouses and fleets of ships and aeroplanes. Financing these enterprises requires capital far above current profits, or the financial resources of all but a handful of households. The financial markets bring together borrowers and savers by financial instruments such as stocks and bonds.

The growth of the corporate form of business organization created a vast quantity of outstanding or previously issued shares of corporate stock, shares that the current owners might wish to convert into cash or to trade for other stock. The stock markets, most closely watched of the financial markets, trade in these shares. The values of these stocks are a function of expected future profits, a subjective measure that can experience wide swings, particularly when psychological factors invade the thinking of stock traders. The values of stocks in modern stock markets fluctuate minute by minute, creating a field for speculative trading and profit, part of the lure that helps to mobilize capital in modern economic systems.

The search for the first beginnings of the modern financial markets leads into the murky recesses of European economic history. In 1141 Louis VII established the *changeurs* on the Pont du Change in Paris. Bills of exchange were traded in this early market which combined a credit instrument with a foreign exchange transaction, providing for payment in a specific currency at a set date and at a certain location. In 1557 the Pont du Change was mentioned in a report the Venetian ambassador sent to his government, describing it as a place where business people meet in the morning and afternoon. In 1572 the king of France required individuals to receive royal permission to deal in securities, which consisted of bills of exchange and various instruments of government debt until the eighteenth century, when stocks were first traded in France.

In the sixteenth century Lyons was the financial centre of France, originally because French kings saw the advantages of privileged access to a financial market, seeing the privileges other monarchs with major financial centres within their territory enjoyed. By the sixteenth century the cost of war had far outpaced the ability of tax systems to generate revenue, and governments turned to credit markets as an alternative preferable to coinage debasement. Bankruptcies of the Spanish crown in the 1570s dealt a hard blow to Lyons, which would lose out to Paris as the financial centre of France over the next century.

Financial markets and commodity and stock exchanges are sometimes called 'bourses' (i.e. the Paris Bourse), a name that originated with the Van der Buerse family of Bruges. During the thirteenth century merchants in Bruges gathered in front of this family's house to negotiate deals and transact business. During the fourteenth and fifteenth centuries Bruges rose to prominence as the crossroads of international trade, acting as a financial centre and transshipment point for trade between the Mediterranean world and Northern Europe.

The end of the fifteenth century saw Antwerp eclipse Bruges as the major European trading centre. Antwerp enjoyed easier access to the sea and was lenient in its regulation of foreign merchants, attracting many from Bruges where regulations were strict. In 1531 Antwerp finished construction of its new bourse, a structure that became a pattern for Amsterdam and England. An inscription reading 'for the use of merchants of whatever nation or tongue', adorned the Antwerp bourse, the first international or world bourse. Commodities and bills of exchange traded at the Antwerp bourse, and governments looked to the bourses at Antwerp and Lyons to float government loans. Antwerp would lose its position as the pre-eminent financial centre of Europe before the appearance of speculation in transferable shares of corporate stock in the seventeenth century.

East Indian spices furnished much of the grist for the speculative mill at Antwerp, exhibiting wide swings in prices driven by the most recent rumours of war or peace. Traders followed the price of pepper as a measure of the pulse of the market, and speculators kept watch on the market's hourly fluctuations. The psychology of speculative markets became clearly evident in the Antwerp bourse. Speculators fluctuating between hope and fear were readily swayed one way or the other, and quickly seized on any piece of information that seemed to give a peek at the future. One market expert, Christopher Kurz, formulated an astrological system that enabled him to forecast a fortnight in advance the prices of pepper, ginger, saffron and bills of exchange.[1] He wrote commercial reports that were popular with leading speculators and merchants who not only read but also made notes on them.

The Netherlands government sought to tame speculative excesses by regulation, and in 1541 banned 'wagers', a favourite trading tool of speculators in the Antwerp bourse. A first speculator wagers (bets) that a foreign exchange rate (the conversion rate of one foreign currency to another) will be at a 2 per cent premium or discount at some date in the future, perhaps at the next trading fair held in Antwerp. A second speculator wagers that the discount or premium will equal 3 per cent. The two speculators promise to pay each other the difference according to the result. Wager speculation was adaptable to commodities and other types of speculative markets.

With the outbreak of war between France and Spain in 1542, European monarchs, particularly the French, the Spanish and the English, became major participants in the financial markets at Antwerp and Lyons, the other international bourse. Monarchs appointed special financial agents who lived in these cities and oversaw their government's efforts to borrow funds and float loans. In 1552 Thomas Gresham, famous as the originator of Gresham's Law in monetary economics, became the English crown's representative at Antwerp. At that time loans to governments paid higher interest rates than commercial loans, and liquid funds from across Europe flowed into Antwerp to invest in government debt instruments, called King's Bonds, Court Bonds or Bonds of the Receivers.

In 1552 Charles V, King of Spain and Emperor of the Holy Roman Empire (which Voltaire described as being neither holy nor Roman nor an empire) again launched a war with Francis I of France. Interest rates on the bourse at Antwerp hit double-digit levels as a mania for investing in government debt rose to fever pitch. The crowns of England, France and Spain were floating loans, mostly secured by government revenue from specific taxes and anticipated shipments of gold and silver from the Americas.

The war of 1552 was shortlived, but in 1557 France and Spain were at war again. Now Charles V's son, Philip II, was king of Spain and the Spanish government was tottering on the edge of bankruptcy. Catholic theologians, voicing the Church's historic disapproval of interest charges, advised Philip II that the credit agreements entered into by the Spanish crown were usurious, absolving Philip of responsibility for repaying them. Armed with this advice, Philip II took a more moderate course, and gave creditors a choice of relinquishing claims for repayment or consolidating the short-term government obligations, paying 10 to 14 per cent interest, into longer-term bonds (rentes) paying 5 per cent interest. Francis I, in no better financial shape than Philip II to weather the cost of another war, also reduced his interest payments. Government debt sold at heavy discounts in Antwerp and Lyons, lifting effective interest rates to 15 per cent, ending the boom in the government securities market and shaking confidence in the markets at Antwerp and Lyons.

Spain and France, unable to afford war, settled their differences at the peace table. Bouts of bankruptcy became a habitual pattern for the Spanish monarchy into the seventeenth century. Amsterdam and London stood to be major beneficiaries when a

Spanish army invaded Antwerp, ending its career as a major European financial centre. Methods pioneered in Antwerp for amassing large amounts of capital, using the lure of speculation, passed down to the financial markets of Amsterdam and London. Amsterdam soon outshone Antwerp. In 1612 the Amsterdam market was the seat of 300 brokers employing 600 people, and conducting business in wide-open spaces. In 1613 Amsterdam saw the completion of a new bourse, modelled on Antwerp, and housing all the commercial activities of Amsterdam with the exception of corn, which was traded on a separate exchange.

In 1602 the formation of the Dutch East India Company as a joint-stock company brought to the Amsterdam market trade in a new type of financial asset, the transferable share of stock. Trade in transferable shares developed slowly and as late as 1670 the stocks of only two companies were traded on the Amsterdam bourse, the Dutch East India Company and Dutch West India Company. Perhaps because of Antwerp's experience with government bankruptcies, Amsterdam was slow to embrace trade in public debts. In 1672 the Dutch government, financing resistance to a French invasion, floated loans, marking the first instance of public funds quoted on the Amsterdam bourse. By 1750, however, Amsterdam had matured into a bustling international financial centre, boasting daily stock price quotations on three Dutch and three English joint-stock companies in addition to quotations on 25 Dutch public funds and thirteen foreign loans, including the public debts of the States General, towns and provinces of the United Provinces, and the British government.

If the market for transferable shares developed slowly in Amsterdam, the same cannot be said about the techniques of speculation, especially futures speculation, which reached an advanced level of sophistication. Traders believing a market was headed up, currently called bulls, were called 'lovers' on the Amsterdam bourse, and traders expecting the market to head down, now called bears, were called 'counterminers'. Futures contracts are agreements to buy or sell a stated commodity, corporate stock, or financial claim (such as US treasury bonds) at a specified price and at a specified period of time. Then, as now, commodity markets accounted for the bulk of futures speculation, but future contracts were traded for the stocks of the Dutch East India Company and the major English joint-stock companies. The first documented appearance of what are now called puts and calls occurred on the Amsterdam bourse during the tulipmania of the 1630s. A put gives a speculator the option to sell at a fixed price a commodity or stock at some future date, and a call gives a speculator the option to buy at a fixed price a commodity or stock at a future date. Rather than take delivery on commodities or stocks, these speculators hoped to resell their contracts for a profit on settlement day. At first a special day of each month, later a special day of each quarter, was designated as the day when all future contracts were settled. Winners collected their profits on settlement day; losers could either pay up or issue a bond to finance losses and remain in the market for another round of speculation. These practices allowed Amsterdam speculators to play the market with minimum capital, giving rise to the term 'windhandel' meaning 'trading in air', a fit description of these speculative manoeuvres. To tame speculative excess the government made several efforts to ban futures speculation, which may explain why Dutch West India Company stock was never traded in futures.

The Amsterdam bourse furnished Europe with its first well-documented episodes of financial euphoria leading to a crash. Viennese travellers to Turkey, struck by the beauty of the tulip, brought the flower to Vienna in the sixteenth century, and cultivation of the tulip spread to Germany, Belgium, and then to Holland. It became a favourite flower at royal courts in Paris and England, and the public followed the aristocratic example, making tulips a booming business, and infecting the tulip market with a passion for trading in tulip futures. By the 1630s tulipmania had enveloped Dutch society from top to bottom, tulip production swallowing up most of the cultivatable land. At first speculators bought and sold tulip bulbs over the winter, but as the euphoria reached frenzy pitch, they took contracts year round for deliveries in the spring.

The chance of fortuitous mutations, caused by tulip bulbs infected with a virus, helped maintain tulipmania. Speculators anxiously waited for new mutations, knowing the public's excitement over new specimens and the high prices growers would pay for mutated specimens they could use as breeders. One rare tulip bulb was exchanged in an even trade for a successful brewery in France. Prices soared and owners of rare specimens could name their price. 'Windhandel', fully exploiting the speculative potential of puts and calls, made itself directly felt in the tulip market. Traders sold tulips they did not own, but promised to acquire in the future, and buyers purchased tulips with money they did not have. Family estates were mortgaged to pay for tulip contracts. When the tulip market crashed in 1637, it brought some of the wealthiest families and oldest merchant firms down with it. The courts were overwhelmed with lawsuits, and Dutch economic activity slid into a prolonged slump.

Such episodes of wild speculation gradually eroded public confidence in Amsterdam. In 1763, and again in 1772, the Amsterdam stock market collapsed amidst a wave of bank failures and deflation. Without discounting banks furnishing additional funds during times of financial stress, Amsterdam was left unprotected from economic cycles. London inherited what Amsterdam lost and became the new financial hub of Europe during the eighteenth century.

Like Amsterdam, London began as a financial centre taking the lead of Antwerp. Visiting the Antwerp bourse in the early 1500s, Sir Richard Gresham, an English adventurer dazzled by what he saw, took back with him to England the idea of building a similar facility in London. He won the king over but never identified a site for the construction. In 1552 his son, Thomas Gresham, received appointment as the royal agent at the Antwerp bourse. He also was swept up with excitement, and decided that London needed a similar trading facility. Drawing heavily upon the architecture of the Antwerp bourse, Gresham began construction in 1566. It was finished in 1568, and Queen Elizabeth, visiting the new trading centre in 1570, proclaimed it the Royal Exchange. Merchants and traders from every industry and country congregated at the Royal Exchange, making it the home of London's commercial activity, centre of trading in foreign exchange, stocks and commodities. Traders in different markets assembled at places called walks: 'Broker's Walk', 'Hamburg

Walk' or 'French Walk'. The Exchange was compared to scenes of Babel with traders speaking many different languages.

In 1666 the Great Fire of London destroyed the Royal Exchange, but a new structure was built, opening in 1669. The stockjobbers moved out in 1698, probably at the invitation of the Royal Exchange, and started transacting business in the coffeehouses of Exchange-alley. In the early history of the stock market, the stockjobber was an unruly sort, regarded as a rather low order of talent and defined by Samuel Johnson as 'a low wretch who gets money by buying and selling shares in funds'. Dealers in foreign stocks remained at the Royal Exchange, and dealers in government securities moved to the rotunda of the Bank of England. Commodity markets moved out as they became specialized, and in the eighteenth century the Royal Exchange became home to London's insurance business. In 1774 Lloyd's of London, getting its name from Lloyd's coffeehouse where it began, set up business in the Royal Exchange. The second Royal Exchange burned in 1838, and a third, completed in 1844, remained a trading centre until 1939.

The number of companies selling stock to raise capital began to proliferate in the last decade of the seventeenth century. Many of them, often without official government charters, aggressively marketed stock, pulling out all the stops, tantalizing potential investors with hopes of huge profits, reinforcing salesmanship with all that showmanship had to offer. One such venture, the Diving Company, proposing to recover precious cargo from sunken ships, regaled spectators with a public demonstration of its equipment, including armoured diving suits.[2] Divers looked out from a helmet through a glass portal resembling the eye of the Cyclops, and breathed through a pipe connected to the crest of the helmet and reaching the surface. London's finest ladies and gentlemen crowded the banks of the Thames at the company's invitation and partook of the company's hospitality while watching divers descend into the river and bring up old iron and ship's tackle.

Concern about the honesty of stockjobbers and stock markets, a familiar subject in an era of insider-trading scandals, surfaced early in the development of stock exchanges. An Act of Parliament provided that no one after 1 May 1697 could act as stockjobber in London, Westminster or within the Bills of Mortality without a licence from the Lord Mayor and Aldermen. The Act addressed the abuses of various brokers, stockjobbers or pretend brokers who bought and discounted 'Talleys, Bank Stock, Bank Bills, Shares, and Interest in Joint Stock and other Matter and Things', and who had conspired to 'raise or fall from time to time' the market prices of these assets. This licence to act as a broker or stockjobber vouched that licensees possessed ability, honesty and an upstanding reputation.

The publication of stock prices began in the late seventeenth century. Apparently the information came from various brokers based upon the deals they had made, and as a result the reported prices varied between publications. The *London Post* of 1-3 January 1699 listed prices of Bank of England stocks, East India Company and African companies, the Orphan Chamber, New East India Company and the Million Bank. In 1725 *The Daily Post* quoted prices on fourteen stocks, a number that grew to 22 by 1741. For most of the eighteenth century newspapers reported the prices of twenty to twenty-five stocks. After 1780 *The Annual Register* listed the monthly highs and monthly lows of individual stock prices.

The London stock exchange took up residence at Jonathan's coffee house, the regular meeting place of stockjobbers, and on 26 March 1714 a list quoting stock prices of outstanding issues was made available in the proprietor's office near Jonathan's coffee house. Stock prices of the East India Company, the African Company, bank stock and the loan of the South Sea Company could be followed on this list, and soon speculative waves of expansion and contraction could be seen rippling through stock prices quoted on this and other lists.

In 1720, within a few months of each other, London and Paris experienced major financial debacles, furnishing an early hint of the interdependence of financial markets that would develop fully over the following two centuries, culminating in the modern tendency for financial crises to take on a global dimension, and manifesting the behaviour of a global financial market that has a life of its own. The crash in the London stock market, the South Sea Bubble, can hardly be understood without an appreciation of the French financial debacle, the

Mississippi Bubble, which preceded the South Sea Bubble by a few months.

The blame for the Mississippi Bubble rests with John Law, a Scottish financier who operated on the assumption that a bank could issue paper money equalling in value all the land a country possessed. Philippe d'Orleans, new regent of France, saw Law's ideas as a possible answer to his government's bankrupt finances and in 1716 gave Law authorization to establish the Banque Generale. This might have led only to an episode of hyperinflation had not Philippe in 1717 conferred a royal charter on the Mississippi Company, a venture that Law organized to exploit the Mississippi basin and to relieve holders of French government debts. Law organized the Mississippi Company as a joint-stock company, sold 200,000 shares of stock at 500 livres per share, and accepted government notes at face value in payment for stock. Up to three-quarters of the value of a stock purchase could be paid for in these government notes, then selling at a third of face value. Holders of government notes rushed to exchange them for stock in a promising, profit-making venture, and the government blessed the project by making taxes payable in paper money issued by the Banque Generale. Emboldened by success, Law's bank purchased the royal tobacco monopoly and all French companies engaged in foreign trade, merging these acquisitions into the Mississippi Company, which then had a monopoly of French foreign trade. By 1720 Law had taken a further step toward consolidation with the merger of the Mississippi Company and the Banque Royale, a reorganized version of the Banque Generale. The Banque Royale assumed the government's debt by exchanging it for shares in the Mississippi Company, setting a fateful example that the South Sea Company in England would soon follow.

The market for shares in the Mississippi Company soon wore the aspect of a speculative mania, prices steadily spiralling upwards, partially fuelled by increases in the Banque Royale's paper money, much of which was used to purchase stock in the Mississippi Company. (It is estimated that 2,700 million livres of banknotes were issued.) Commodity prices also took off, advancing 100 per cent between 1716 and 1720, faster than wages, creating a deep distrust of paper money and big banks in the minds of the French people. By 1720 profit expectations from the Mississippi Company had dimmed, reflecting the failure to find precious metals and to attract families willing to immigrate to the Mississippi basin. As the market for Mississippi shares crumbled, sending prices into a steep downward spiral, the Banque Royale printed more paper money to bid up the prices of the shares. The Banque Royale became the scene of a panic that killed several people as besieging holders of paper money demanded redemption in gold or silver.

The next financial debacle, not involving paper money, was the South Sea Bubble of 1720, the London stock exchange's first major crash following a mania of stock speculation. It was largely driven by speculation in the stock of the South Sea Company, from which the episode got its name. In 1711 Parliament had confirmed a royal charter granted to the South Sea Company, conferring upon the company an exclusive privilege to monopolize trade with Spanish colonies in America and the Pacific Isles. Early joint-stock companies always enjoyed special relations with governments and, in 1719, the South Sea Company, borrowing a page from the Mississippi Company in France, put forth a plan, with the government's blessing, that let holders of government debt obligations swap these obligations for South Sea Company stock. The plan would put a significant share of the government's debt in the hands of the South Sea Company, which intended to charge the government less interest than it was currently paying. With the government a beneficiary of the plan, King George I let himself be made governor of the South Sea Company, and the government lent a hand in strengthening investor confidence and talking up the profits that future shareholders of the South Sea Company would reap, in light of the exclusive monopoly privilege. The offer to swap government debt for stock had been on the table only six days when two-thirds of government debt had been exchanged for South Sea Company stock.

The stock exchange saw the market for South Sea Company shares rally significantly amid this interest, lifting the price from £77 to £123.5 in 1719. As its stock price climbed, the South Sea Company floated new stock issues, taking advantage of the favourable market for raising cash. On 12 April an offer to sell additional shares at £300 per share drew a crowd of people of all social classes, sending the price to £340 in a few days. On 21 April an announcement of a 10 per cent summer dividend threw more fuel on the frenzied speculation, and the company exploited the public's eagerness, floating another round of new stock issues at £400 per share on 23 April. June saw South Sea Company shares climb to £800.

In July investors watched the price of another new issue of South Sea Company stock hit £1,000 per share. The boom lost its upward momentum when word reached the market that Spain was restricting the company's trade with America. Market downdrafts began to outweigh updrafts with the burst of the Mississippi Bubble in France and the failure of smaller companies. In August South Sea shares tumbled to £700, and in September the bottom fell out of the market as they plunged to £131. Bank failures and bankruptcies mounted as repercussions of the crash spread throughout the English economy, and the Bank of England had to fend off a run on its bank after announcing a plan to ease the crisis by purchasing shares of South Sea stock.

Fever for South Sea stock had spilled over into the market for stocks in general, touching off a burst of speculation in new stock issues of start-up companies. To attract stock-hungry investors, ventures were organized to fish for shipwrecks off the Irish coast; to insure horses and other cattle; to insure losses from servants; to render salt water fresh; to build hospitals for bastard children; to extract oil from sunflower seed; to improve malt liquors; to recover seamen's wages; to extract silver from lead; to make iron from pit coal; to import large jackasses from Spain; to trade in human hair; to fatten hogs; and to market a wheel of perpetual motion.[3] One morning an enterprising promoter sold subscriptions for two guineas a piece to finance a secret venture whose details he promised to reveal in the afternoon. After selling one thousand subscriptions the promoter disappeared without revealing the details of the venture.

The South Sea Company, seeing potential South Sea stockholders enticed into investing in stock of other companies, became a supporter of the Bubble Act of 1720, the major piece of legislation that emerged from this speculative debacle. Since the most speculative ventures were joint-stock companies acting without an official charter from Parliament, the Bubble Act sought to tame speculative excesses by making it illegal for a group of persons to organize as a joint-stock company without a charter confirmed by an act of Parliament. The Act was particularly aimed at unchartered companies promoting public subscriptions of company shares transferable by a simple sale. It also raised more hurdles for groups of individuals seeking to obtain official charters approved by Parliament. The Bubble Act, often criticized for acting as a restraint on investment spending, would remain in effect until 1825. In the name of regulating the incorporation of new companies, it may have prolonged the importance of family-based business organization at the expense of public corporations.

Despite the Bubble Act the South Sea debacle inflicted serious damage to the public's confidence in transferable shares of joint-stock companies, haunting the market in transferable shares for nearly a century, and retarding the rate of economic growth and technological innovation until the Industrial Revolution. The Mississippi Bubble helped draw the attention of the French government to the stock market, leading to the establishment in 1724 of an official exchange, formed as a separate legal entity subject to special regulations. The home of the new exchange was the Rue Vivienne, near the Palais Royal, where it remained until the Revolution. Sixty individuals were given government permission to act as brokers of stocks and loans.

Like Amsterdam, England tried to ban speculative practices that enabled speculators to earn vast profits with little capital, and left many less expert investors feeling cheated. In 1733 the English Parliament passed Sir John Barnard's Act directed against futures trading, an act that outlawed 'all wagers, puts and refusals'.[4] It aimed to ban speculative transactions, like 'puts', where no stock was expected to change hands.

Before the enactment of the Barnard legislation, individual brokers sent lists to customers of stock prices that included the prices of puts and refusals for specific times, such as twelve months, six months and three months. Sir John Barnard's Act levied a penalty of £500 against brokers, agents, scriveners and other persons found guilty of negotiating and writing contracts of puts, wagers or refusals, and imposed the same penalty on those individuals guilty of 'the frequent and mischievous practice' of selling and disposing of stock which they did not possess, a practice no doubt much more startling then than today. The Act had the effect of driving the practice underground, helped by court cases that quickly diluted its effectiveness, and was long considered obsolete when Parliament repealed it in 1868.

Speculation again reached a high pitch in the 1750s and 1760s, leading to discussions in Parliament about legislation aiming to tame speculative forces, but nothing materialized during the remainder of the eighteenth century. The speculation of the 1760s prompted charges of lenders selling stock held as collateral, against the wishes of stockowners. The practice of financing stock purchases using stock as collateral is now called 'buying on the margin', a reference to the share of the stock paid for out of hard cash and the share purchased on credit backed by the stock as collateral. The lender holding stock collateral always had the authority to sell the stock if the borrower (the speculator) defaulted on the loan, or if the stock price fell sufficiently to disable it as source of collateral. In the late 1760s lenders, using stock they were holding as collateral, borrowed funds themselves on the strength of this stock, transferring the possession of the stock to a second lender, a business transaction one step removed from the speculator who first borrowed money to purchase the stock. This second lender in turn took the stock held as collateral and borrowed funds from a third lender, transferring possession of the stock to a third lender. In 1769 the price of East India stock crashed, removing an essential linchpin in a fragile structure of credit and leading to a rash of defaulted loans. Parliament studied the problem but never addressed the issue.

France appears to have been slower in trying to regulate speculative practices. A passion for gambling, a favourite sport of the French nobility, grew to fever pitch in the last quarter of the eighteenth century, attaching itself to any suitable vehicle, at first lotteries, horseracing, chess, dominoes, and later to speculation in the stock market. In 1785 Russia's ambassador to Paris wrote to his government of the frenzied speculation on the Paris Bourse, making references to unscrupulous speculation, the foolishness of people beguiled into risking their fortunes in the stock market, the insidious manoeuvres of speculators operating without owning stock or having money, the pursuit of immoderate profits, and the likely damage these activities would have on the good reputation of the Paris Bourse in Europe.

A comparison of regulation of financial markets with regulation of interest rates in France reveals how policy instincts formed in a simpler time often miss the most important policy issues facing an economy steadily growing in complexity. While the French remained unconcerned about the wisdom and fairness of speculative practices in financial markets, they were anxious lest they should violate church doctrine on usury, by charging interest. In 1665 Louis XIV was considering the issuance of an edict capping the maximum lawful interest rate at 5 per cent. Since even this low interest rate troubled the royal conscience, Louis called an informal meeting with five of the most learned doctors of the Sorbonne, and piously laid the matter before them, perhaps praying for a theological loophole. The dean of the faculty spoke first and said that a question of such gravity must be brought before a meeting of the entire faculty. The faculty of Sorbonne gravely took the matter under consideration, reviewing Scripture, the writings of Church fathers, the decisions of various councils and decrees of Popes. After weighing the evidence carefully, one of the doctors reported the faculty's findings, saying that no doctor of the Sorbonne could approve the proposition that one could take interest on money or set the rate thereof. Despite this, however, Louis XIV issued the edict limiting interest to a maximum of 5 per cent.

None of the methods of speculation developed in Amsterdam and Paris would appear in the German exchanges until the nineteenth century. Nevertheless, Frankfurt had already embarked upon the meandering path it would follow before becoming the second largest exchange in Europe, next to London. The Frankfurt Stock Exchange can boast of a history hardly inferior to the other major stock exchanges in Europe, dating back to 1585. In the beginning bills of exchange accounted for the main business, but merchants also floated loans at Frankfurt. The exchange first published a listing of publicly offered shares in 1727. Joint-stock companies developed more slowly in Germany; trading in shares of joint-stock companies only coming to Frankfurt in 1820 after the Austrian National Bank issued shares. London was not the only stock exchange that benefited from Amsterdam's fall from grace as an international financial market at the end of the eighteenth century. Amsterdam's loss was at least partly Frankfurt's gain, marking the time when Frankfurt began to take on the character of an international financial centre. Frankfurt was already headquarters for the House of Rothschild, one of the largest and most prestigious international banking institutions. In the mid nineteenth century Frankfurt was the dominant commercial and banking centre in Germany, and held that position until 1866.

Spurring the growth of financial markets during the eighteenth century was the growth in respectability of public debt. The Spanish government had not helped the market for government obligations by suspending interest payments on its debts in 1557, 1575, 1596, 1607, 1627 and 1647. In 1797 a government of the French Revolution would repudiate two-thirds of the public debt of France. Nevertheless the eighteenth century saw rapid development in markets for public securities, and national debts became a mark of prosperity. Montesquieu, in his famous book *The Spirit of Laws*, published in 1748, echoed this view, observing, 'Some have imagined that it was for the advantage of a state to be indebted to itself: they thought that this multiplied riches by increasing the circulation.'[5] Alexander Hamilton sounded a similar theme in his *First Report on the Public Credit*, pointing out that safe government obligations gave merchants and planters a place to invest idle capital, enabling them to get by with lower profits on merchandise trade. Hamilton went so far as to argue that a public debt lowered interest rates because the public held government obligations as a substitute for gold and silver, freeing the gold and silver to be loaned out.

In England Parliament had approved the issuance of long-term government obligations in 1693 and 1694. These obligations took the form of lifetime annuities, sometimes stretching up to three lives, and tontine loans. Tontine loans resembled an annuity, but were purchased by a group of investors and interest payments were divided among them, increasing the payment to each investor as the number of surviving investors dwindled. In 1696 Parliament approved the issuance of short-term government obligations called Exchequer Bills. At first these interest-paying bills were in small denominations, around £20, and convertible into cash on demand at the Bank of England. Later in the eighteenth century the government turned to interest-paying bills redeemable after a fixed time. Tax revenue from particular sources was dedicated to the payment of interest on these bills.

As the markets for government obligations grew in efficiency, governments financed a larger share of their spending out of public borrowing. A comparison of England's public finance for the years 1702–13 against the years 1776–83 shows that the share of government spending financed by public borrowing grew from 31.4 per cent to 39.9 per cent. France was much slower in developing financial instruments and markets to float a national debt, which may explain why the French monarchy struggled with the management of a heavy public debt, eventually leading to government bankruptcy that helped push France into revolution. The methods developed to market government obligations that were transferable and could be traded, making them convertible into cash on short notice, helped make possible the growth in stock markets that financed the Industrial Revolution.

By the beginning of the nineteenth century finance assets had begun to compete with land as an attractive means of holding wealth, and both Britain and France opened the century with plans for building new stock markets. In 1773 London brokers had organized themselves as the London Stock Exchange, and in 1802 the London Stock Exchange moved to its present location in a new structure purposely built close to the Bank of England. In 1807 Napoleon issued the order for the construction of the Palais Brongiart, the home of the Paris Bourse since 1827. The nineteenth century also began with Wall Street emerging in the United States as a market for financial assets. A tree in front of 68 Wall Street furnished a shaded meeting place for early traders.

In the beginning, government obligations accounted for the bulk of Wall Street trading activity. The new US government had issued federal bonds paying 6 per cent to redeem state bonds issued during the Revolutionary war and individual states issued new bonds to finance internal improvement. In 1792 twenty-four Wall Street brokers organized themselves as a group specializing in the brokerage of financial instruments, establishing minimum rates and agreeing to favour each other. The next year the Tontine Coffee House at the corner of Wall and Williams streets became the seat of the Wall Street stock market. In 1817 Wall Street brokers established themselves in a more formal body, the New York Stock and Exchange Board, an organization that operated as a private club with initiation fees, consisting at first of eight firms and nineteen individual members. New members had to be voted in and three negative votes blackballed a potential member. The New York Stock Exchange is sometimes called the Big Board, a reference to a blackboard that was used to post the prices of securities in the early days. There were no reporting requirements that companies had to meet before their stock could be listed, and prices were set from offers to buy or sell tendered when the name of a stock was called out. In the 1830s volume rose to one thousand shares traded per day, a number that would rise to over one million on 15 December 1886. Before 1840 payments on most trades were not settled for six to twelve months after the transaction, minimizing the capital that brokers needed to play the stock market, and encouraging speculation. Thereafter for a while settlements were customarily made at sixty days; gradually following day settlements became customary.

The Panic of 1837 established Wall Street as the financial centre of the United States. New York's major rival was Philadelphia, headquarters for the First Bank of the United States (the first US experiment with a central bank), and home to some of the largest merchant bankers of the day. The English merchant banker John Baring, later of Baring Brothers and Company, had opened a Philadelphia office in 1783, founding what would be the largest banking house in America before the Civil War, handling such deals as financing the Louisiana Purchase for the US government. In the Panic of 1837 the state of Pennsylvania suspended payments on its state bonds, throwing into confusion the numerous Pennsylvanian banks that held these bonds and shaking the public's faith in the financial markets of Philadelphia. The state of New York met its obligations to pay interest on its bonds, and from that time began to overtake Philadelphia as the financial centre of the United States.

As New York displaced Philadelphia in the United States, London came to subsume all the regional markets in Britain, creating the most highly organized market in the world, and becoming the premier world financial market in the nineteenth century. The bulk of the trade on the London Stock Exchange involved government securities, mostly British, but there was trading in stocks and shares of joint-stock companies engaged in insurance, banking, gas and water works, docks, canals and railways, and a few miscellaneous companies. As late as 1840, however, nearly 90 per cent of the issues traded were obligations of British and foreign governments.

At first London had been just the largest among a number of regional markets, trading largely in companies headquartered in London. As late as 1840 only 37 per cent of the Scottish securities in existence had been heard of in London, and that percentage existed only because of the amount of information that was routinely copied from lists supplied by Edinburgh brokers. Regional markets in Manchester, Glasgow and Edinburgh traded in ignorance of market conditions in London, and fluctuated in step with regional shifts in supply and demand. A study of stock prices in London and Glasgow in 1846, the year before the telegraph linked these two markets, showed that only in 30 per cent of the stocks was there any overlapping or matching of closing prices between the two markets. For the remaining stocks, the lowest price on the London market was higher than the highest price on the Glasgow market, or vice versa. The divergence of prices of individual stocks between the two markets averaged 10.5 per cent.

The late 1840s saw major British cities linked by telegraph service, too unreliable at first for brokers to incorporate it into routine business. By the early 1850s, however, the telegraph was making itself felt in security markets, and over the remainder of the century special wires were set up connecting regional stock exchanges.[6] Telegraph offices were opened either within or adjacent to stock exchanges. Between 1870 and 1899 the number of special wires linking the London Stock Exchange with regional exchanges grew from eleven to almost sixty, and the number of daily telegraph messages sent from the London Stock Exchange office increased from a maximum of 2,884 to 28,142. A comparison of two stocks common to the London and Glasgow markets, the Caledonian Railway and the Grand Trunk Railway of Canada, revealed that these stocks closed with matching prices on these markets 2.6 times more often in 1860 than in 1846. The divergence in prices had also narrowed by 1860 to only 7 per cent of what it had been in 1846, forcing the conclusion that the markets were beginning to fluctuate in step with each other.

A second development contributing to the integration of the British stock market was the growth in securities traded on multiple markets. Railway companies serving numerous towns and cities attracted investors from a broad range of regions, and their stocks found a market on more than one exchange. Railway firms that acquired other companies saw their stocks listed on numerous exchanges. By the end of 1845 the Glasgow Stock Exchange quoted the stocks of 110 railway companies, of which 23 were also quoted on the London Stock Exchange. Because of mergers and acquisitions, the number of railway stocks quoted on the Glasgow Exchange had fallen to 46 by 1860, but 27 of those were listed on the London Stock Exchange, a significant percentage increase in Glasgow railway stocks traded in London. By 1910 only a small fraction of British railway securities were listed on just one exchange. With improved communication between regional exchanges and increasing numbers of securities listed at more than one exchange, the London Stock Exchange became the centre of an integrated British market in financial securities. Local shifts in supply and demand for securities caused flows of securities to other regional markets rather than fluctuations in local security prices.

Another improvement in communication came with the introduction of the ticker, an American invention that printed out lists of ticker symbols and prices. In 1867 Edward A. Calahan, an operator for the American Telegraph Company, patented the first version of the ticker. The Gold and Stock Telegraph Company, formed with Calahan's help, began manufacturing and leasing ticker machines to brokerages for $6 a week in the United States. Ticker symbols had evolved quickly, soon after the telegraph service had appeared in financial markets, the result of telegraph operators saving wire space by making up abbreviations for firms, sometimes using one-letter symbols for actively traded stocks. For a subscription fee the ticker furnished a continuous record of prices, with only momentary delay, to those not on the floor of the exchange, including brokers and clients in private offices, and market participants at other exchanges. The ticker tape made its appearance on the London Stock Exchange in 1872.

The following decade saw market participants adopt the telephone as a common tool of trading. Anyone with a telephone could have instant access to the floor of the stock exchange, creating an extended market, beyond the confines of the stock exchange floor, and enabling trades to take place outside the stock exchange at prices that closely followed prices at the exchange. The market was no longer made up of traders who happened to be on the floor at the time. At first these extended markets were kept within city boundaries by the awkward, slow and unreliable nature of long-distance telephone services connecting regional exchanges. In Britain the development of long-distance telephone services was further hampered by the Post Office's monopoly of telecommunications.

During the 1890s direct lines connecting the London Stock Exchange with regional exchanges came into service. The use of direct lines caught on immediately, notwithstanding many complaints about quality of service, and quickly overburdened a fledgling system. In London members of the exchange had to make reservations in advance to use a direct telephone line to a provincial exchange, and in Glasgow access to the London line had to be rationed, in addition to limiting each member to one call every six minutes. By 1900 an artery of inter-market lines bypassing public telephone lines linked the London Stock Exchange and provincial exchanges. Traders could access this through their office telephones, connecting members of the London Stock Exchange with members of the provincial stock exchanges. In 1908 the month of October saw 81,883 outgoing calls from the London Stock Exchange and 23,916 incoming, averaging one call made every six seconds and one received every 21 seconds during the working day. These calls went through stock exchange telephones linked to brokers' offices.

With the full development of telephone communication between provincial markets, a revolution in communications was complete, leaving geographical separation of provincial markets a minor factor in Britain, the forces acting on the market now national in scope. Prices in all provincial markets could be monitored simultaneously, enabling speculators to engage in profitable arbitrage whenever a security sold for a lower price in one market than in another, keeping the national market in equilibrium and creating a more receptive market for all securities. These arbitrageurs became known as 'shunters', and buying securities on one market and selling it on another market was called 'shunting', a practice that in London came to be concentrated in the hands of a few members of the London Stock Exchange. A similar specialization evolved on the provincial markets. The profit made on shunting deals was shared equally between the shunter where a security was purchased, and the market where it was sold. Shunters in each market kept their correspondents in other markets constantly informed of local prices, price discrepancies were quickly exploited, and London dealers quoted prices and maintained an active market for many securities primarily traded on provincial markets.

As the British securities market evolved towards complete integration, provincial markets lost their role as self-contained regional security markets trading in a broad range of securities, and began to specialize in specific sectors of a national market. Glasgow specialized in iron and coal, Cardiff in shipping, and Liverpool in insurance. The location of a specialist market was unimportant, since shunting operations and the operations of London dealers gave investors throughout the country equal access to the market through their local brokers. The market for government debt, such as British Consols, remained at the London Stock Exchange, where all orders were directed. As late as 1900 government securities, British and foreign, accounted for more than half of the paid-up capital of securities quoted on the London Stock Exchange. Foreign and British railway stocks quoted on the London Stock Exchange, measured in paid-up capital, equalled about 80 per cent of the value of the government securities. Remaining sectors: mining, financial services and other services accounted for less than 15 per cent of the value of securities. At the same time railway securities accounted for nearly two-thirds of the value of securities quoted on the Glasgow Stock Exchange.

With growth in security trading, in the number of securities, and technological advancement, the number of members of the London Stock Exchange grew from 864 in 1850 to 2,000 in 1875, and reached 5,567 in 1905. Much of the income to the London Stock Exchange came from subscription fees paid by members, giving the exchange an incentive to attract new owners and keep fees low enough to discourage the formation of a rival exchange.

As the London and the New York stock exchanges grew in the nineteenth century, the Frankfurt Stock Exchange saw itself sidetracked. In the later nineteenth century Berlin, capital of the newly unified Germany, grew rapidly as a commercial and financial centre, eclipsing Frankfurt as financial capital of the German Empire. Berlin did not have a stock exchange until the early decades of the eighteenth century. The growth of Berlin seemed to be a case of financial power following political power. Banks formerly headquartered in Frankfurt moved to Berlin, and the Reichbank, the central bank of the German Empire, resided in Berlin. The concentration of banking gave an edge to the Berlin stock market, which gained ascendancy over Frankfurt. Then Berlin experienced a boom in real estate and stock prices and in 1872 and 1873 a frenzy of stock market speculation ended in a crash. Apparently a speculative debacle in Germany had never been followed by so many suicides. Frankfurt remained a regional financial centre of international importance. In 1914 the Frankfurt exchange listed about 1,500 securities, including stocks of 51 foreign corporations, and 388 foreign bonds.

The same forces shaping the growth and development of the London Stock Exchange during the nineteenth century made themselves felt in the growth and development of the European stock exchanges and New York Stock Exchange. On both Frankfurt and London stock exchanges railway stocks dominated trade in corporate stocks and technological improvements in communication were rapidly assimilated. London and Frankfurt quoted stocks from companies headquartered in foreign countries, but the New York Stock Exchange remained a centre for trading in stocks of American companies. On 15 December 1886 the New York Stock Exchange saw more than 1 million shares change hands in one day for the first time.

Unlike London, the New York Stock Exchange took on the characteristics of an exclusive club, restricting membership to a fixed number which never exceeded 1,100 before 1914.[7] In 1866 membership cost $10,000, and in 1868 memberships became property saleable by their owners, forcing new members to pay membership costs plus the cost of an existing member's seat. The price of seats fluctuated with the prosperity of the market, but rose in cost over time, ranging between $4,000 and $4,500 in 1870, and between $64,000 and $94,000 in 1910. The members of the New York Stock Exchange owned the building and facilities, and were eager to introduce the telegraph, ticker machine and telephone as a means of keeping members informed when they were not on the floor. In London the owners of the exchange were a different group from the members and not as interested in sharing what was transpiring on the floor with people who had not paid membership fees. The New York Stock Exchange fixed the commissions charged by its members, leaving no room for price competition, while the London Stock Exchange, until 1912, allowed brokers flexibility in fees charged to clients, allowing special deals for large clients such as banks, financial institutions and the like.[8]

The restrictive nature of the New York Stock Exchange explains the emergence of rival exchanges in New York, a phenomenon that never occurred in London to a significant extent because of its relatively open membership policies.[9] In the 1840s the corner of Wall Street and Hanover Street became the scene of trade in unlisted securities, creating what was called the Outdoor Curb Market. The market gradually shifted south along Broad Street and survived informally until the foundation of the New York Curb Agency in 1908 and the organization of the New York Curb Market with official trading rules and ticker in 1911. In 1921 this market equipped itself with ticker tape service, moved indoors at 86 Trinity Place, and later changed its name to the New York Curb Exchange before becoming the American Stock Exchange in 1953.

The New York Stock Exchange, unlike London, allowed members to join other exchanges outside New York City, and brokering firms in cities with regional exchanges joined both their regional exchange and the New York Stock Exchange, putting them in a position to capitalize on temporary stock price differences between exchanges, and facilitating the integration of a national stock market.[10] Intra-firm arbitrage was not looked upon with favour by the New York Stock Exchange, prompting periodic actions to discourage it, including banning the continuous transmission of security prices in 1898.

By 1912, the roster of New York Stock Exchange members included 106 out-of-town stock brokering firms headquartered in 22 different cities, and 258 New York firms had branches in other cities. Transactions originating out-of-town accounted for an estimated 48 per cent of all transactions on the New York Stock Exchange in 1913. London was a major competitor for the New York Stock Exchange, even in the market for United States securities, and in 1911 New York took steps to prevent New York brokering firms from participating in shared deals that split commissions with members of the London Stock Exchange.

Aside from membership the restrictive philosophy of the New York Stock Exchange also manifested itself in limitations on the kinds of securities quoted. London, consistent with its open approach to membership, was much more open to types of securities quoted, and size of companies. Early in the nineteenth century neither exchange tried to regulate the types of securities quoted, but as the number of securities grew the exchanges felt pressure to be selective. London imposed a rule of excluding firms with paid-up capital of less than £100,000, but made numerous exceptions, particularly for firms headquartered in London. In practice any security that commanded a significant market was quoted on the London Stock Exchange. The New York Stock Exchange followed a much more exclusive policy, helping to explain why, in 1902, the value of the securities traded on its exchange equalled only about one-third of the value of the securities traded in London.[11] By 1914 the average value of the stock issues of commercial and industrial companies quoted on the New York Exchange equalled $24.7 million, while the average size of the stock issues for commercial and industrial firms quoted on the London Stock Exchange was £1.03 million, suggesting that companies quoted on the New York Exchange were on average about five times larger than companies quoted on the London Exchange. New York refused to quote securities of state and local governments if they were too small, and refused to quote the securities of mining and petroleum companies because they were judged too risky, a judgement never made on the London Stock Exchange. The New York Stock Exchange accepted companies for listing that had developed beyond the formative stage, and whose securities already enjoyed a market outside the exchange. The privileged access to the floor of the New York Stock Exchange given to capital intensive and well-established companies may have accelerated the movement towards mergers and ever larger corporations in the United States, since these companies had much greater potential to raise capital than their smaller brethren, whose stock was not as marketable or as useful as collateral. In Britain, around the turn of the century, the trend toward mergers and bigness was not quite so pronounced, partly because small companies still had access to the London Stock Exchange, making their stocks, quickly convertible into cash, more valuable to stockholders.

On 3 July 1884 Charles Dow published his first market average, the beginning of what would become the Dow Jones Industrial Average (DJIA), one of the most influential stock market barometers in the world. In 1882 Dow, an established financial reporter, joining with Edward D. Jones and Charles M. Bergstresser, had formed Dow, Jones & Company, which began by publishing a daily financial newsletter, but was soon publishing a two-page newspaper, the *Customer's Afternoon Letter*, which became the *Wall Street Journal* in 1889. The first Dow average (apparently Jones and Bergstresser had nothing to do with developing the DJIA) was calculated from the stocks of eleven companies: nine railroad and two industrial companies, one of which was General Electric, the only stock on the original

list that remains on the DJIA until the present day without changing its name. In 1885 the number of railroad stocks grew from
nine to eleven, adding Pacific Mail Steamship and Western
Union, but industrial stocks remained at two, increasing the
concentration of railroad stocks, which dominated the Dow at
first, being the most actively traded stocks at that time. In 1896
Dow cut back the number of stocks to twelve, where it remained
until 1916, long after Dow's death in 1902. Industrials gradually
took on a larger role in the calculation of Dow's average and on
26 May 1896 Dow published the first all-industrial average.[12]

Dow's average was an unweighted arithmetic mean, calculated by summing the values of the stocks and dividing by the
number of stocks. In 1916 the number of stocks listed on the
DJIA grew to twenty and, in 1928, thirty, where it has remained
until the present day. The composition of the DJIA has changed,
of course. Currently it remains an unweighted average, but the
sum of stock values is divided by a divisor adjusted for stock
splits and changes in the composition of stocks. This method
attaches greater importance to higher-value stocks, but not to
companies with larger numbers of outstanding shares. The
company with the smallest number of outstanding shares exerts
the same influence as that with the largest.

Panics on the stock market invariably left some investors feeling swindled and cheated, and reinforced feelings that markets
were rigged and could be manipulated. In the US the panic of
1907 raised strong concerns about stock market manipulation,
and both the State of New York and the United States Congress
launched investigations. John Pierpont Morgan Jr had organized a group of investors to inject liquidity into markets, perhaps further fuelling suspicion that groups of insiders had much
better information about the prospects for the stock market.
Morgan testified before a congressional committee, but World
War I diverted attention before action could be taken.

The stock market crash of 1929 sparked renewed concern
about the operation of stock markets, and the potential for fraud
and dishonesty. The US Congress, against vigorous lobbying
from Wall Street, enacted the Securities and Exchange Act of
1934, a far-reaching piece of legislation that forms the basis for
the regulation of US stock exchanges and stock trading today.

This Act provided for the establishment of the Securities and Exchange Commission (SEC), composed of five members and a chairperson.

Companies whose stocks are listed on one of the thirteen largest US stock exchanges must furnish the SEC with detailed financial reports. Even unlisted companies must file a detailed financial report if they have a million dollars in assets and at least five hundred stockholders. Newly issued securities cannot be publicly offered for sale until they are registered with the SEC, furnishing the SEC with a detailed financial report and the proposed prospectus advertising the stock to potential investors. SEC accountants will examine the prospectus in light of the financial statement, and can halt the sale of the stock if it is misleading.

The SEC requires that companies submit reports to the exchanges disclosing information that might expose manipulation or rigging of stock prices. Wash sales, sales between members of the same group, are expressly prohibited. These sales were a means of registering artificially high transaction prices and deceiving less informed investors about the value of a stock. The SEC also banned aggregations of funds or pools that exist for the purpose of manipulating stock prices. The SEC receives monthly reports on stock transactions of officers, directors and major stockholders of corporations, and requires that short-term profits of these transactions stay with the corporation. The SEC also regulates elections for Boards of Directors of corporations, including the use of proxy votes.

In 1975 the Securities and Exchange Commission forced the New York and other exchanges to give up the practice of fixing minimum commission rates for all brokers, freeing brokers to engage in price competition. Major brokerage firms went out of business as commission rates plummeted. Deregulation opened the field for discount brokers who provided minimal service but charged low commissions for speculators not needing the help of full service brokers, starting a trend that received substantial impetus from computing and the Internet in the 1990s.

The Securities and Exchange Act of 1934 declared it 'unlawful for any person to engage in any act that operates as a fraud or deceit upon any person, in connection with purchase or sale of any security', intending to ban the kind of insider trading that became a scandal in the 1980s. Insider trading occurs when company insiders use information that is useful for speculation but not available to average investors. The early 1980s saw a burst of insider-trading scandals, prompting the SEC to bring 51 cases to court between 1980 and 1984. Lawyers, accountants, corporate executives and relatives took advantage of knowledge of planned mergers and acquisitions to engage in insider trading, knowing that a company's stock would go up when it became a known target of a takeover. A law firm typist earned $50,000 in one day's speculation from inside information.

At centre stage of the most notorious insider-trading scandals of the 1980s stood Ivan Boesky. Boesky specialized in buying up stocks of companies he regarded as good takeover targets, holding the stock while he and corporate raiders drove up the price, and selling out for huge profits just when the price had become high enough to entice the majority of stockholders to sell out. Boesky's speculation remained legal as long as he was acting without insider information, or was not spreading false rumours that a company was about to become a takeover target. However, it was learned that Carl Icahn, Chairman of TWA, had conspired with Boesky to propagate the rumour that Gulf and Western Corporation was a takeover target, solely for the purpose of driving up its price. Boesky also received insider information from Michael Milkin, senior executive vice-president of Drexel, Burnham, and Lambert of New York City, and an early promoter of junk bonds, the low-grade, high-interest bonds that corporate raiders used to finance takeovers. Milkin's involvement in raising vast sums of capital to finance corporate takeovers gave him the kind of insider information that could guarantee huge profits in the stock market; information that he illegally shared with Boesky. Boesky was secretly holding stock for Drexel at Milkin's request, allowing Drexel to speculate in stock with insider information. It was later learned that Milkin, known as the king of junk bonds, averaged over $10 million per week during his insider-trading activity. In September 1988 the SEC filed charges against Drexel and Milkin, charging fraudulent manipulation of stock prices in sixteen different takeover situations. Milkin paid a heavy fine and spent time in prison, and

Drexel, also facing heavy fines, went out of business.

As insider-trading scandals topped business stories in the 1980s, Congress acted, passing the Insider Trading Sanctions Act of 1984 and the Insider Trading Securities Enforcement Act of 1988. These acts raised legal obstacles to insider trading, codifying previous insider-trading law, and clearly defining insider trading as a breach of trust.

After World War II the London and New York stock exchanges remained premier global financial centres, but two new markets arose to rival them. Frankfurt Stock Exchange did not take a straight path to become the second largest stock exchange in Europe. We have seen how Berlin eclipsed Frankfurt as the financial capital of Germany after German unification, though Frankfurt remained as an international market of lesser importance. The worldwide depression of the 1930s brought a brief suspension of trading on the Frankfurt Stock Exchange, and in 1944 an air raid destroyed the trading floor. However, Berlin's situation after World War II, as a divided city geographically positioned in East Germany, ruined its career as financial capital of Germany. The part of Germany occupied by the Allies encompassed three regional financial markets of approximately equal size and importance. Two, Hamburg and Dusseldorf, fell in the British zone, Frankfurt in the American zone.

Frankfurt pulled ahead to become the financial capital of West Germany, and later unified Germany. One factor giving Frankfurt the advantage over Hamburg and Dusseldorf was its role as administrative capital of the American zone, including the headquarters of the American military forces. American multinational corporations reopened their German offices in Frankfurt. Also weighing in Frankfurt's favour was the decision to locate the headquarters for the Deutsche Bundesbank, the central bank of West Germany, in Frankfurt.

After World War II the West German economy was the fastest growing economy in Europe, with one of the best inflation records, winning worldwide respect for the Deutschmark, and lifting Frankfurt to the stature of one of the world's leading financial centres. The attraction of banking and multinational corporations probably gave the impetus of strong growth to the Frankfurt Stock Exchange. After the unification of

Germany, Frankfurt accounted for nearly 70 per cent of total share trading volume in Germany, the remaining volume occurring at seven other regional exchanges in Germany, the largest at Dusseldorf which accounts for about 12 per cent of share trading in Germany.

Foreign investors are active in the Frankfurt stock market. The participation of foreign investors falls in the 20 per cent range for all German shares, and in the 30 to 40 per cent range for blue-chip German shares. Institutional investors from Britain account for the largest number, followed by investors from the rest of Europe and the United States. The influence of foreign investors is directly felt on German share prices. In 1998 the London Stock Exchange and the Frankfurt Stock Exchange announced plans for a merger, a decision that did not please other regional exchanges in Germany; these plans have now been cancelled.

The Tokyo Stock Exchange, the second largest stock exchange today after New York, graduated to its position as a world-class financial market after a relatively brief history. During the last quarter of the nineteenth century Japan began developing financial institutions patterned after Western models, at least after the way these models were understood by the Japanese. In May 1878 Tokyo became the seat of a newly created exchange, the Tokyo Stock Exchange Co. Ltd. It was a profit-making institution and would remain in business until the beginning of World War II. The unique brand of finance capitalism developed in Japan may have restricted the growth of the Tokyo stock market at first. Shares were often held by banks and cross-holding of shares tied Japanese corporations together, practices that have continued to the present day. The banks exerted their influence largely to avoid speculative swings.

At the beginning of World War II the Nippon Securities Exchange, a semi-government organization, superseded the Tokyo Stock Exchange Co. Ltd., and enjoyed a brief existence for the duration of the war. After the dissolution of the Nippon Securities Exchange in 1945, all stock trades took place in an over-the-counter market until 1949, when the government inaugurated new stock exchanges in Tokyo, Osaka and Nagoya, and subsequently in Kyoto, Hiroshima, Fukuoka, Niigata and

Saporo. The Tokyo Stock Exchange, modelled after the New York Stock Exchange, accounts for about two-thirds of all stock transactions in Japan.

Post World War II the Japanese economy experienced robust growth to such an extent that economists felt a need to explain the secret of the 'Japanese Miracle'. During the first three decades following World War II, however, Japan's international stature as a global financial centre remained modest, mainly because its Ministry of Finance clung to isolationist policies as far as foreign access to Japanese financial markets was concerned. During this time the Ministry of Finance stood firmly in favour of low interest rates, stable financial markets and minimal competition between financial institutions. To maintain these policies the Ministry subjected domestic interest rates to rigid regulation, and restricted foreign access to Japanese financial markets, policies that added up to the complete isolation of Japanese financial markets from the forces at work in global financial markets. Foreign companies hoping to raise capital in Japanese equity markets also faced grim hurdles defined in terms of minimum profits, minimum dividends, specification of number of shares available to Japanese investors, and other conditions. As late as 1976 these kinds of barriers kept to a tiny handful the number of foreign issues traded on the Tokyo Exchange.

In the 1970s Japan began lifting regulations on its financial markets, and continued to take major steps towards deregulation of its financial markets to 1984. By 1981 foreigners owned about 20 per cent of shares traded on the Tokyo Stock Exchange, a percentage that declined in the 1990s after a major retreat in stock prices. The liberalization of Japanese financial markets, combined with the Bank of Japan's easy monetary policy, sent the Japanese stock market into speculative frenzy from 1986 to 1990, lifting the Nikkei index, the most important index of stock prices on the Tokyo Exchange, from 12,000 to 39,000. In 1990 stock prices began a prolonged retreat, reaching a low level of 15,000 in 1992. The crash led the Japanese economy into an era of economic sluggishness from which it had not recovered by the end of the century.

THREE

Gold and Silver: Aristocrats of Monetary Standards

The varied monetary standards fall cleanly into one of two categories, commodity monetary standards and inconvertible paper standards. A commodity monetary standard exists when some tantalizing commodity circulates as a lubricating instrument of exchange and acts as a measuring unit of account, a means for rating goods and services, expressing prices and comparing values. Jingling gold and silver come immediately to mind because of the shining history they enjoyed as monetary metals, but a substantial range of commodities have filled the shoes of money. In the 1800s the Canadian trading posts of the Hudson Bay Company kept accounts and measured profits and sales in terms of furs.[1] In the early twentieth century a goat standard prevailed in Uganda and each district commissioner of Uganda as part of his official duties adjudicated disputes arising when a creditor regarded a particular goat as too old or scraggy for acceptance as a standard goat in the payment of a debt.[2] Tobacco acted as a medium of exchange in colonial Virginia, officially sanctioned to the extent that public officials and clergy received wage payments in tobacco.[3]

During the Middle Ages gold and silver virtually disappeared in Europe, but silver reappeared in the late medieval period. Pepin the Short, Charlemagne's father, around 755 established a silver standard, sometimes called the Carolingian system. Under this system one pound of silver equalled twenty shillings, which in turn equalled 240 pennies. The Carolingian coinage system spread throughout Europe with the conquest of Charlemagne, the last vestige of it surviving until 1971, when England became the last European country to abandon the Carolingian system in favour of a decimalized currency.

Perhaps the disappearance of precious metals during the Middle Ages created the lust and worship for gold evident many generations later in the gruelling expedition of 1896, in which 30,000 prospectors crossed a US mountain range in Arctic conditions, and founded Dawson City, where they held out against hunger and starvation as salt rivalled gold in value. Long before that heroic trial of endurance, Spain explored and conquered much of the Americas in search of the mythical city of El Dorado, fabulously rich in gold according to Indian legend. And then there was Sir Isaac Newton, one of history's towering scientific geniuses. Perhaps it is only coincidental that Newton, master of the London mint from 1699 to 1726, was an energetic student of alchemy, searching for a means to transmute base metals into gold. For years he patiently performed experiments in alchemy, leaving manuscripts of 100,000 words. King Charles II of England built his own laboratory for experimentation in alchemy. The laboratory was connected to his bedchamber by a secret staircase. Even artists fell prey to the idolization of gold. During the seventeenth century Dutch and Northern European painters often featured metallic coinage in scenes of bankers counting money, tables adorned with coins, men procuring women with coins, and women weighing gold in balance scales. Scenes of alchemists at work, and group pictures of mint masters and assistants, also figured in the works of Dutch painters. Taken together these morsels from the history of gold remind us of the power it wielded over the minds and souls of governments and peoples until recent times.

In the mid thirteenth century Florence and Genoa began the coinage of gold and Venice adopted the gold standard during the fourteenth century. After the reintroduction of gold into Europe, many European countries minted both gold and silver coins but remained officially on a silver standard, or a bimetallic monetary standard that made use of both gold and silver at official rates of conversion. The almost universal acceptance of the gold standard during the latter part of the nineteenth century ended the bimetallic monetary systems.

An inconvertible paper monetary system is a system in which paper money circulates as a medium of exchange, and is not convertible into a commodity such as gold at an official rate.

The economic factors favouring the adoption of paper money can be easily gleaned from a relatively short span in the monetary history of Sweden, one of the first countries to introduce paper money. In 1625 Sweden monetized copper, creating a bimetallic standard of copper and silver, which replaced a silver standard that Sweden, with the rest of Europe, had inherited from the medieval period. The motivation for the adoption of copper lay in the desire to increase the demand for this resource of Sweden, where copper mining was a major industry. The Swedish government reasoned that drawing copper into circulation as money reduced the copper available for industrial purposes, driving up copper prices. As happened in most bimetallic systems one metal, in this case copper, was overvalued, thus driving out the other metal and creating a de facto single metallic standard, copper in the case of Sweden.

Because an ounce of silver was worth about a hundred times the value of an ounce of copper, copper coins were large, approximately a hundred times the size of silver coins of comparable value. People carried coins on their backs, and horse carts carrying money were not uncommon. Probably the heaviest coin in history came out of a Swedish mint in 1644, a ten-daler copper plate weighing over 43 lb. Swedish copper mines discovered the convenience of paying miners in copper notes, redeemable into copper, rather than bulky copper. These notes were preferred above copper itself, and traded at a premium over copper coins. In 1661 the Riksbank, a private Swedish bank formed in 1656, issued Europe's first banknotes redeemable into a precious metal. Despite the bank's difficulty in maintaining convertibility, the public showed a decided preference for banknotes over heavy copper coinage. In 1668 the Swedish government assumed ownership of the Riksbank, establishing the world's first central bank, still in existence today. Between 1741 and 1743 war with Russia put a severe strain on Sweden's financial resources, pressuring the Swedish government to resort to the printing press, an expedient often repeated by future governments in similar straits. Despite vast increases in the quantity of banknotes, Sweden was able to remain on a copper standard until 1745 because the costs and inconvenience of transporting copper discouraged holders of banknotes from converting them, reducing the drain on copper reserves.

The Swedish government clung to the practice of rapid banknote expansion, and by 1745 the copper standard was no longer tenable, leading to the government's suspension of banknote convertibility and putting Sweden on an inconvertible paper standard. The public accepted the suspension of convertibility without panic, but domestic inflation and currency depreciation in foreign exchange markets advanced to the forefront of economic and political issues. Currency depreciation increased the prices of imported goods while domestic inflation drove up the prices of goods produced at home.

During the time of Sweden's monetary disorder, two parties, the 'Hats' and the 'Caps' vied for power in Sweden's parliamentary government. The Hats promoted inflationary policies to finance the government expenditures needed to maintain Sweden's position as a European power. The Caps, originally called 'Nightcaps' because they wanted to sleep while the rest of Europe passed Sweden by, favoured disinflationary policies. Sweden alternated between inflation and disinflation, the political environment soon mirroring the economic turmoil, and in 1772 a bloodless *coup d'état* overthrew Sweden's parliamentary government, replacing it with a constitutional monarchy. In 1776 the new government adopted the silver standard, discontinuing the issuance of inconvertible banknotes and severing all links with the copper standard. Banknotes remained in circulation, convertible into silver.

Until the twentieth century inconvertible paper standards existed mainly as wartime expedients. England suspended the convertibility of the pound sterling during the Napoleonic Wars, and France issued inconvertible paper money during the French Revolution. Governments around the world suspended convertibility during World War I. When the depression of the 1930s forced governments to suspend convertibility again, metallic monetary standards lost credibility and inconvertible paper money became issued on a permanent basis. The US government continued to convert paper money into gold at the request of finance officials of foreign governments until 1971. Today the inconvertible paper standard, reigning supreme throughout the world, boasts no serious rivals.

The eighteenth century would find much of Europe officially on a silver standard with gold gaining ground on silver,
particularly in England. England reformed its currency in 1696,
restoring the silver content in the coinage that had been lost due
to clipping and wear. This restoration increased the silver content relative to the face value of each silver coin, which
increased the amount of silver that could be purchased with
gold coins. It also increased the amount of silver needed to purchase gold, essentially raising the price of gold in England. The
result of this currency reform was to cause gold to flow into
England, and silver advanced in payment for gold flowed out.
Gold coinage replaced silver coinage, paving the way for
England's official adoption of the gold standard early in the
nineteenth century.

France shared with England the common inheritance of the
Carolingian monetary reform of the eighth century. In France
the system set one livre (originally a pound of silver) equal to
twenty sols, and each sol equalled twelve deniers. France began
reforming its monetary system during the French Revolution,
but the implementation of the reforms was lost in revolutionary
chaos, and they were not carried out consistently until
Napoleon's government consolidated them in the Monetary
Law of 1803. This law changed the French monetary unit of
account from the livre to the franc, and replaced the
Carolingian coinage system with a decimalized currency in
which one franc equalled ten dixiemes, which in turn equalled a
hundred centimes. Only Russia and the United States preceded
France in the adoption of a decimalized currency.

More importantly, the Monetary Law of 1803 established a
silver equivalent of the franc, and a gold equivalent, a bimetallic
monetary system. The precious metal contents of the silver
franc and the gold franc established an official price between
gold and silver based upon a ratio of 15.5 to 1, meaning that a
gram of gold was 15.5 times as valuable as a gram of silver. Both
gold and silver coins circulated and anyone could bring gold or
silver to the mint for coinage. The official conversion ratio of
15–16 to 1 remained in effect until 1870 when silver began to
lose value significantly, forcing France and other bimetallic
countries to shift to the gold standard. Until the 1870s France

remained a strong proponent of the bimetallic system, while Britain advanced the gold standard.

After a century of operating an unofficial gold standard, Britain officially adopted it when Parliament enacted the Liverpool Act of 1816. Parliament had tacitly approved the unofficial gold standard, which existed because the market price of silver under Britain's official bimetallic system was above the mint price in Britain, which meant that no silver was brought to the mint for coinage, leaving only gold coinage in circulation. In 1785 the market price of silver tumbled, triggering an inflow of silver to the mint and threatening to derail Britain's de facto gold standard. Parliament immediately took action prohibiting the Mint from purchasing silver for coinage, but baulked at taking further steps to reform the coinage without more study. War with France intervened, putting pressure on the financial system and leading to the introduction of an inconvertible paper standard by 1797. Coinage questions advanced to the front ranks of political issues largely out of mistrust for the inconvertible standard and agitation for a reinstatement of the gold standard. There was also a call for the reform of the silver coinage.

In 1798 Parliament formed the Committee of the Privy Council on the State of the Coinage to study reform, but this Committee opted not to make recommendations until the end of the war with France. After the defeat of Napoleon it issued a report recommending the establishment of a gold standard, the unlimited coinage of gold brought to the mint, and the limited coinage of silver as a subsidiary coinage. Parliament immediately approved the Committee's recommendations in the Liverpool Act of 1816.

The Committee had recommended that the weight and denominations of the gold coins remain unchanged, but the silver coins took on rather a token coinage aspect. Under the recommendations, the Mint was to purchase silver for 62 shillings per pound, and issue silver coins with face values of 66 shillings per pound, reducing the silver content relative to the face value. The modest reduction in silver content removed the incentive to melt down the silver coins without giving counterfeiters an incentive to manufacture fake coins. These silver coins were legal tender for amounts up to 40 shillings. The creation of a subsidiary silver coinage set a precedent that would spread to most other countries as the gold standard displaced the bimetallic standard in the latter part of the nineteenth century.

While the Act of 1816 put Britain officially on a gold standard, it did not provide for the resumption of banknote convertibility into gold specie, a necessary condition for the gold standard to become operational. In 1819 Parliament enacted legislation providing for resumption by 1823, but the Bank of England was able to resume convertibility by 1821. In the course of the nineteenth century Britain developed a gold standard in which the Bank of England became the custodian of the nation's gold reserves, maintaining the convertibility of Bank of England banknotes into gold, and using its bank interest rate and open market operations to regulate the inflow and outflow of its gold reserves. An outflow of gold reserves could be stemmed by increases in the bank rate, which acted to attract foreign capital convertible into gold. An inflow of gold allowed the Bank of England to lower interest rates, reducing the attraction to foreign capital and giving domestic capital an incentive to search for higher rates of return abroad. Commercial banks held Bank of England banknotes as reserves, and the Bank of England held gold as reserves to support its own banknotes.

The next 50 years of European monetary history turned into a vigorous rivalry between the gold standard and the bimetallic standard based on gold and silver. Britain championed the cause of the gold standard and the United States and France were the chief proponents of the bimetallic standard. In 1792 Congress had put the United States on a bimetallic system, and France became the dominant force in the Latin Monetary Union, a group of European countries cooperatively maintaining a bimetallic standard.

The bimetallic system was unable to surmount the difficulties created when the prices paid for precious metals at official mints differed from free market prices, the situation more often than not. If the ratio of the values of silver and gold at mint prices was 15 to 1, and the ratio of the values at free market prices was 16 to 1, then speculators carried silver to the mint for coinage, and exchanged new silver coinage for gold coinage. The gold coinage thus obtained could purchase more silver on the free market than was taken to the mint in the first place. With no incentive to bring gold to the mint at mint prices, gold coinage disappeared from circulation, and the bimetallic standard became an unofficial silver standard.

From 1792 until 1834 the United States maintained a silver to gold mint ratio of 15 to 1 while the free market ratio was 15.5 to 1, causing gold to disappear from circulation. In the Coinage Act of 1834 Congress increased the mint ratio to 16 to 1, and gold coinage displaced silver, putting the United States on a path of monetary development favouring the gold standard.

In 1866 France, Italy, Switzerland and Belgium (later joined by Greece and Bulgaria) formed the Latin Monetary Union, agreeing to a standardized coinage system, and a silver to gold mint ratio of 15.5 to 1. The members of the Latin Monetary Union sponsored a world conference to discuss the establishment of a uniform world currency based upon a bimetallic system. Britain was decidedly unsympathetic, and the conference met without making headway. In 1878 the United States arranged another international conference hoping to persuade the major powers to adopt an international bimetallic system.

The United States argued that if the bimetallic system was adopted worldwide, uniformly establishing a mint ratio between gold and silver, then mint prices of precious metals would dominate the free market prices, and discrepancies between mint ratios and free market ratios would disappear, delivering the bimetallic system from its major source of disturbance. As the holder of large silver deposits, the United States favoured a bimetallic system if it could be adopted worldwide as a cooperative initiative, but did not consider it feasible for an individual country to operate a bimetallic system in isolation. A strong populist movement in the United States, the Free Silver Movement, nudged the US government towards a pro-bimetallism stance. Germany refused to attend the international conference, and other European delegates suggested that the use of silver as money was more appropriate for less developed countries.[4] Britain was maintaining a silver standard in India while maintaining a gold standard for itself.

Britain's commercial success may have given the gold standard an edge over the bimetallic system. A war indemnity from the Franco-Prussian War furnished Germany with the gold reserves to support a gold standard, which Germany established in 1873. As countries began to favour gold and sell off silver reserves, silver prices plummeted in world markets and bimetallic countries such as France had to severely limit silver coinage, effectively putting an end to the bimetallic system. The major trading partners either officially or unofficially adopted the gold standard: the United States in 1879, Austria-Hungary in 1892, and Russia and Japan in 1897. The Latin Monetary Union survived, in name only, until the 1920s. The strains of wartime finance and the dangers of transporting gold forced countries to suspend the gold standard at the outset of World War I, bringing to a close the era of the classic gold standard, lasting from 1870 until 1914, when gold standard furnished the world with a bulwark against paper money inflation, and a stable, self-equilibrating financial system.

Perhaps the most visible cultural legacy of the struggle to enthrone the gold standard survives in the classic movie, *The Wizard of Oz*, still shown regularly. The movie is based upon a book of the same title published in the United States in 1900. The author was Frank Baum. One wonders how many fans of the movie know that the Emerald City represents Washington DC, and its green tint symbolizes the suggestion that in Washington everything was seen from the point of view of money. In the book everyone in the Emerald City wears green-tinted glasses. The word *Oz* is the 'oz' that is an abbreviation of ounce, as in ounce of gold. The yellow brick road represents the gold standard, which leads the heroine Dorothy from home to the Emerald City. The movie makes an important departure from the symbolism when it substitutes ruby slippers for the silver slippers that Dorothy wears in the book. The silver slippers represented silver, and Dorothy was able to return home when she discovered the power of her silver slippers, clicking them together. The role of the silver slippers suggested the United States would return to normality, recovering from the storm of economic depression, when it learned to use its huge silver deposits. The clicking together of the two silver slippers suggested the various silver interests must cooperate to achieve this objective. Dorothy represented traditional American values, the rusty-jointed tin man the unemployed industrial workers, the scarecrow the debt-ridden farmers ruined by deflation, and the cowardly lion represented three-time Democratic presidential candidate William Jennings Bryan, famous for his colourfully embroidered oratory in favour of bimetallism. In a speech that won him the Democratic nomination for the Presidency in 1896, Bryan compared the gold standard to the crucifixion of mankind on a cross of gold. Apparently Baum regarded Bryan's bark worse than his bite.

Under the world gold standard between 1870 and 1914, international flows of gold aided in the stabilization of prices in individual countries. If residents of country A saw domestic prices escalate faster than prices in country B, country A residents shifted expenditures in favour of the cheaper goods from country B, making payment in gold, which flowed out of country A and into country B. As gold flowed from country A to country B, the money supply in country A shrank, exerting downward pressure on prices in country A. The inflow of gold into country B expanded the money supply, exerting upward pressure on prices in country B. As prices fell in country A and rose in country B, the flow of gold from A to B ended, and prices stabilized in both countries. The Franco-Prussian Indemnity illustrates the stern operation of the gold standard. In February 1871 Germany extracted from France a brutal five billion franc indemnity as a price for peace and a return of French territory. France paid part of the indemnity in silver, but a handsome sum in gold, enabling Germany to switch from a bimetallic standard to a gold standard. The infusion of money infected Berlin with a frenzied boom in construction, and an index of wholesale prices in Germany, which stood at 103 in 1870, reached a height of 141 in 1873. The indemnity transfer left France depressed when other countries in Europe were experiencing inflationary expansion. Prices held steady in France, making it a cheaper place to purchase goods, particularly compared to Britain and Germany, increasing French exports relative to French imports. The excess of French exports over imports represented the actual payment of the indemnity in goods and services, which probably took place over a three to five-year period.

When gold production failed to keep pace with economic

expansion, restricting the supply of money relative to production, prices fell, increasing the purchasing power of gold, and increasing the incentive for the discovery of gold. The discipline of the gold standard put the world through an era of mild deflation in the 1880s, lasting into the 1890s, until the discovery of gold in Alaska, Canada, South Africa and Australia. Between 1890 and 1900 gold stocks doubled in the United States, and world deflationary trends disappeared.

The hazards of war put an end to international gold transportation after 1914, forcing countries to abandon the gold standard, at least unofficially. All European belligerents to some degree helped finance the war with expansion of paper money supplies, but England was less guilty than other European countries and suffered less post-war inflation. Even in England the 1920 price level was three times higher than the 1913 price level. At the close of World War I, Britain and France launched major efforts to re-establish the pre-war gold standard, striving to accumulate gold reserves that would enable them to maintain the convertibility of domestic currencies into gold at pre-war rates.

In 1922, at a Genoa conference, Britain advanced a proposal for an international monetary system in which the world's major trading partners held gold as reserves, leaving little or none available for coinage, and remaining nations held leading foreign currencies as reserves. Such a system, called the gold exchange standard, economized on the use of gold at a time when the demand for gold was rising faster than the supply. Although it was never officially adopted as an international monetary system, many countries adopted it individually. Britain officially returned to the gold standard in 1925, but never resumed the coinage of gold for circulation.

The effort to reinstate the gold standard forced countries towards domestic economic polices of tight money and high interest rates, policies that lifted the value of domestic currencies and encouraged an importation of capital, attracting the resources necessary for the re-establishment of the gold standard. Overvalued currencies made imported goods less expensive relative to domestically produced goods, and exported goods more expensive in foreign markets, depressing the vitality of domestic economies, and giving Europe an advanced taste of deflation and economic recession that would become chronic worldwide in the 1930s.

The death knell of the gold standard as a domestic monetary standard sounded in the economic debacle of the 1930s. In the face of downwardly spiralling domestic economies, governments commandeered control of domestic monetary supplies, conferring upon themselves the ability to expand and contract monetary supplies in an effort to stem the tide of depression. With the British government's suspension of gold payments on 19 September 1931, ratified on the following Monday with Parliament's adoption of the Gold Standard Amendment Act of 1931, the international gold standard suffered a severe blow. Preceding Britain in the abandonment of the gold standard were Australia, New Zealand, Brazil, Chile, Paraguay, Uruguay, Venezuela and Peru. Most of the world's trading partners followed Britain's example over the following year, the major exceptions being the United States, France, Belgium, Switzerland and the Netherlands. The United States abandoned the gold standard in 1933; the remaining European countries held out until 1936.

After abandoning the gold standard the United States devalued the dollar from $20.67 per ounce of gold (a value that had existed for nearly 100 years) to $35.00, a value that would only become effective for purposes of official international transactions. A dollar equivalent to gold at a rate of $35.00 per ounce became the basis of the international monetary system during the post-war era, in which the dollar served as an international currency.

The groundwork for the new international monetary order began in March 1933 when President Roosevelt closed all commercial banks for four days, banned the export of gold, recovered all gold and gold certificates from commercial banks, and called for lists of all persons who had withdrawn gold and gold certificates since 1 February. A month later the government banned individual ownership of gold and gold certificates, and the Federal Reserve issued Federal Reserve Notes in exchange for them.

Soon after Congress passed the Gold Reserve Act of 1934,

nationalizing all monetary gold in the United States and giving sole authority to the Treasury to own, buy and sell gold. Under the provisions of the Act, Roosevelt reduced the gold equivalent of the dollar to $35.00 per ounce the day after the Act was passed. The Act also provided for a $2 billion stabilization fund to finance the Treasury's purchase and sale of foreign currencies as needed to stabilize the value of the dollar in foreign exchange markets.

By the early twentieth century gold had largely replaced silver as a monetary standard, but two relatively large countries, China and Mexico, had remained on a silver standard. The discovery of huge silver deposits in the New World infused the world trading system with vast amounts of silver. In the early nineteenth century Mexico boasted one of the world's largest mints, and Spanish silver coinage flowed directly from Peru and Mexico to the Far East. After winning independence from Spain in 1821, Mexico began minting its own peso with a bit more silver than the Spanish dollar it replaced, and the new coin was called the Mexican dollar in Far Eastern trade, where it became the most popular coin throughout the nineteenth century. In the later nineteenth century the United States and Britain, both on the gold standard, minted special silver dollars specifically designed to compete with the Mexican dollar in the Far East, the English silver dollar bearing inscriptions in English, Chinese and Malay-Arabic. These dollars were called yuan, meaning 'round things', by the Chinese, and yuan became the standard monetary unit in China and modern Taiwan. The word for Japan's unit of money, the yen, is a corruption of yuan.

After Europe opened up trade with China in the mid nineteenth century, China became a major attraction for foreign investment, and China invariably ran balance of trade surpluses with the rest of the world, accounting for the large influx of silver enabling China to accumulate the reserves needed to support a silver standard. China, the birthplace of paper money, reintroduced paper money in the form of banknotes at the close of the nineteenth century. Chinese banks held reserves in silver, and banks not maintaining convertibility of banknotes into silver saw their banknotes depreciate rapidly. From 1916 until 1922 the Chinese government, confiscating silver reserves for its own purposes, enforced a system of inconvertible paper money, but met with significant resistance. At one point the Manchurian government decreed the death penalty for anyone not accepting inconvertible banknotes at par, but heavy discounts continued to disadvantage irredeemable banknotes.[5]

The silver standard countries weathered the early phases of the Depression in better condition than the gold standard countries. At first silver prices fell along with the prices of everything else besides gold, the price of which was a matter of official policy in gold standard countries. As silver prices fell, the exports of silver standard countries became cheaper in gold standard countries while foreign imports became more expensive in silver standard countries, boosting the demand for domestic production in silver standard countries, and sparking a modest boom in countries such as China and Mexico as the rest of the world slid into depression.

As the Depression deepened, countries abandoned the gold standard, allowing domestic currencies to devalue relative to gold and silver, causing silver prices to reinflate. China and Mexico and other silver standard countries were already feeling some of the effects of the Depression when the US Congress enacted the Silver Purchase Act of 1934, authorizing the US Treasury to purchase silver until either the US monetary stock of silver equalled one-third of the value of US monetary gold, or until the market price of silver had reached $1.29 per ounce. The US government also nationalized domestic stocks of silver. The US Treasury accumulated so much silver under this policy that it built a special depository for its silver holding on the grounds of West Point.

The Silver Repurchase Agreement significantly raised the world price of silver, making the exports of silver standard countries more expensive in foreign markets, and foreign imports cheaper. Silver standard countries began experiencing the same deflation seen in countries formerly under the gold standard, and the largest countries, China and Mexico, abandoned the silver standard in 1935. In 1936 and 1937 the US government allowed silver prices to fall, but the trend towards demonetization of silver had gathered too much strength and the handful of countries still on the silver standard abandoned it. Paradoxically, by reducing the monetary demand for silver, the

Silver Repurchase Act probably did not increase the world demand for silver, or help the silver-producing interest in the long run.

With the demise of precious metal standards, the world monetary system functioned with varying degrees of intervention from individual governments, but without formal agreements, until the end of World War II when the concept of a gold exchange standard was revived in a modified form, called a gold bullion standard. Under a gold bullion standard governments own all the monetary gold, strictly using it to settle international transactions while private ownership of gold is limited to industrial purposes, such as dentistry or jewellery manufacture. As in the gold exchange system following World War I, countries without significant gold reserves under the gold bullion standard maintained reserves of currencies from countries with gold reserves, particularly US dollars. By the end of World War II the United States had accumulated most of the non-communist world's gold.

The gold bullion standard came into being in 1946 after an international conference of monetary officials held in Bretton Woods, New Hampshire, giving the new monetary system the name of the Bretton Woods System. Under this system the value of the US dollar remained fixed at $35.00 per ounce of gold. Other countries also officially established the value of domestic currencies, either in a fixed weight of gold or in terms of US dollars. Upon request from official agencies of foreign governments, the US government stood ready to redeem dollars for gold at a rate of $35.00 per ounce. Individual governments bought and sold foreign currency in order to maintain the official value of their domestic currency relative to gold or major foreign currencies, maintaining a fixed exchange rate between individual currencies.

Just as Britain had tended to suffer balance of payments deficits under the post-World War I gold exchange system, the United States experienced balance of payments deficits under the Bretton Woods System. A balance of payments deficit results from foreign claims on domestic currency growing faster than domestic claims on foreign currency, creating pressures for the redemption of dollars into gold, and a subsequent outflow of gold. By 1971 only a significant devaluation of the US dollar could hope to salvage the Bretton Woods System. The United States chose to discontinue the redemption of dollars into gold, closing the final chapter on the gold standard as a monetary standard in the world economy.

In the nineteenth century the gold standard favoured globalization by strengthening the security of foreign investments, guaranteeing that they could be cashed in for gold. In the twentieth century the gold standard, by limiting growth in global liquidity, had begun to exert a restraining influence on globalization. After 1971 global trade, unfettered by the monetary constraints of a gold standard, was free to develop at a faster pace, governments growing money stocks as needed to promote economic growth and consequently global trade.

FOUR

The Triumph of Paper Money

For domestic purposes most countries rushed to inconvertible paper standards during the 1930s, but gold remained a hidden prop to monetary discipline until 1971 when the adoption of inconvertible paper standards became universal. While adoption of inconvertible paper money on a lasting basis occurred in the later twentieth century, the history of passing experiments with inconvertible paper standards stretched back at least to the eighteenth century. The circumstances in which Sweden between 1745 and 1776 furnished Europe with its first example of an inconvertible paper standard has already claimed our attention.

Paradoxically the New World, generously endowed with alluring deposits of precious metals, also deserves credit for some of the earliest, boldest and sometimes most dubious experiments with paper money. Colonial governments in North America enjoyed and abused the privilege to issue paper money. In 1676 the colonial government of the Massachusetts Bay Colony authorized the issuance of Treasury receipts under the expectation that these receipts would circulate as currency. The Massachusetts paper money was legal tender for the payment of taxes, and some issues were legal tender for the payment of all debt. Pressure of wartime expenditure led the colonial government to over issue paper money and, in 1748, after receiving a large reimbursement from England for war expenses, it redeemed the paper money with specie (gold and silver coinage) at 20 per cent of its face value. Most American colonies mishandled paper money, resulting in the Constitutional Convention conferral upon the Congress of the Federal Government the sole privilege to coin money. Before the American Revolution English investors and merchants, not wanting American debts to English creditors to be payable in depreciated colonial paper currency, had persuaded England's Parliament to restrict the issuance of paper money in the American colonies.

The American Revolution itself was financed with the issue of paper money, first authorized by the First Continental Congress in June 1775. Officially called bills of credit, they became known as 'continentals'. The Continental Congress had power neither to tax nor to borrow, and since resentment of taxation had helped spark the revolution, printing paper money appeared the only choice. Many colonial governments complied with the request of the Continental Congress to declare the continentals legal tender. Inflation remained in bounds until 1776, but by 1781 the ratio of continentals to specie in face value had risen to 100 to 1, the rate at which the Continental Congress later voted to redeem the continentals into interest-bearing, long-term bonds. New England colonies imposed wage and price controls, and the Continental Congress gave its blessing, hoping other colonial governments would take similar action. The Continental Congress passed resolutions castigating individuals who refused to accept continentals in payment, characterizing them as lost to virtue and an enemy of the country, but stopped short of imposing legal penalties for refusing to accept them.[1]

The continentals were not banknotes, but state notes, theoretically acceptable in payment of taxes that colonial governments were expected to impose to redeem them. The colonial governments refused to levy taxes to redeem the continentals, the fundamental reason for their failure. By the time of the War of 1812, the paper money in the United States was banknotes, each bank issuing its own banknotes individually. The banking system had allowed banknote circulation to grow rapidly before 1812, and soon succumbed to the pressure of war, suspending the redemption of banknotes into specie. This suspension of payments lasted until 1817 and, while the banknotes depreciated in value, the United States avoided the excesses of inflation that had accompanied the American Revolution.

Britain's first experience with inconvertible paper money began in 1797 and lasted until 1821, roughly spanning the period of intense war with France, including the Napoleonic Wars, when Britain was under severe financial stress. With approval from Parliament the Bank of England suspended the convertibility of Bank of England banknotes into specie after rumours of an invasion of Ireland had caused runs on banks, significantly drawing down the Bank of England's gold reserves. Indices of inflation were not available at that time, but exchange rates between currencies could be examined for evidence of currency depreciation. The British pound sterling maintained its value until 1809 when it sharply plunged on the Hamburg foreign exchange market and the pound price of gold bullion rose. Parliament formed a commission to study the problem, and opened a debate on the proper course of monetary policy for Britain. The most famous economists of the era, Thomas Malthus and David Ricardo, urged a return to convertibility of banknotes into specie, but financial conditions would not permit it even after the Napoleonic Wars ended in 1815. On balance it seems that England was spared a severe bout of inflation, probably because it had developed long-term capital markets for financing large government deficits, and had enacted an income tax, relieving pressure to print money as a means of paying government expenditures.

With much more disastrous consequences than Britain experienced, France turned to inconvertible paper money from 1789 to 1796, amid the French Revolution and wars with Britain. France allowed its paper money experiment to deteriorate into an inflationary riot, though interestingly enough this was not the first paper money debacle suffered by France in the eighteenth century – the Mississippi Bubble has been discussed in an earlier chapter. Nevertheless in October 1789 the financially hard-pressed National Assembly, the first government of revolutionary France, confiscated Church lands and issued *assignats*, certificates of government indebtedness, bearing 5 per cent interest, to be accepted in payment for Church land sold to private buyers. Later the Assembly converted the *assignats* to banknotes, removed the payment of interest, and began issuing *assignats* to finance deficit spending. Prices soared, and in 1794 the government imposed a system of price controls, the Law of the Maximum, in an effort to contain the situation. Individuals faced the death penalty for withholding goods from the market,[2] but hopes of higher prices in the future tempted sellers to hoard goods. Each night paper money came off the press for issuance the following day, farmers hoarded goods, famine threatened the cities, and *assignats* fell to 3 per cent of face value when the government lifted price controls in December 1794.

Inflation now ravaged the French economy. Speculation created a new class of rich, known for ostentatious ways, while inflation destroyed creditors and savers. Prices rose hourly, leaving wages behind, and paper money continued to multiply. The government tried issues of other variants of paper money but the public had lost confidence in it, forcing the government in July 1796 to return to specie. Inflation was finally put to rest after Napoleon came to power in 1799. Apparently Napoleon's wars, at least his early ones, generated a greater inflow than outflow of revenue, enabling France to build up monetary reserves to support a sound currency.

The nineteenth century saw numerous experiments with inconvertible paper standards, usually without devastating inflation, the Confederate hyperinflation in America being the exception. During the Civil War the US federal government issued legal tender, fiat paper money called greenbacks. Prices doubled during the Civil War, but nothing in the order of hyperinflation. The greenbacks continued to circulate, with Congressional approval, in peacetime, and the question of the constitutional right of the government to issue legal tender paper money came before the Supreme Court. In 1870 the Court ruled that Congress did not have the power to issue legal tender notes; in 1871 that Congress did have the right to issue legal tender notes in wartime, but left in doubt Congress's right to issue notes in peacetime. In 1884 it ruled that Congress had the right even in peacetime to issue paper money, legal tender for the payment of all debts, public and private.[3]

From 1866 to 1881 Italy suspended the convertibility of the paper lira, an episode of Italian monetary history called *Corso Forzoso* – 'forced circulation'. The *Corso Forzoso* replaced a bimetallic standard based upon gold and silver. The financial strain necessitating the *Corso Forzoso* lay in the costly wars waged to unify Italy, disorderly public financing owing to the fiscal consolidation of individual Italian governments, and heavy public works expenditures in the pursuit of industrialization. A crisis in the Italian bond market sparked a wave of requests from foreign bondholders for bond redemption in gold, draining Italy of its monetary gold reserves and forcing the government to establish an inconvertible paper standard. Inflation was kept in bounds, only lifting the wholesale price index from 0.897 to 1.051 for the period 1866–71. An index of the price of gold inched upwards from 1.046 to 1.137 in the same time interval. After 1871 the government began taking steps to restore convertibility and inflation remained in check until the return to convertibility in 1881.

Between 1883 and 1914, a time when the gold standard was thought to be the cornerstone of monetary probity, Spain operated an inconvertible paper standard even more successful than the Italian experience during *Corso Forzoso*. In 1868, immediately before the world's major trading partners rushed to the adoption of a gold standard, Spain adopted a bimetallic standard similar to that of France and other countries in the Latin Monetary Union. This standard set the official price of silver to gold at 15.5 to 1. After the Bank of Spain received a government-approved exclusive privilege to issue banknotes in 1874, Spain possessed the conditions ideally suited for the successful operation of an inconvertible paper standard, remembering that a monopoly, in this case the Bank of Spain, can maintain the value of any commodity with a demand by restricting its supply. In the 1870s, beginning with Germany in 1873, the world's major trading nations began adopting the gold standard, a trend that would spread even to Japan by 1897. As monetary institutions around the world began selling silver and acquiring gold, the price of silver fell, increasing the free market ratio of silver to gold to 18 to 1 by 1876. Spanish holders of gold could only purchase 15.5 ounces of silver for each ounce of gold at the official price in Spain, but 18 ounces of silver for each ounce of gold on the world market, triggering an outflow of gold from Spain and draining the gold reserves of the Bank of Spain. Between 1874 and 1883 gold currency in Spain decreased from 1,131 million pesetas to 736 million pesetas.

In 1883 an international financial crisis, including a stock market crash in France, and a deteriorating Spanish balance of trade, pushed Spain over the financial abyss, draining gold reserves to 60 per cent of their 1881 level, and forcing the Spanish government to suspend convertibility of pesetas into gold. Despite the circulation of inconvertible paper money, Spain's inflation remained in check, even turning mildly negative in the 1880s and early 1890s when deflation was a worldwide trend owing to pervasive economic depression. The two decades before World War I saw gently rising prices in Spain, lifting the Spanish wholesale price index to a level of 100, only 11.5 points above where it stood in 1883. The Spanish inflation rate between 1883 and 1913 averaged less than 1 per cent annually, a sound record of monetary stability only disturbed briefly when the exchange rate of pesetas relative to British pounds sterling plunged during the Spanish-American War. The Spanish experience cast doubt on the gold standard's role as the bulwark against inflation in the last quarter of the nineteenth century.

The years between World War I and World War II were the most influential for the development of inconvertible paper money. During World War I belligerent powers adopted inconvertible paper money as a wartime necessity, mainly because of financial strain, and partly from the risks of transporting gold. The rapid growth of inconvertible money stocks during the war rendered impossible a quick return to the gold standard. During World War I only Russia experienced hyperinflation, but in the years immediately following the war hyperinflation broke out in Austria, Germany, Hungary and Poland. By the 1930s the monetary pendulum had swung from inflation to deflation, and the gold standard which countries had laboriously struggled to re-establish after World War I, thought to be the best insurance against inflation, became a barrier against economic recovery and disappeared within the decade.

The German hyperinflation following World War I may constitute the most fantastic case in history, the best documented case of inflation reaching fantastic levels, and one that stands as a constant reminder of the potential for insanity residing in an inconvertible paper standard. The German government financed World War I by increasing money stocks rather than borrowing in capital markets or levying new taxes. During the war money stocks grew five-fold while prices only doubled. After the war Germany, needing to restock its warehouses with imported raw materials and pay war reparations, continued to increase money stocks, which increased nearly four-fold by December 1921. By that time prices began to catch up with monetary growth, rising to thirteen times their 1914 level. During 1922 money stocks in Germany leaped forward another ten-fold, and inflation, particularly after June 1922, entered a phase of fantastic growth, exceeding all expectations. Prices climbed to 1,475 times their 1914 level by December 1922 and to 19,985 times their 1914 level by June 1923. Workers received payments for wages at half-day intervals, and rushed to spend those wages before buying power was lost to inflation. Consumers came to the grocery store pushing wheelbarrows laden with sacks of money, and surplus bills were bailed and used for fuel. A newspaper selling for 1 mark in May 1922 brought 1,000 marks in September 1923, and 70 million marks by 17 November 1923. In December 1923 the German government stabilized the money supply, replacing the mark with a new currency, the Rentenmark, each Rentenmark equalling 1 trillion marks, and prices stabilized.[4]

The inflation problem in the immediate aftermath of World War I added a sense of urgency to the need for restoration of the gold standard. In the nineteenth century it was Britain's commercial and financial leadership that had established the gold standard in the confidence of an international community that anxiously awaited their return to the gold standard after World War I. In 1918 the British Parliament, seeking recommendations for reconstituting its monetary and financial system, appointed the Cunliffe Committee, named after Lord Cunliffe, Governor of the Bank of England. The twelve members making up the committee, nine of whom were traditional bankers, regarded the gold standard as the absolute standard of financial probity, assuming without question that Britain should return to it, and that the gold value of the pound sterling should be fixed at pre-war levels. Acting upon the recommendations of this committee, Britain began marshalling the monetary reserves needed, a goal finally achieved with the Gold Standard Act of 1925. With the help of loans from the Federal Reserve Bank of New York, and a US banking syndicate, Britain returned to the gold standard at pre-war parity, committing the Bank of England to sell gold for pound sterling at pre-war prices.

By 1930 the world was on a gold exchange standard in which countries maintained monetary reserves in the form of gold bullion or major foreign currencies, mainly British pounds and American dollars, both regarded as good as gold. Britain itself never minted gold coins for circulation after 1914, only holding gold for the redemption of pounds into gold in support of the gold standard. The public could convert Bank of England banknotes into gold bars, but could not demand the convertibility of banknotes into gold coins. Some gold coins were available for settling international transactions.

Under the post-war gold exchange system Britain and France (at least in the beginning) kept their currencies, the pound sterling and the franc, overvalued, regarding the return to pre-war parities as a matter of prestige. Overvalued currencies however, reduce the costs of imports while increasing costs of exports, depressing the demand for domestically produced goods relative to foreign produced goods. The maintenance of overvalued exchange rates required high interest rates in order to attract the foreign capital necessary to maintain gold reserves and discourage requests for the redemption of currency in gold.

With overvalued exchange rates and high interest rates the economies of Britain and France settled into a sluggish, lethargic recession, though not nearly as severe as in the 1930s. British industry could not compete with cheap German imports and strikes and labour-management clashes became common as unemployment spread. The Bank of England was caught between conflicting goals, between the need to lower domestic interest rates in an effort to revive the domestic economy, and the need to maintain high interest rates for preserving the value of the pound sterling at pre-war levels. As economic difficulties mounted worldwide, the pound came under greater pressure in foreign exchange markets. With declining world trade many smaller countries, unable to export domestically produced goods, began to pay for imports out of foreign currency reserves. When bank failures in Austria and Germany undermined confidence in foreign currencies, requests for redemption of foreign currencies into gold increased, putting further pressure on the pound.

As the crisis of confidence in the pound deepened, Britain experienced a gold outflow, cutting into its gold reserves and threatening the viability of the pound as a convertible currency. Hoping to weather the confidence crisis, Britain sought to strengthen its gold position by negotiating loans with the central banks of France and the United States. Later, private lenders granted another loan to the British government, but it came with strings attached, including requirements to restrict deficit spending, unemployment compensation expenditure and wages of government workers. These loans failed to restore confidence, and Britain continued to face an outflow of gold reserves, forcing it off the gold standard in September 1931.

France contributed to the pressure on the pound by taking every opportunity to convert pounds and dollars into gold. France was apparently sensitive to the perception that foreign currency reserves were most suitable for secondary powers, while major powers were expected to hold reserves in gold. Whatever the reason, by bolstering its gold reserves France was able to remain on the gold standard until 1936.

London was the site of the World Economic and Monetary Conference during June-July 1933, held within months of the United States suspending the gold standard. The conference was organized to negotiate an agreement for the stabilization of international currencies and eventual resurrection of the international gold standard. President Roosevelt undermined the conference and sealed the fate of the international gold standard when he announced that the United States would be guided solely by the needs of its domestic economy in the management of monetary policy, even if that meant ignoring conditions set for international monetary cooperation.[5]

As far as domestic economies were concerned the world's major trading partners emerged from the 1930s on inconvertible paper standards, permanently depriving citizens engaged in domestic trade the privilege of converting currency into gold (or silver). A gold standard was reconstituted as the foundation of an international monetary system, providing the basis for the conversion of national currencies into other national currencies. The United States stabilized the value of the dollar and accumulated gold reserves, enabling the dollar to supply the foundation of a new international monetary system. This, the Bretton Woods System, lasted from 1946 until 1971, during which time the United States, at requests from official foreign holders of dollars, redeemed dollars into gold at the official rate. When the United States suspended the convertibility of dollars into gold in 1971, the world's major trading partners made the final break with the gold standard, putting these countries on inconvertible paper standards for domestic and international purposes.

The breakdown of the Bretton Woods System began with the robust growth in world trade following World War II, forcing the world's trading partners to accept dollars as monetary reserves in the light of slow growth in gold reserves. Given the eagerness of the rest of the world to absorb dollars as monetary reserves, the United States was at first able to run balance of payments deficits without triggering a major outflow of gold reserves. The ability to run balance of payments deficits without creating a confidence crisis in the dollar was convenient for the US government at the time because of its worldwide military and political involvement.

The mid 1960s saw a significant shift away from confidence in the US dollar. With the Vietnam War, and other expenditures abroad arising from the Cold War, US balance of payments deficits were growing, and the rest of the world became increasingly concerned that the supply of foreign-held dollars far exceeded official gold stocks in the United States. Official foreign holders of dollars increased demands for the redemption of dollars into gold, and by the early 1970s the official gold stock of the United States had fallen to $12 billion, down from $25 billion in 1949. Redemption requests had reached crisis levels when President Nixon announced in August 1971 that official foreign holders of dollars could no longer convert dollars into gold at the US Treasury. The major trading partners tried to save the Bretton Woods System by moderately devaluing the dollar, raising the official price of gold into the $40 range, but the effort failed, and international trade began to function in an environment of freely fluctuating exchange rates.

The exchange rate regime that has existed since 1973 allows foreign exchange rates for major currencies to vary with conditions of supply and demand. The system is sometimes called a managed float, because governments intervene to smooth out short-term fluctuations, but not to reverse long-term trends determined by imbalances between supply and demand. Some countries, particularly countries that have had a problem with inflation, maintain the convertibility of their currencies into US dollars at an official rate, and countries maintain reserves of major currencies to support their own currencies at times in foreign exchange markets. None of the major currencies, however, the Deutschmark, Japanese yen, French franc, US dollar and British pound, are convertible into gold at official rates, which means the world has been on an inconvertible paper standard since 1973.

Suspensions of convertibility into gold have often occurred during wartime and the suspension in 1971 shares that characteristic. It appears to be the most permanent of suspensions that have occurred up to now inasmuch as adherents of the gold standard or other commodity standards are not in the mainstream of current political or economic thinking. The suspension of convertibility was followed by a decade of worldwide inflation, a problem associated with inconvertible currencies, but strong monetary discipline tamed inflation worldwide in the early 1980s, and for nearly two decades the world has enjoyed subdued inflation with an inconvertible paper standard.

FIVE

The Passage from Free Banking to Central Banking

Central banks meet the banking needs of commercial bankers and government, safely holding deposits of commercial banks, quietly lending funds to commercial banks and courteously holding deposits for the Treasury. Central banks act as a heroic lender of last resort to commercial banks during financial crises, and may grudgingly purchase government bonds directly from the government if the government treasury labours under heavy pressure to raise funds, as in wartime or when the private sector has lost faith in government, unwilling to purchase government bonds or loan money to government. Governments relying too heavily upon central banks to purchase government bonds are asking for serious inflationary difficulties. Central banks enjoy a lordly monopoly on the issuance of paper money. These central banks hold a large place in the global financial system, injecting liquidity into the global financial system when financial crisis threatens, smoothing out fluctuations in foreign exchange markets, cooperatively pursuing solutions to economic and financial problems that impact the global financial system as one unit. Topping the list of central banks worldwide are the Federal Reserve System in the United States, Deutsche Bundesbank of Germany, Bank of England, Bank of France, Bank of Japan and now the European Central Bank.

Central banks wield power and control processes that could turn a royal profit, if that was their mission, but it is not. They borrow funds interest-free, issuing non-interest bearing banknotes, which the public is eager to hold because these notes are legal tender in the payment of all debts public and private. By issuing banknotes, and incurring liabilities payable in these notes, central banks can marshal funds for the purchase of income-earning assets, such as bonds. While they possess the unrealized potential to earn lofty profits, central banks are public institutions, intended to faithfully serve the public's interest. At the onset of an economic recession or depression, a central bank infuses additional money and credit into the economic system, easing forces pulling the economy down. When an economic boom shows signs of reaching a feverish pitch, a central bank withdraws money and credit, slowing the momentum of expansion. Commanding a monopoly on the issuance of paper money and commercial bank reserves, central banks are in a position to control money stocks, interest rates and credit conditions.

Currently all highly developed countries can boast a central bank. Banks faintly resembling modern central banks appeared in Italy in the period just preceding the Renaissance. Sweden and Britain had banks bearing a strong resemblance to central banks by the end of the eighteenth century. Only a handful existed, however, until the latter portion of the nineteenth century, which saw the beginning of an explosion of growth in central banks. In 1873 the number of central banks worldwide remained in single digit territory, but by 1990 over 160 operated around the world.

The main competitor for central banking systems was the free banking system, which flowered in the early nineteenth century, when *laissez-faire* economics enjoyed its greatest prestige. Under systems of free banking, individual banks issued their own paper money subject to the requirement that each bank maintain the convertibility of its paper money into gold and silver specie. Free banking systems are only functional under a gold or silver standard, which limits the amount of paper money that will be issued by a myriad of banks. Under some variations of free banking systems, any individual or group of individuals could open a bank upon meeting certain capitalization requirements, removing the importance of political connections as a factor in starting a bank.

Scotland can lay claim to the credit for pioneering the development of free banking. The Scottish Banking Act of 1765 authorized all banks, banking companies and bankers, to issue banknotes in Scotland, establishing a principle that made the issuance of banknotes and banking synonymous in Scotland for a century. At that time the Bank of England enjoyed a monopoly on the privilege to issue banknotes in London and the Bank of Scotland and the Royal Bank of Scotland had lobbied hard for the exclusive privilege to issue banknotes. The political forces favoured the small banks and the Act gave Scotland a decentralized banking system that conferred upon each and every bank the privilege to issue banknotes. A shortage of specie may have encouraged Scotland to adopt a free banking system.

Adam Smith poured profuse praise upon the Scottish free banking system in his famous *Wealth of Nations*, not discouraged by some of the failures of the Scottish system. Smith himself describes in detail the episode of the Ayr Bank that failed in 1772. Under free banking systems banks easily succumb to greed, issuing paper money in excess, beyond the bank's resources for maintaining convertibility. Smith thought Scotland owed its rapid commercial expansion at the time to the adoption of its free banking system.[1] During the Napoleonic Wars, Parliament ordered the suspension of convertibility of banknotes into specie for the Bank of England and the Bank of Ireland, protecting the gold and silver reserves of those two banks. The banks of Scotland maintained the convertibility of their banknotes and never had to appeal to Parliament for protection.

The success of the Scottish system of banking, and Adam Smith's lavish praise of it, led England to experiment with free banking, temporarily retarding the development of the Bank of England as a central bank. In 1709 Parliament had made the Bank of England the only joint-stock bank with more than six partners that could issue banknotes. Permission to practise joint-stock banking was a special privilege because it limited the liabilities of the owners in the event of bank failure. By 1780 the Bank of England enjoyed a virtual monopoly on the issuance of banknotes in London. Things changed in 1826 when Parliament deprived the Bank of England of its nationwide monopoly on joint-stock banking, reserving the monopoly within a 65-mile radius from the centre of London, but outside London authorizing the formation of note-issuing banking corporations without limit on the number of partners. Parliament allowed the Bank of England to open branches in cities outside

London, but these branches faced competition from other joint-stock banks. The trend towards free banking in Britain was shortlived, however. In 1833 Parliament made Bank of England notes legal tender, and in 1844 took steps to concentrate the privilege to issue banknotes in the hands of the Bank of England, ending Britain's flirtation with free banking.

Free banking struck deeper roots in the United States, flourishing particularly in the two decades prior to the Civil War. Before the era of free banking the establishment of a bank in the United States required a bank charter granted by a state legislature that usually acted out of political favouritism. The First Bank of the United States and, later, the Second Bank of the United States, provided some of the monetary regulation expected from central banks. The banking system lost what regulation there was with the demise of the Second Bank of the United States in 1833. After a wave of inflation between 1834 and 1837 ended in a severe money panic and widespread bank failures, the public grew angry at a system that effectively reserved bank-opening privileges for those with political connections.

The legislature of New York led the states in the movement toward free banking, enacting the Free Banking Act of 1838 that allowed any person or group of persons to receive a bank charter upon meeting certain objective criteria. These criteria required that banknotes receive 100 per cent backing by mortgages and state bonds, and in addition that gold and silver specie reserves be maintained equalling 12.5 per cent of banknotes. This forced banks to hold reserves sufficient for maintaining convertibility of banknotes into specie. The requirement that outstanding banknotes receive 100 per cent backing in mortgages and state bonds gave state authorities sound assets that could be liquidated in case of a failing bank, the proceeds of the liquidation going towards redemption of outstanding banknotes.

The New York example spread, legislatures in eighteen states eventually adopting free banking legislation. Free banking laws provided that anyone, without receiving a special charter from a legislature or even having political contacts, could obtain a bank charter by depositing suitable financial securities, often federal or state bonds, with a state banking authority. The new bank then had authorization to issue banknotes in an amount equal in value to the financial securities deposited with the state authority.

The free banking system in a vast country such as the United States had its faults. With no one bank or government agency exercising controls over the money supply, inflation was a constant danger, at least in the eyes of the public. As banks multiplied, a perplexing assortment of banknotes circulated, trading at various discounts, depending upon the issuing bank's reputation for soundness. Merchants had to consult periodicals that published the discounts on all the known circulating banknotes. Some newspapers published lists of good notes and bad notes. Trade between regions suffered because a currency equally acceptable in all regions was lacking. The free banking system allowed the formation of 'wildcat banks' established in remote areas, perhaps in the midst of an Indian reservation.[2] In physical structure these banks were practically nothing, sometimes lacking office furniture, not expecting or wanting customers to find them. They wanted to issue banknotes without facing requests to redeem the notes in gold and silver specie.

In some cases individuals started up wildcat banks with only enough capital to purchase engraved plates and dies and to defray the cost of printing the banknotes. A state auditor's office agreed to accept delivery of federal or state bonds from a broker after the wildcat bank had already printed up its banknotes. The banknotes were delivered to the broker in payment for the bonds, and the broker delivered the bonds to the state auditor's office. Experiences with wildcat banks help explain why the fledgling Republic of Texas in 1845 adopted a provision in its constitution that flatly outlawed banks.[3] By 1857 four other states had enacted similar legislation.

Free banking was actually an interlude in the development of modern central banks. While the development of central banks accelerated in the later nineteenth and twentieth centuries, banks bearing some central bank characteristics have a much longer history, stretching back to the late Middle Ages. The Bank of Venice developed informally after the government of the Republic of Venice in 1171, needing help to finance a war, forced its wealthiest citizens to loan specie to the government.

Instead of receiving bonds, IOUs or other certificates of indebtedness, each citizen had a record of his loan to the government kept in a government record book registering the amount the government owed. The government made no effort to pay down the principal, but paid each citizen 4 per cent interest.

Venetians soon learned that government obligations were readily acceptable as a medium of exchange in private transactions. Transferring the ownership of government obligations was simply a matter of transferring funds from one account to another, a bookkeeping transaction that involved no coined money changing hands. When large sums were involved, a money transaction settled by entries in a record book was much more convenient than transactions requiring the exchange of coinage, a point not lost on the business community of Venice. Venetians began depositing specie with the 'government bank', accepting transferable bookkeeping entries in return.

The government's record of its debt functioned informally as a bank for two centuries, using the debt as an instrument of exchange. In 1374 a committee of scholars suggested that the government's banking and debt management activities be organized into a public bank. It took another two centuries before the government organized the Bank of Venice as the Il Banco dell' Piazza del Rialto, in 1587. Other Italian cities had already established public banks by then, stealing Venice's glory as the founder of the first public bank. Venetians, however, pioneered modern banking practices, and the informal Bank of Venice, creating a public debt that circulated as money, is the oldest ancestor of modern central banks.

Another step in the evolution of banks performing central bank functions occurred in the Italian city-state of Genoa, financial headquarters for Europe between 1557 and 1627. In the fourteenth century Genoa, at war with Venice, raised specie from its citizens, issuing promissory notes in exchange. At the war's end Genoa pledged the customs dues (taxes levied at its port for imports and exports) for the redemption of the promissory notes. In 1407 the government's creditors, holders of the promissory notes, organized themselves into a public bank, the Casa di San Georgio, or House of St George, appointing a board of eight directors to direct the affairs of the new bank.

Officially the establishment of the House of St George predates the official establishment of the Bank of Venice, which existed for several centuries as an informal organization. The House of St George began collecting the custom dues and advancing loans to the government. The Renaissance palace that housed the bank can still be seen in the Piazza Caricmento.

The House of St George developed into a bank of deposit, accepting coin deposits from around the world. Depositors of coin received what was called bank money, a bookkeeping entry representing ownership of a deposit. The entries switched funds from one depositor's account to another depositor's account without coinage ever leaving the bank. To transfer funds from one account to another, bank depositors came to the bank and observed the bookkeeping entries in the presence of a notary. Ownership of the bank was vested in stockholders, and stock shares also served as a form of money, changing hands through bookkeeping entries. Holders of the public debt received interest payments in three-year instalments, creating accounts of accrued interest that also acted as a medium of exchange.

Banknotes owe their origin to the House of St George. These banknotes were not printed up in mass, as modern banknotes, and were not for specific denominations. Each note was individually written out for a specific amount, representing a deposit of gold or silver or shares of bank stock. By endorsing the note the holder could pass ownership to another party.

The next step in the evolution of central banks occurred in Sweden with the establishment of the Riksbank or Bank of Sweden, an institution that has enjoyed continuous development from its inception in 1656 until the present day, making it the oldest central bank in the world. The Riksbank began as a private bank, operating as a lending bank in one branch, and in another branch creating transferable bank deposits on the basis of coin and precious metal deposits. One hundred per cent reserves of precious metals backed the bank deposits, making these deposits readily acceptable in exchange, just like money.

When the Riksbank issued the first known banknotes in 1656, bills of exchange had long been in existence, and in England banknotes were evolving from the receipts issued for deposits at goldsmiths. The practice of issuing banknotes would spread to the rest of Europe quickly, and in 1720 France showed Europe its first inflationary episode of paper money. While the motivation for the issuance of banknotes in other countries lay in the need to keep precious metals safely stored, protected from theft, Sweden turned to banknotes because the chief currency was heavy, bulky copper, inconvenient to transport even in small values.

The Swedish government assumed ownership of the Riksbank in 1668, making it the oldest central bank still functioning today, predating the Bank of England by 26 years. The year 1789 saw the Riksbank first issue government currency, and a century later in 1897, the Swedish government conferred upon the Riksbank the exclusive privilege to issue paper money in Sweden.

The Bank of England, the institution that has shaped the development of central banking more than any other, received its founding charter from Parliament in 1694. Engaged in a costly war with France, the English Parliament chartered the Bank of England as a means of borrowing money for the government, hoping to float a loan of £1,200,000 at 8 per cent interest. A special duty or tax was placed on tonnage or shipping, and the proceeds of the tax pledged to servicing this new debt burden. As an added sweetener to attract as many funds as possible at the moderate interest rate, Parliament bestowed on the subscribers to the new loan the privilege of pooling their funds and incorporating under the name of the 'Governor and Company of the Bank of England'. The act chartering the Bank of England did not glide through Parliament without turbulence. According to Macaulay opponents portrayed the bank as an instrument of tyranny more threatening than 50,000 soldiers of Oliver Cromwell, the High Chamber or the Star Chamber. They saw it as a plot to advance the moneyed interest at the expense of the landed interest, and predicted the ruin of the monarchy.[4]

The original charter provided for a governor, deputy governor, and 24 directors. These officials were elected annually by the stockholders and bore responsibility for overseeing and directing the affairs of the bank. The charter authorized the bank to trade in gold and silver bullion and bills of exchange, but prohibited trade in merchandise, excepting for the sale of merchandise held in security for defaulted loans. The Bank's charters were invariably of fixed duration, the first one for ten years. Parliament always renewed the charters, usually on the condition that the government received another loan, perhaps at a lower interest rate. In 1709 Parliament approved a new charter for the Bank of England, this time adding the provision that no other joint-stock company with more than six partners could issue banknotes, the first step that would eventually give the Bank of England a monopoly on issuing banknotes. In 1751 the bank assumed responsibility for management of the national debt. By 1780 it monopolized the issuance of banknotes in London, and was the major holder of deposits for smaller banks, putting it in the position of banker's bank in London. The Bank of England now began to fit the description of a central bank. It was around this time that Alexander Hamilton proposed the establishment of the First Bank of the United States, patterned after the Bank of England.

Conceived as an innovative measure of public finance amid war, the Bank of England acquired valuable central banking experience during the period of the French Revolution and Napoleonic Wars. The government pressed the bank to accommodate the financing needs of the war over the protests of the bank's directors. Heavy government borrowing drew the bank's reserve position to dangerously low levels and, in 1797, the bank, with the approval of Parliament, suspended the convertibility of banknotes into specie. Parliament acted to protect the bank against depositors making a run on the bank. The bank also issued small denomination banknotes, compensating for a coinage shortage.

The Bank Restriction Act of 1797 officially suspending the convertibility of Bank of England notes was intended as a temporary wartime measure. It was continually renewed, remaining in effect for 24 years, much longer than originally intended. This suspension of payments, Britain's first experience with an inconvertible paper standard, dominated monetary discussions for over two decades. During the era of suspended payments the Bank of England managed monetary affairs without touching off an episode of hyperinflation, an important development in the history of inconvertible paper money. No accurate measures of inflation existed at the time, but the exchange rate between the British pound sterling and other foreign currency was readily observable. However, the famous economist David Ricardo joined a chorus of critics urging the government to return to convertibility after 1809.[5]

Two things contributed to Britain's ability to dodge the inflationary pitfalls of paper money. First, London was the seat of a highly developed capital market, capable of marketing long-term government debt. Second, Parliament in 1799 took the historic step of enacting an income tax, substantially increasing the government's ability to pay for the war. With Parliament's willingness to impose heavy taxation, coupled with access to long-term borrowing opportunities, the Bank of England felt less pressure to accelerate the inflationary printing of banknotes as a means of financing government expenditure. The British government continued to accept Bank of England banknotes at face value in obligations owed to the government, helping the banknotes maintain value.

It was always assumed that when the struggle with Napoleon came to a close the Bank of England would return to convertibility of banknotes into specie. When the Napoleonic Wars finally ended in 1815 the Bank of England, however, continued to face an outflow of gold reserves, forcing Parliament to postpone the resumption of convertibility. Only in 1819 did Parliament enact legislation calling for resumption by 1823, and also officially putting England on the gold standard. The Bank of England's gold reserve position began to improve, and convertibility of banknotes into gold resumed in May 1821.

After resumption of convertibility, Bank of England banknotes began to command the same respect as gold itself, enabling banks in the countryside to hold Bank of England banknotes as reserves, as acceptable gold specie in the eyes of the public. Amid financial crises country banks began to turn to the Bank as a source of liquidity, a lender of last resort, a role that it resisted at first.

With the Bank Charter Act of 1833, Britain ended a trend towards free banking, and resumed a historical trend towards concentrating the privilege to issue banknotes in the hands of the

Bank of England. The Act allowed other joint-stock banks to open for business in London, something not allowed by previous legislation, but reserved for the Bank of England the privilege to issue banknotes. Under the Act Bank of England banknotes of more than £5 became legal tender everywhere in England and Wales but not in Scotland or Ireland. The legal tender provision, the first time banknotes passed as legal tender in peacetime England, remained conditional upon the Bank of England maintaining convertibility of its banknotes. Country banks could now hold Bank of England notes as reserves instead of gold, stemming the outflow of gold reserves in financial and liquidity crises. Bank of England banknotes were not legal tender for payments owed to the Bank of England, which caused a gold inflow to the Bank of England, centralizing gold reserves in its vault and making it custodian of Britain's gold reserves.

The Bank Charter Act also exempted bills of exchange payable within three months from usury laws, laying the groundwork for the development of the famed 'bank rate', a short-term interest rate that the Bank of England controlled for policy reasons. The Bank of England raised the bank rate to stem an outflow of gold, attracting funds abroad by higher interest rates. Its adjustment of the bank rate to maintain Britain's gold reserves made it a powerful policy instrument for the operation of the gold standard. The Act also called for the Bank of England to furnish statistics on note issues and bullion reserves, requiring weekly reports to the Treasury and monthly summaries to the *London Gazette*. The additional power and responsibility vested with the Bank came at the price of added emphasis on public disclosure of the bank's activities.

After the financial crisis of 1847 the Bank of England gave up resistance to the idea of being lender of last resort. It had clung to a perception of itself as a bank competing with other commercial banks, and adjusted its bank rate to compete with them. After the crash of 1847, the Bank of England discovered the destabilizing effects of adjustments in the bank rate made to keep it in step with interest rates charged at other banks. It also discovered the need for a lender of last resort. The Bank began to emphasize the stabilization of financial markets, using its power to act as a lender of last resort, and adjusting the bank rate to meet the needs of the economy rather than to maximize its own profits.

By the eve of World War I, the Bank of England had developed the bank rate and open market operations into highly effective instruments for regulating market interest rates. Open market operations have to do with a central bank's purchase and sale of government bonds to influence interest rates. Today open market operations are the most important item in a central bank's arsenal of weapons for managing financial markets and economic systems.

Before World War I the Bank of England saw itself as the chief custodian of a gold standard that was the premier monetary standard, representing the height of perfection in monetary respectability. While individual countries complained about the gold standard's deflationary effects, worldwide loyalty to the gold standard was regarded as another mark of progress in an age mesmerized with progress. During World War I most governments, including the British, either officially or unofficially abandoned the gold standard. The British government banned the export of gold, preventing foreign countries from exchanging Bank of England notes into gold.

The close of World War I touched off an almost international struggle for a return to gold, a reinstatement of the gold standard. In Britain, Lord Cunliffe, Governor of the Bank of England, chaired the Cunliffe Committee, which was charged with making recommendations for the post-war reconstruction of the financial system. We have already read how the British endured innumerable economic woes to reinstate the gold standard, only to see it collapse in the 1930s.

During the Depression years the Bank of England suffered a lack of direction from a government that had abandoned the gold standard but was unable to provide monetary leadership in a post-gold standard era. During World War II Britain subjected its economy to a strict regimen of controls, and compared to the Depression years the British economy seemed to thrive under strict government direction, enhancing the prestige of heavy government involvement. At the end of the war the British electorate returned a Labour government to power and the new government began nationalizing major industries. The

Bank of England, whose policies bore some of the blame for the Depression, had little defence for warding off nationalization and in 1946 the Bank of England yielded to nationalization, becoming an arm of the Exchequer (British Treasury).

In 1957 Parliament formed the Radcliffe Committee, named after its chair, Lord Radcliffe, for the purpose of studying monetary policy. In 1959 the Committee issued its findings, which played down the significance of controlling the growth rate of the money supply, citing many other factors that can override the influence of monetary growth. The report recommended that goals of monetary policy be defined in terms other than money stock growth rates, relaxing some of the discipline in monetary policy.

The strong voice elected officials commanded in the affairs of the nationalized Bank of England, coupled with the findings of the Radcliffe committee, contributed to the higher inflation rates of the post-World War II era. In the late 1980s and 1990s a capitalist revolution in Britain led to the privatization of formerly nationalized industries, and the Bank of England has been mentioned as a possible candidate for privatization.

The development of central banking in Britain appears smooth and continuous compared with the trials and tribulations that France experienced in the course of developing central banking institutions. The first French bank bearing a significant resemblance to a central bank was established as the Banque Generale in 1716 and reorganized as the Banque Royale in 1718. The Banque Royale spawned such a financial disaster (see Chapter 2) that the word *banque* was banished from the names of financial institutions in France for nearly a century. It was the first bank in France to issue legal tender paper money.

The French public not wanting to have any more to do with banks, the next French institution bearing the marks of a central bank was called the Caisse d'Escompte, established in 1767. The Caisse was authorized to purchase commercial paper and government securities paying 4 per cent interest, raised to 5 per cent in wartime. It enjoyed a monopoly on the issuance of coinage. This institution failed but the famous French finance minister, Turgot, established by government decree another Caisse d'Escompte in

1776. In addition to acting as the government's bank, it was authorized to discount bills of exchange and commercial paper at 4 per cent interest, trade in gold and silver, accept deposits from the public and issue non-interest-bearing banknotes. It could not issue interest-bearing banknotes or bonds, borrow funds from the public at interest, or engage in commercial or maritime enterprises, including insurance, factors thought to have contributed to the debacle of the Banque Royale.

The Caisse d'Escompte was one of the early casualties of the economic chaos and fiscal bankruptcy that pushed France over the edge of revolution. In February 1783, six years before revolution broke out, the *Ancien Régime*, desperate for money, granted the Caisse the privilege to issue banknotes for 50 years in return for a loan of 70 million livres, absorbing virtually all the Caisse's financial capital. In August 1783 the Caisse faced a major crisis of confidence that erupted into a panic, forcing the redemption of 33 million livres in banknotes before order was restored. The government, unable to offer financial assistance or repay any part of the 70 million livre loan, offered to declare the banknotes legal tender, but the governing council of the Caisse rejected the offer. Close association with the government continued to erode public confidence in the Caisse, and panic erupted again in August 1788. This time the Caisse suspended the convertibility of banknotes into coinage after paying out half of its 50 million livres in coin reserves. The government declared the Caisse's banknotes legal tender, and authorized the Caisse to redeem banknotes in discounted commercial paper.

As the fiscal crisis deepened the Caisse continued to advance funds to the government, including the revolutionary government that took over after July 1789. The National Assembly (1789–91), the first governing body of the French Revolution, issued its own paper money, legal tender notes called *assignats*, and made payments to the Caisse in these notes. The *assignats* became famous for touching off one of the most extreme hyperinflation episodes in history. Proposals to convert the Caisse into a national bank came before the National Assembly, but no action was taken. As governing bodies of the revolution changed the Caisse continued to advance funds to the government. In August 1793 the revolutionary government took over the assets of the Caisse, ending France's second major effort at developing a central bank, both ending in disaster.

The Bank of France, the central bank of France for two centuries, owes its origin to Napoleon, who created it in 1800 because he needed a financial institution to purchase government bonds. By then the government of France, having no credibility in financial circles, found it very difficult to borrow. The fact that the new institution was called a 'bank' was significant in itself, as it was the first major French financial institution so called since the Banque Royal had discredited the term. The Bank of France itself was formed out of the dissolution and reorganization of the Caisse des Comptes Courants, an institution in Paris that purchased financial assets by issuing banknotes, what could be called a discount bank. In 1802 the French government forced the Caisse d'Escompte du Commerce, the main competitor to the Bank of France as a note-issuing institution, to merge with the Bank of France. In 1803 the government conferred upon the Bank of France the exclusive privilege to issue banknotes in Paris, required other note-issuing institutions in Paris to withdraw their notes before a certain date, and prevented the opening of new note-issuing banks in the provinces without government approval. The Bank of France was capitalized at 30 million livres, equivalent to 30 million francs after monetary reform replaced the livre with the franc in 1803. Public subscriptions, government funds and capital of the dissolved Caisse d'Escompte du Commerce furnished the funds for capitalization of this new institution.

Napoleon soon witnessed the difficulties of using a central bank as a ready source of cheap credit for the government, an institution that will purchase low-interest government bonds when no other market for them exists, and pay for them by issuing banknotes. In 1804 the Bank of France, succumbing to government pressure, bought too much government debt, issuing excess banknotes in the process. Rumours that Napoleon had shipped metallic reserves to Germany in payment of military expenses sparked a confidence crisis, forcing the Bank of France to partially suspend specie payments. Bank of France banknotes depreciated 10 to 15 per cent while the Bank of France accepted blame for the difficulties, covering the government's role in pressuring it to pursue unsound policies. The year 1814 saw another partial suspension of payments. Napoleon constantly encouraged the bank to err on the side of low interest rates, keeping the bank's discount rate in the 4 to 5 per cent range, a practice that became customary until mid century. Napoleon also encouraged the bank to act as a lender of last resort. In the 1850s the Bank of France turned its discount rate into a policy tool, raising and lowering it as needed to regulate the flow of specie into and out of the country. An increase in the discount rate halted a specie outflow by increasing the interest money could earn inside France. In 1857 the government exempted the Bank of France from a usury law that put a 6 per cent ceiling on interest rates, giving the bank more flexibility in discount rate adjustments.

At first stockholders elected a committee responsible for the management of the Bank of France. In 1806 the governance of the bank was put in the hands of a government-appointed governor and two deputy governors, strengthening the position of the government in the management of the bank, and streamlining the management. Compared to Britain, France developed a much more centralized control over monetary affairs, as shown by the importance of branches in the Bank of France's organization. The French government authorized the Bank of France to open up branch banks in the provinces, and after 1840 ceased granting charters for the establishment of new private banks in the provinces with authority to issue banknotes. Between 1841 and 1848 fifteen branches of the Bank of France opened up in the provinces, often with a provincial monopoly on the issuance of banknotes. By 1900 over four hundred French towns could boast some kind of office of the Bank of France; as many as 120 towns were the seats of a full-size branch. In comparison the Bank of England only operated eight branches at that time. Critics have charged that the pervasive presence of the Bank of France throughout France and its tight control over French money and banking may have restricted the availability of credit and retarded French economic development in the nineteenth century. Napoleon's preference for centralization and government control exerted a strong influence on the evolution of the Bank, which in turn influenced the evolution of central banks around the world.

In the 1848 political upheaval, the French government turned to the Bank of France for financial support. The public began to hoard specie out of a fear of paper money, still haunted by memories of the Revolution's *assignats*. The Bank, trying to avoid a run on banks with requests to convert banknotes into specie, received the protection of the government, which rendered Bank of France banknotes legal tender nationwide. The government also limited the issuance of Bank of France banknotes to a fixed amount. The private provincial banks, whose banknotes were legal tender in their respective regions, now lost ground to the Bank of France, leading to their merger with the Bank of France, yielding to the Bank of France an exclusive privilege to issue banknotes.

During World War I the French government, wanting help financing the war, looked to the Bank of France for the purchase of government bonds and the issuance of banknotes. France avoided the post-World War I inflationary fiascos of several European countries by spreading post-war inflation over several years, with less devastating results for the middle class. A similar policy of war finance was pursued during World War II, increasing banknotes 400 per cent between 1940 and 1944. The Bank of France, an early target for the nationalization fever that followed World War II, surrendered to nationalization in 1945.

In 1993 the government of France enacted measures to increase the independence of the Bank of France, freeing it from short-term economic and political considerations and reinforcing its commitment to price stability relative to minimization of unemployment and other economic goals. Now the Bank of France has a representative on the General Council of the European Central Bank (ECB), and is one of the larger subscribers to the capital of the ECB.

The Deutsche Bundesbank, a relatively new member of the ranks of European central banks, is the central bank of Germany. While the Bundesbank has a relatively short history, beginning in 1948, it inherited a long tradition of central banking in Germany, predating World War I. In 1948, the allied occupation authorities in West Germany introduced a new currency, the Deutschemark, and erected in place of the Reichsbank, the central bank of Nazi Germany, a regional system of autonomous central banks called *Landeszentralbanks*. The exclusive privilege to issue banknotes lay with the Bank Deutscher Lander, which stood at the apex of the system of West German central banks. This bank could also act as a lender of last resort. Perhaps one of the flaws of the system was that the banks at the base of the pyramid were legally independent entities.

Organizational reform came with the Bundesbank Act of 1957, which provided for the merger of the independent *Landeszentralbanks* with the Bank Deutscher Lander. This new system was incorporated as the Deutsche Bundesbank with only one stockholder, the West German government. Headquarters for the Bundesbank remained at Frankfurt and presided over a system of eleven *Landeszentralbanks*, each the focal point of a system of regional branch banks which could include as many as fifty. The unification of Germany led to the integration of the state banking system of East Germany with the Bundesbank in 1990, creating a single central banking system responsible for monetary policy in Germany.

Fear of inflation shaped the philosophy of the Deutsche Bundesbank, conditioned by the two hyperinflation episodes in the twentieth century that had left the German economy severely crippled. The law providing for the creation of the Bundesbank conspicuously ignored any economy goals besides regulating the money stock and credit conditions and safeguarding the integrity of the currency. Maintaining an inflation free economy took precedence over maintaining a fully employed, rapidly growing economy.

Characteristic of the philosophy shaping the Bundesbank, the governing officials enjoy a high degree of independence from the elected officials, who in all countries are often suspected of nudging central banks towards inflationary policies. The Central Bank Council, the supreme policy-making body of the Bundesbank, includes a president, a vice-president, the presidents of eleven *Landeszentralbanks* and up to eight additional members of a directorate. The President of the Federal Republic of Germany appoints the President and Vice-President of the Central Bank Council and the eight members of the directorate, each appointed for secure terms lasting eight years. The presidents of the *Landeszentralbanks* owe their appointments to the President of the Federal Republic, who acts after receiving recommendations from the directorate of the Central Bank Council.

The independence from government officials that marked the organization of the Bundesbank gave Germany an advantage during the 1970s when inflation ravaged most Western countries. The Bundesbank could focus solely upon taming inflation when other central banks, less independent of government authorities, had to keep one eye on unemployment, often at the expense of controlling inflation. The Bundesbank steadily rose to become the premier central bank in Europe, in a strategic position to play a key role in the organization of the European Central Bank, which became active in 1999.

The central bank exerting the most influence on the global financial markets today is the Federal Reserve System, the central banking system of the United States. The Federal Reserve System was the final product of an effort to find an acceptable banking system for a vast country where regional concentrations of power were invariably resisted. The history of central banking in the United States begins with the presidency of George Washington. One of his administration's early accomplishments was the establishment of the First Bank of the United States, a banking institution patterned after the Bank of England. Washington's Secretary of Treasury, Alexander Hamilton, one of the *Federalist Papers* authors, was known for his partiality to English institutions, an attitude slightly out of step with some American revolutionaries. Over Thomas Jefferson's objections, Hamilton persuaded Washington to sign a bill providing for the establishment of the First Bank of the United States. In 1791 the bill authorizing its incorporation became law.

In December 1790 Hamilton had sent a report to Congress, calling for it to enact enabling legislation for the establishment of the First Bank, drawing many of his ideas from the role the Bank of England played in the English economy.[6] He argued the bank would increase the banknotes in circulation, easing the currency shortage of the colonies, and would assist the US government in raising short-term capital and in foreign exchange transactions arising from payments to foreign holders of the national debt. The proposal triggered a hot debate, some members of Congress baulking at a proposal to grant a charter of incorporation when the Constitution had not expressly given it the power to grant such charters. The constitutional issues raised in the debate continued to supply fuel for critics of the First Bank, contributing to its demise in 1811 after Congress failed to renew its charter.

The First Bank performed its central banking function, controlling the money supply and credit conditions, by varying the pressure on commercial banks to maintain convertibility of banknotes into specie. With varying degrees of aggressiveness it sent incoming banknotes back to the issuing commercial bank for redemption. As a bulwark against currency inflation, the First Bank won the support of the large commercial banks, but the small country banks resented the intrusion, costing it much public support.

The First Bank was a public corporation, responsible to its stockholders. Four-fifths of its stock was held in the private sector, largely by foreign investors, and one-fifth by the US government, giving the government only a modest influence on bank policies. When the bill for re-chartering the First Bank came before Congress in 1811, it lost by one vote in the House of Representatives, and failed to pass in the Senate after the Vice-President broke a tie by voting against the bill.

The US government soon had reason to miss the regulating function of the First Bank. In 1814, six months before the end of the War of 1812, commercial banks stopped the redemption of banknotes into specie, the exigencies of a wartime economy catching up with the US financial system. Following the war the government, eager to restore the soundness of the financial system, found itself without means for pressuring commercial banks to resume convertibility of banknotes into specie. Practical considerations began to outweigh the constitutional objections levelled against the First Bank, and on 10 April 1816 President Madison signed a bill approving a charter for another bank closely resembling the First Bank. It would be called the Second Bank of the United States.

Again the US government owned only one-fifth of the voting stock, enabling the government to appoint five out of the 25 directors responsible for management of the bank, but provisions in the charter limited the voting rights of large stockholders, and foreign stockholders had no voting rights. At first the Second Bank suffered from poor management, making loans to investors for the purchase of Second Bank stock (using the stock as collateral for the loan), and allowing bank officers to speculate in the bank's stock. It was slow in demanding specie payments on banknotes issued by other banks, and barely avoided suspending payments on its own banknotes. In 1823, however, an individual assumed the Bank presidency who thoroughly understood the role a central bank could play in the management of an economic and financial system if the bank put public responsibility ahead of the goal of maximizing stockholder profits. His name was Nicholas Biddle. Under his leadership the Second Bank regulated the circulating money stock, accumulating specie to decrease the money stock, and granted loans more generously to inject additional specie into circulation.

The practice of forcing commercial banks to redeem banknotes on demand aroused the resentment of banks in the West and South, the political power base of Andrew Jackson, elected President in 1828. Banks in the West and South seemed particularly prone to issue notes beyond what their resources in specie could support and redeem. Biddle and his advisors saw opposition to the Second Bank gathering strength and decided to ask Congress to approve a re-charter of the Bank in 1832, four years before the existing charter expired. Biddle hoped Congress, with his persuasion, would re-charter the bank before opposition grew strong enough to block approval of a second charter. The House and Senate approved a bill renewing the charter, but President Jackson vetoed the bill, siding with critics of the bank who charged that it put too much power in the hands of officials neither elected by the people, nor appointed by elected representatives of the people. The Second Bank continued in operation until its charter expired in 1836.

With the Second Bank of the United States out of the picture, the United States experimented with free banking operating under a variety of laws in individual states. Public and private schemes emerged to meet some needs normally met by a central bank. In Boston the Suffolk Bank established the Suffolk System in 1819. This system, which added six other Boston banks by 1824, required country banks in the surrounding area to maintain reserves in the form of $5,000 in deposits at the seven Boston banks participating. The reserves could be deposited in one or spread over all seven banks. The reserve deposits guaranteed that Boston banks could always redeem country banknotes into specie. Largely because of the Suffolk System New England boasted the soundest currency in the United States between 1825 and 1860.

The state of Louisiana adopted the Forestall System in 1842, amid the depression that followed the Panic of 1837. A government-sponsored system, it required banks to maintain reserves in specie equal to 30 per cent of outstanding banknotes, and forbade loans of customer deposits for periods longer than 90 days. When banks across the nation suspended payments amid the Panic of 1857, Louisiana banks continued to redeem banknotes in specie, a testimony to the success of the Forestall System.

Trying to remedy some flaws of a free banking system without embracing a central banking system, in 1864 Congress passed the National Bank Act, providing for a system of note-issuing national banks operating under national charters. Under this system, national banks all issued uniform banknotes received from the Comptroller of the Currency in exchange for US government bonds. (Under the free banking system each bank had had its own banknotes printed, and the banknotes were redeemable at the issuing bank.) The National Bank Act gave the country a unified currency system instead of a medley of state banknotes trading at various discounts. Separate legislation put a tax on state banknotes, putting an end to that form of money in the United States.

One, perhaps fatal, weakness inherent in the system of national banks, was its provision for a hierarchy of reserve banks. Country banks held a share of reserves in the form of deposits at banks located in eighteen large cities designated as redemption centres. In turn, banks in redemption centres kept a share of reserves in the form of deposits in New York banks. The system led to a dangerous pyramiding of reserves, and the apex of the pyramid stood in New York City, the seat of the largest stock and bond markets. Funds held in New York City banks as reserves flowed into the New York money market and became part of the reservoir of capital available to finance stocks purchased on the margin. Fluctuations in agricultural production or any economic disturbance in the agricultural hinterland risked a sudden withdrawal of reserves from New York City, draining funds from the New York money market, and forcing the sale of stock purchased on credit with a marginal down payment. This forced sale often triggered a collapse in the stock market, which could easily plunge the country into a major economic downturn.

Concern about recurring economic crises led the United States to revert to the central banking model of monetary organization. In 1913 Congress adopted the Federal Reserve Act, one of numerous economic reforms enacted during the first year of the Woodrow Wilson administration. This act provided for the establishment of a central banking system called the Federal Reserve System, its name a reference to the role central banks play in holding reserves of liquidity for commercial banks. The Federal Reserve System is composed of twelve regional central banks spread across the United States in such diverse cities as New York City, San Francisco, Dallas, Atlanta and Denver. The New York Federal Reserve Bank is the largest and most important component bank of the Federal Reserve System, but none of the banks exert a dominant force. One reason the United States postponed the adoption of a central banking system was the fear that such an institution would be located in New York City, reinforcing Wall Street domination of the financial affairs of the country, something other regions resisted. The system of regional central banks, as opposed to one large central bank, defused the fear.

At the apex of the Federal Reserve System rests the Board of Governors of the Federal Reserve System, the governing body responsible for monetary policy in the United States. The board is composed of seven members, each appointed for a fourteen-year term. The terms are staggered such that one member's term expires every two years. The President of the United States makes the appointments, subject to Senate approval. The staggered terms are intended to remove politics from the composition of the board, limiting the power of a President serving the maximum eight years in office to stack the board with individuals of one persuasion or political affiliation. The Chairperson of the Board of Governors serves a four-year term, also appointed by the President of the United States, subject to Senate approval. This person can be reappointed, which often happens when a chairperson has firmly established themselves in the confidence of the banking and financial community. Neutralizing the political factor in monetary policy has helped to allay the fears of those who consider politicians incurably biased in favour of inflation. Decisions regarding open market operations are in the hands of the Federal Open Market Committee. This twelve-member committee is composed of the seven members of the Board of Governors, plus five of the twelve presidents of the Federal Reserve Banks. These presidents take turns serving on the Federal Open Market Committee.

While the Board of Governors is a public body appointed by government officials, the individual Federal Reserve Banks are owned by commercial banks, members of the Federal Reserve System. Commercial banks with charters from the federal government must join the Federal Reserve System, while commercial banks with charters from state governments may join the Federal Reserve System at their own discretion. The Federal Reserve Bank in each Federal Reserve District acts as a bankers' bank for the member commercial banks of that district. The Federal Reserve Bank of New York conducts open market operations.

The political insulation of the Board of Governors enabled the Federal Reserve System to doggedly pursue anti-inflation policies in the 1980s, pushing the US economy into its worst recession since the 1930s.[7] By the late 1980s prosperity with stable prices had returned. As central banks and governments around the world searched for non-inflationary monetary policies in the 1990s, the US dollar became the standard for currencies in other parts of the world. Particularly in Latin America, governments defined domestic currencies in terms of a fixed number of dollars.

Three decades before the United States finally resigned itself to tolerating a central bank, Japan, struggling to modernize its economic and financial system against a background of feudalism, formed the Bank of Japan, patterned after the European model of central banks. The money supply of feudal Japan consisted of gold and silver coins and a medley of paper money issued by feudal lords and merchants. Stores of rice, rather than gold or silver, often backed paper money. After the Meiji Restoration in 1868, Japan entered upon a path of accelerated economic development along Western lines. In 1872 the Japanese government adopted a national banking system resembling the national banking system in the United States that predated the Federal Reserve System. Under this system, banknotes were convertible into precious metal, and banks held government bonds as collateral for banknotes, making banks a ready customer for government bonds. In 1877 the Japanese government, financing the costs of suppressing a rebellion, allowed commercial banks to issue inconvertible paper money, inducing a raging inflation that lasted until 1881.

In 1881 the Japanese Minister of Finance toured Europe on a mission to study European models of central banks. The National Bank of Belgium, which Belgium had created as a central bank in 1850, caught the eye of the Japanese as the most advanced institution of that kind. It became the model for the Bank of Japan, created by the Bank of Japan Act of 1882. Organized as a private joint-stock company, the bank raised capital by selling shares of stock. Half its capital came from the government, accounting for the strong influence the Japanese treasury exerted on bank policies. Government officials appointed the governor of the Bank of Japan and supervised the bank's operations and administration.

The Bank of Japan began with a monopoly on the issuance of banknotes, and the capacity to act as a lender of last resort to commercial banks. It assumed responsibility for stabilizing seasonal and regional fluctuations, holding specie reserves, financing international trade and acting as the fiscal agent for the government. Bank of Japan banknotes were convertible into silver until 1897, when Japan adopted the gold standard after receiving a large war indemnity from China, enabling it to substantially enlarge its gold reserves. Most Western countries had adopted the gold standard between 1875 and 1900, while countries in the Far East, except Japan, remained on the silver standard until the Depression of the 1930s virtually abolished precious metal standards.

Japanese society adapted quickly to the development of modern banking. The percentage of the money supply composed of precious metal coinage decreased from 75 per cent in 1868 to 20 per cent in 1881. Bank deposits, which had represented 7 per cent of the money supply in 1882, grew to represent 44 per cent by 1914, putting Japan squarely on the road to a highly monetized economy. As late as June 1997 the Japanese Diet enacted the Bank of Japan Law, a piece of legislation requiring the government to respect the Bank of Japan's autonomy. In 1998 the Bank undertook a programme of reorganization aimed at streamlining operations and scaling down real estate and other unnecessary holdings.

Europe saw the formation of a new central bank, the European Central Bank (ECB) after leaders of the European Union agreed on 3 May 1998 to establish the European Monetary Union (EMU).[8] The ECB launched a common EMU currency, the Euro, on 1 January 1999. The management of the ECB rests in the hands of a president serving an eight-year term, a vice-president, and a four-member board with representatives from Germany, Italy, Spain and Finland. The first president, Dutchman Wim Duisenberg, has promised to step aside after four years, allowing Frenchman Jean-Claude Trichet to ascend to the presidency. A Frenchman, Christian Noyers, holds the position of vice-president.

The ECB faces a difficult task establishing an all-European monetary policy, with a single European interest rate, that will satisfy the individual needs of the economies involved. Currently eleven countries, Germany, France, Italy, Spain, Portugal, Belgium, Luxembourg, the Netherlands, Austria, Finland and Ireland, have joined the new monetary union represented by the ECB.

The universal acceptance of central banking systems added momentum to trends towards globalization. The major financial headquarters of the global economy, New York, London, Tokyo, Frankfurt, Paris, are seats to central banks constantly taking the temperature and pulse of financial markets and economic systems, reacting as needed to promote stability and growth. The central banks communicate with each other and employ similar methods to achieve similar goals.

SIX

The Birth of World Currencies

Almost from the outset of coinage and foreign exchange markets, certain coins and coinage systems rose to the stature of international coinage, lubricating and unifying international trade, nurturing the subterranean forces of economic law that led to the current racy pace of globalization. The Persian Empire coined 'Darics' after King Darius, gold coins mentioned once in the Bible, which held court over Middle Eastern trade during the sixth and fifth centuries BC. The Athenian 'Owls,' principal coins of the Athenian silver standard, presided over Mediterranean trade during the later fifth century. Arnold Toynbee mentions the Athenian Owl as an example of a coin that remained in circulation in remote corners of the world long after Athens ceased to exist as an independent state.[1] Alexander the Great's coinage superseded the Athenian as the international coinage of the time, and his coins belong with the most ancient examples discovered in England. Constantine I introduced the solidus, a gold coin popularized by the sound money policies of the Byzantine government, becoming the foundation of the international monetary system during the Middle Ages, faithfully maintaining its purity and weight for nearly 1,000 years, a record for any currency, even today.

During the Middle Ages gold and most silver coinage disappeared from Europe even while the solidus remained as the money of account. Around AD 755 Pepin the Short, father to Charlemagne, introduced the Carolingian Reform, establishing a currency system that reigned in Europe until the end of the eighteenth century, and exerted an influence that could still be felt in the twentieth century. The Reform established a silver standard in which the fundamental unit was a pound of silver, equal to 20 shillings or 240 pennies (pence). For the next 300 years, the silver penny was the only coin minted in Europe.

Pounds and shillings acted as ghost money, a money of account useful for keeping books and defining debts but not circulating as coins. Rather than write '2,400 pennies', it was much more convenient to write '10 pounds'.

The Carolingian system spread throughout Western Europe, a legacy of Charlemagne. The Norman Conquest took the Carolingian system to England, where it survived until 1971 in the pound-shilling-penny relationship. The Latin word for pound furnished the root for the Italian lira and the French livre. The Italian money of account is still called a lira. The French livre was the unit of account in France until the French Revolution when the franc replaced it in a decimal currency system. Under the French Carolingian system 1 livre equalled 20 sols or sous, and 20 sols equalled 240 deniers. The French Empire under Napoleon propagated the decimal currency systems, accounting for present-day Swiss and Belgian francs.

Pennies suffered from debasement, a reduction in the silver content of 240 pennies to less than a pound of silver, a deterioration accelerating after the break up of the Carolingian Empire. Several states in Italy began minting silver coins in larger denominations.

Towards the end of the Middle Ages European coinage returned to play an important role in international trade. In 1252 Florence issued the florin, a gold coin weighing 3.53 gm (or 72 grains) of fine gold, bearing on one side an image of the fleur-de-lis, which gave the coin its name. During the second half of the thirteenth century and the first half of the fourteenth, the florin circulated as the predominant currency in international trade, equivalent to the dollar post World War II. The Florentine government launched the florin with the intention of grooming it to act as an international currency. Like many subsequent international currencies, the florin owed part of its success to the strength and expansion of the economy it represented. Florence issued both gold and silver currency, but gold currency was reserved for international merchants, money-changers, cloth and silk manufacturers, grocers and furriers, who were allowed to keep books and transact business in florins. Retail trade, payment of wages and small purchases were transacted in silver currency. The government made efforts to fix the exchange rates between gold and silver but without success, always yielding to overriding market forces.

During the fifteenth century the Venetian gold ducat supplanted the florin as the international currency of the trading world. The florin lost stature as an international currency after other governments began striking inferior imitations and the Florentine government minted issues of florins at a lighter weight. The Venetian ducat, first introduced in 1284, soon after the florin, enjoyed a prestige that embraced both Christian and Muslim countries, setting the standard followed wherever currency reform was instituted. It furnished the model for the Mamluk ashraftil, the Ottoman altun and the Castilian ducat. The Venetian ducat may owe part of its success to the Venetian government's commitment to maintaining the integrity of its coinage. From its inception in 1284, until the end of the Venetian Republic in 1797, the weight and purity of the gold ducat remained constant, at 3.5 gm of gold at 0.997 fineness.

The political history of Venice reveals the underlying forces that help governments maintain commitment to their currencies over time, resisting the temptation to depreciate in times of financial distress. Feudal monarchies, often overextending themselves on military and court expenditures and sparing a hereditary aristocracy much of the burden of taxes, all too readily turn to currency devaluations, debasements and seigniorage to pay for government expenditures. In Venice the landowning aristocracy lost its grip on political power and social prestige, yielding to a class of hereditary mercantile families who had a vested interest in protecting the special place Venice commanded in international trade. The mercantile oligarchy that ruled Venice saw a sound currency, one that always maintained its value, as a means of promoting Venice as a world financial centre, knowing international trade would follow. A sound currency symbolized Venetian respect for fairness in commercial dealings. To protect its currency, the government manned the mint with Venetian citizens only, excluding foreigners from access to stamp patterns that could be duplicated. Governments caught issuing imitations of Venetian ducats incurred the wrath of the Venetian government.

With the discovery of precious metals in the New World, leadership passed to Spanish coinage, particularly the *de a ocho reales* 'pieces of eight', a silver coin, immediate forebear of the US dollar and the Mexican peso. The pieces of eight was called the Spanish dollar in the United States, where it remained legal tender in much of the pre-Civil War era of the Republic. Ferdinand and Isabella, Spanish monarchs famous for financing Columbus's expedition in search of a western route to the Indies, introduced the *de a ocho reales* as part of a plan to furnish Spain with a unified coinage system. *Reales*, Spanish for royal, was sometimes called a 'bit' in English, which explains why a quarter is two bits, or three quarters six bits. The term bits may be a reference to a practice of cutting a pieces of eight into eight bits, which circulated as coins. Charles V spread the Spanish coinage system in Europe, where the pieces of eight was equal in value to the Bohemian or Saxon thaler. In the United States the thaler became the dollar.

Vast silver deposits in Peru and Mexico enabled Spain to infuse the world trading system with a steady stream of reals. Mexico City became the seat of the largest mint in the world, turning out a piece of eight coin called the 'pillar dollar', a reference to the symbol of the Pillars of Hercules stamped on the obverse. One purpose of the coin was to advertise the New World, and the Pillars of Hercules, the strait that opens the Mediterranean into the Atlantic Ocean, was regarded as the door that led to the New World. The '$' sign probably evolved as a bookkeeping symbol for the dollar with the vertical line or lines representing the pillars and the S sign representing a banner hanging from one pillar.

Towards the end of the sixteenth century Spanish coinage, and particularly pieces of eight, emerged as the leading international currency, and remained so through the seventeenth and eighteenth centuries, dominating international trade between the Far East, the Mediterranean and the New World. The British pound sterling supplanted Spanish reals in the nineteenth century as the principal international currency, but Mexico's version of the pieces of eight, called the peso, launched in 1821 after Mexico won independence from Spain, remained a popular coin in the Far East throughout the nineteenth century.

The pound sterling assumed the role of an international currency in trade between European colonial empires. Trade within the colonial empires was transacted in currencies of those empires, the French franc financing trade between France and French colonies, the Deutschmark between Germany and German colonies. The continental European currencies largely froze out the pound sterling as a major currency between countries on the European continent, but the pound sterling became the dominant international currency for trade between the colonial empires, for instance between the French colonies and England or Germany.

The pride of the British currency during the nineteenth century was the gold sovereign, a gold coin equal to twenty shillings or one pound. The sovereign and half sovereign remained in circulation until the beginning of World War I. It was a gold coin because Britain had officially adopted the gold standard in 1816, and the enabling legislation, Lord Liverpool's Coinage Act, provided for the coinage of a twenty-shilling gold coin consisting of 123.3 grains of gold. This coin, the sovereign, became the last coin to circulate as an international currency before the metallic currencies yielded the field to more elastic paper money, able expand and contract with the needs of trade.

Mints in Britain, Sydney and Bombay supplied the world with sovereigns. A strong demand drew many of them to foreign countries, causing the coins to leave England permanently. Whenever the value of sovereigns fell in foreign exchange markets, speculators bought up sovereigns, melted them down into bullion, and sold the gold bullion to the British mints. British officials were known to deplore the burden of keeping the world supplied with coins, but also recognized the commercial advantages of furnishing it with a sound circulating medium that promoted international trade.

In 1914 gold coinage ceased to circulate in Britain. Following World War I sovereigns were minted periodically as a hedge against inflation, but never returned as a circulating medium. The pound sterling continued to act as a major international currency, the last currency whose international prestige originated with a precious metal coin of unquestioned weight and purity. After World War I Britain valiantly struggled to restore the gold standard at pre-war parity, which was 3 pounds, 17 shillings and 10 pence per fine ounce of gold. The Gold Standard Act of 1925 put the pound sterling back on the gold standard, but made no provision for the domestic circulation of gold coins, instead allowing the British public to convert Bank of England banknotes into gold bars.

The return to pre-war parity left the pound overvalued, making British exports too costly in foreign markets, and foreign imports too cheap in British markets. As an added depressant to the British economy, the Bank of England, discouraging the conversion of pounds into gold, leaned towards high interest rates. The economic suffering that the British endured to maintain the value of the pound at pre-war parity helps to explain why the British pound sterling has a longer continuous history than any other major currency, surviving 1,300 years as the currency unit of Britain, never discontinued in favour of a 'new pound', or any other change of name reflecting a need to restore credibility.

By 1931 the conversion of pounds into gold was accelerating and British economic conditions were too depressed for the Bank of England to contemplate raising interest rates, leading to the abandonment of the gold standard with the Gold Standard Amendment Act. Other countries were left with three choices, maintain themselves on the gold standard; keep their currencies linked to the pound sterling, maintaining the conversion of their currencies into sterling at a fixed rate; or pursue an independent policy. A 'sterling area' emerged composed of countries choosing to maintain a fixed convertibility ratio between their currencies and sterling. Prominent members of the sterling area were the Commonwealth countries (except Canada), the English colonies, Portugal and the Scandinavian countries.

The US dollar advanced to the forefront of international currencies following World War II, supported by the United States' vast gold stock and production facilities unscathed by war. Immediately after the war the pound sterling ranked second after the US dollar, but in the 1950s the prestige of the pound suffered from currency crises and devaluation. Long before the post-World War II era the dollar had filled an important niche in international trade. The American colonists had called the Spanish pieces of eight the 'dollar', the term for

Scottish currency. Probably its anti-British and anti-authoritarian connotation made the term popular in the American colonies. The term 'dollar' had evolved from thaler, a name for coins minted in Germany and Eastern Europe dating back to the sixteenth century. England had prohibited the coinage of money in English colonies, but Spanish colonies made the coinage of money a major industry and Mexico became the seat of the world's largest mint. Variously called dollars, pesos or reals, Spanish coinage dominated trade in the New World and the Pacific Basin, areas within the Spanish Empire's sphere of influence. In the New World, aside from the United States, dollars became the official currency in Anguilla, Saint Kitts and Nevis, Antigua and Barbuda, Montserrat, Dominica, Saint Lucia, Saint Vincent, Guyana, the Bahamas, Belize, Barbados, the Cayman Islands, the British Virgin Islands, Trinidad and Tobago, the Turks and Caicos Islands and Jamaica. Mexico and numerous Latin American countries adopted the peso, the Spanish name for the same coin. Currencies named dollars sprung up in every part of the world except Europe, where the word dollar in connection with currency originated. By 1994 the term dollar denoted the official currencies in 37 countries and autonomous territories.

US dollars remained the principal world currency under the system of managed float exchange rates that has continued since 1973, and banks around the world offered deposits denominated in dollars. European banks and foreign branches of US banks began holding deposits of US dollars, called Eurodollars, in the late 1950s, but the practice really took off in the 1970s. From 1976 until 1992 Eurodollar deposits mushroomed from $14 billion to $56 billion. The former Soviet Union during the Cold War maintained deposits of dollars in European banks as a protective measure, keeping its dollar deposits out of the reach of the US government, which might freeze the assets in a political dispute.

Eurodollar deposits were dollar deposits in US banks, but the deposits belonged to either foreign banks or foreign branches of US banks. Dollar deposits held in US banks may belong to individuals living in foreign countries, in which case they do not count as Eurodollars. Foreign banks and foreign branches of

US banks pay interest to attract dollar deposits, usually held in the form of interest-paying time deposits, usually in large amounts. Businesses from around the world, including the United States, contract for loans of dollars from banks holding Eurodollar deposits. The growth of Eurodollar deposits made dealing in dollars an ongoing activity during normal business hours in European time zones.

European banks got into the business of loaning dollars because US interest rate ceilings on deposit interest rates, so-called Regulation Q, put a limit on the interest rate US banks could pay to attract dollar deposits, making it possible for European banks, outside the orbit of US banking regulations, to offer higher interest rates than US banks. Given this advantage in attracting dollar deposits, European banks found lending dollars a lucrative business. The United States' deregulation of banking in the 1980s removed much of the attraction for Eurodollar deposits, but the Eurodollar market had established itself and continued to thrive. Headquarters for the Eurodollar market is in London, but banks worldwide, from the Bahamas, Cayman Islands and Canada to Hong Kong and Singapore, share in the market, holding dollar deposits and making dollar loans.

Other currencies have never quite achieved the status of a dominating currency, but have played important roles in certain regions or spheres of influence. The French franc, Europe's first decimalized currency, an innovation of the French Revolution and Napoleonic period, was the most influential currency in Western Europe during the nineteenth century. The British pound sterling dominated international trade during the era, but the French franc dominated trade on the continent. The history of the Belgian franc and the Swiss franc can be traced to the spread of the French monetary system during the nineteenth century.

Napoleon's government was the first to coin francs. France had suffered two episodes of hyperinflationary paper money during the eighteenth century, strengthening the commitment of the French government to uphold the metallic content of this new currency. For 125 years the metallic equivalent of the franc would remain constant. The French Monetary Law of 1803 had established the franc on the bimetallic system at a ratio of 15.5 ounces of silver to 1 ounce of gold. One franc equalled 5 grams of silver. Silver coins ranged from one-quarter-franc to five-franc pieces, and the smallest gold coin was a ten-franc piece.

Napoleon's victories brought war indemnities to France, building up gold and silver reserves that helped France launch and maintain the franc on a sound basis. Throughout the Napoleonic struggle between Britain and France the franc remained a stronger currency than the pound sterling, fluctuating less in foreign exchange markets. During the Revolution of 1848 the French government suspended convertibility of the franc into gold and silver, but the franc only depreciated mildly, suggesting its strength as a currency. The government resumed convertibility in 1850. During the Franco-Prussian War (1870–71), the French government again suspended convertibility, this time the suspension lasted until 1878. Following the war France paid heavy war reparations to Germany, supplying Germany with the gold reserves to establish itself on a gold standard. The episode of the Paris Commune infused additional uncertainty into the future of French monetary affairs. Despite these difficulties the franc suffered only mild fluctuations before the restoration of convertibility.

In 1865 France, Italy, Switzerland and Belgium organized the Latin Monetary Union, based upon a unified bimetallic coinage system. These countries waged a campaign to preserve a worldwide bimetallic system based upon gold and silver, but history was on the side of the gold standard, which seemed to be vindicated by Britain's commercial success. As countries abandoned silver in favour of gold, silver prices plummeted, and France was forced to drop silver in 1873. By 1878 France had officially adopted the gold standard. The French franc's reputation for soundness floundered slightly under the gold standard, partly because France jealously hoarded its gold reserves and often redeemed francs in badly worn ten-franc gold coins and five-franc silver coins.

World War I brought the operation of the gold standard to a halt in Europe, most countries suspending the redemption of paper money into gold and banning the export of gold. Like most European countries, particularly on the continent, France increased domestic money stocks substantially to help finance the war effort. After the war the franc sustained an onslaught of speculative waves and in 1926 finally stabilized around one-fifth of its pre-war parity, leaving it undervalued, particularly compared to the overvalued pound sterling, and easing the downward speculative pressure on the franc.

By the eve of the 1930s Depression the world's major trading partners, including France, had reinstated the gold standard, but it lasted only briefly. As the Depression gathered momentum, Britain, Japan and the United States suspended the gold standard, allowing the value of their currencies to depreciate, increasing the amounts of their own currencies needed to purchase an ounce of gold. These devaluations made each country's exports cheaper in foreign markets, and left foreign imports more expensive in domestic markets, on balance increasing the demand for domestically produced goods relative to foreign. Depression-torn countries devalued currencies to stimulate domestic economies.

Because the franc was undervalued at the onset of the Depression, France was able to remain committed to the gold standard well into the Depression. The French franc became the leading currency of the Gold Bloc, a group of countries (Belgium, France, Holland, Italy, Poland, Switzerland) that stayed on the gold standard until September 1936. France began the Bretton Woods era with the franc overvalued, forcing the government to undertake a series of official devaluations of the franc, the last in 1968. A strong Deutschmark in the decades after World War II tended to eclipse the franc as the leading currency on the continent. As for the pound sterling, escalating inflation rates sapped confidence in the franc. As France demonstrated success on the inflation front, the franc regained some of its lost ground, beginning to rival the Deutschmark in the 1990s. With Germany and several other European countries France agreed to the eventual adoption of an all-European currency, the Euro, which will replace the franc along with other major European currencies.

The Swiss franc also won itself a place in the leading currencies of the world. While it never acted as principal international currency in any sphere of world trade, the Swiss have long enjoyed a reputation for financial probity, making the Swiss franc a safe currency for a store of wealth. The Swiss franc may owe part of its strength to the fact that the Switzerland is the seat of the world's largest gold market. Unlike the United States, the government of Switzerland never banned or restricted the ownership of gold during the years before and after World War II, and Swiss banknotes are backed by gold reserves equalling 40 per cent of outstanding notes in face value.

When Switzerland, along with the belligerent countries, suspended the gold standard during World War I, the Swiss franc appreciated relative to other currencies, including the US dollar, which remained relatively strong during the war. After the war Switzerland re-established its currency on the gold standard at pre-war parity without the struggle that Britain faced with the pound, and was one of the last to suspend the gold standard during the Depression. Switzerland was one of the Gold Bloc countries that resisted devaluation. Only after France suspended the gold standard in September 1936 did Switzerland give up the standard. Both France and Switzerland devalued their currencies 30 per cent.

During World War II the record of the Swiss franc was not quite as sound as during World War I, but it maintained its reputation, trading at 3 per cent premium over the US dollar by July 1945. Under the fixed exchange rate regime of the Bretton Woods System, the rate between Swiss francs and US dollars was set at four francs per dollar, and the demand for Swiss francs relative to US dollars remained so strong that the Swiss government took measures to discourage holding Swiss francs. When the exchange rates were allowed to float early in the 1970s, the Swiss franc steadily gained ground relative to the US dollar, trading at 1.5 francs per dollar by the late 1990s.

A relatively new currency, the Deutschmark can boast a distinguished ancestry. In 1873 when only two European countries, Britain and Portugal, were on the gold standard, Germany adopted it after extracting a large war indemnity from France over the Franco-Prussian War, which furnished Germany with the gold reserves necessary. The mark as the monetary unit of Germany only dates back to 1871 when the Reichstag established it as part of a plan to provide a single monetary unit for the newly unified Germany, formerly split into six currency areas. Germany's hyperinflation after World War I put an end to Germany's reputation for monetary probity and towards the end of 1923 the Rentenmark replaced the gold mark as part of the anti-inflation monetary reform. The Rentenmark was later renamed the Reichmark, discontinued after World War II in favour of the Deutschmark.

The Deutschmark burst onto the scene on 20 June 1948, its introduction a secret military operation of the Allies, Operation Birddog.[2] The Allied Powers kept the Soviet Union out of the operation, fearing that Soviet authorities could not be trusted with printing plates that would enable them to print extra Deutschmark notes and impose an inflation tax on Germany. The German currency of World War II, the Reichsmark, had lost all credibility, ceasing to function as a medium of exchange because shortages and price controls emptied all shelves and stocks, leaving no goods to be purchased. An underground barter system, depending heavily upon cigarettes and coal, helped the economy function immediately following the war. City dwellers carried what they had to the countryside and traded it for food with farmers. Goods returned surprisingly soon after the introduction of the Deutschmark, suggesting much had been held in the underground economy.

The Allies decreed that one Deutschmark equalled ten Reichsmarks, and all government debts, bank loans, insurance policies, bank deposits and balance sheets of businesses, both the assets and the liabilities, were adjusted downward on a 10:1 basis. All new debts had to be contracted in Deutschmarks. Authorities established a central banking system, organizing the branches of the Reichsbank into a system modelled after the Federal Reserve System in the United States. First called the Bank of Deutscher Lander (Bank of German States), the bank was transformed into the Deutsche Bundesbank in 1957. The charter of the Deutsche Bundesbank emphasized the maintenance of price stability as the bank's mission, without mentioning the importance of full employment or economic growth, an important consideration at a time when governments around the world were assuming responsibility for maintaining full employment.[3] Credited with keeping West Germany's inflation rate low when inflation became a worldwide scourge in the 1970s, the Bundesbank emerged to become the most prestigious central banking system in Europe, in the process lifting the Deutschmark to the stature of a major currency.

As the movement towards economic integration progressed in Europe, the Bundesbank played an increasingly dominant role in European monetary affairs, leading Europe through the disinflation period of the 1980s, and maintaining the reputation of the Deutschmark as the most stable currency in Europe. In the 1990s the challenges of merging the economies of East and West Germany distracted Germany from its priority of monetary stability, and confidence in the Deutschmark suffered. By then France seemed firmly committed to a course of price stability, and the franc developed a reputation for currency soundness rivalling the Deutschmark, which will nevertheless remain the leading currency of Europe until its replacement by the Euro.

Another currency that gained strength relative to the US dollar and came to play a major role in global financial system is the Japanese yen. The yen, modelled after the nineteenth century US and Mexican dollars that circulated in East Asian trade, has been the monetary unit of account in Japan since 1871. Originally its silver content was comparable to that of US and Mexican silver dollars. The yen price of an ounce of gold was 20 yen, while the US dollar price was $20.67. Like the dollar and most European currencies by that time, the yen was a decimal currency, a sen equaling a hundredth of a yen. Officially on a bimetallic standard, Japan was on a de facto silver standard till the Sino-Japanese War (1894–5) won Japan a large reparation payment from Russia, paid in gold.

Japan suspended the gold standard and banned gold exports at the onset of World War I, by no means an unusual action at the time. The European powers took similar action, partly to give more freedom for expanding domestic stocks of paper money, and partly because of the risks of exporting gold. Japan, facing more than the usual obstacles to returning to gold, briefly re-instituted the gold standard in 1930, but suspended it again in 1931, owing to the pressures of the developing worldwide Depression. Through the Depression and World War II

Japan maintained strict government regulation of its currency, trying to maintain its reserves of gold and foreign exchange.

During World War II Japan turned to inflationary finance, increasing paper money stocks far ahead of what could be justified on the basis of gold and foreign exchange reserves. Following the war, occupation authorities reformed the Japanese currency, withdrawing old yen notes, issuing new ones, and fixing the exchange rate between yen and US dollars at 360 yen per dollar, a rate that remained constant without devaluation or revaluation under the Bretton Woods System. Under the Bretton Woods System the yen was undervalued, leaving Japanese goods highly competitive in world markets, and Japanese consumers paying high prices for imported goods. A significant excess of exports over imports brought substantial additions to Japan's gold and foreign exchange reserves, leading to the abolition of Japanese restrictions on foreign exchange transactions.

After the Bretton Woods System of fixed exchange rates was dismantled in 1973, the yen steadily appreciated in value relative to the US dollar. From the 360 yen required to purchase a dollar under the Bretton Woods System, the number of yen required fell to 272 in 1973 and to 219 by the end of the decade. This also meant that more dollars were required to purchase a yen, leaving Japanese-produced goods more expensive in US markets. Despite the appreciation of the yen, US producers continued to face stiff competition from Japanese goods. In 1984 the world's major trading partners initiated a plan to further appreciate the yen in foreign exchange markets through cooperative intervention. In 1985 its value stood at 239 yen per dollar but had fallen to 128 yen per dollar by 1988. Towards the later 1990s economic depression in Japan cost the yen some of its appreciated value, putting it in the 140 yen per dollar trading range in 1998. The yen regained its strength in 1999, trading at 120.65 yen per dollar on 7 June.

Like the US dollar, the international currencies of the second rank developed extra-territorial markets comparable to the Eurodollar. The extra-territorial markets, including the Eurodollar, are collectively referred to as the Eurocurrencies, and include the yen, Deutschmarks, British pounds sterling,

French francs and Swiss francs. Paris and Brussels share the market in Eurosterling, and the market for Euromark deposits is in Luxembourg.

An important financial innovation of the Bretton Woods System, surviving to the present day, is Special Drawing Rights (SDRS), a species of fiat international monetary reserves awarded the same status as gold by the members of the International Monetary Fund (IMF). The IMF proposed the issuance of SDRS at an annual meeting in 1967, hoping to ease problems created by a growing shortage of international gold reserves, which eventually led to an end of the Bretton Woods System. Countries held gold reserves and dollars to redeem their own currencies at official rates, effectively pegging the market value of their currencies. In 1969 members of the IMF ratified an agreement to allocate SDRS to member countries at a rate proportional to each country's IMF quota of funds, based upon such factors as national income and involvement in international trade.

Created with the stroke of a pen, SDRS, sometimes called 'paper gold', because originally their value was fixed in gold, commanded the same purchasing power as gold of equal value. They are actually only bookkeeping entries in the IMF accounts. After the break up of the Bretton Woods System, the IMF stopped defining the value of SDRS in gold and turned to a system of defining their value in terms of a weighted basket of major international currencies. In 1981 the basket was fixed with five currencies, the US dollar, Deutschmark, French franc, Japanese yen and British pound. The significance of each currency in the composite make-up of SDR is determined by the weight attached to each currency, a factor that is adjusted every five years by the IMF; the last adjustment was in 1995.

By international agreement, SDRS are treated as gold or foreign exchange for settling intergovernmental transactions. Assume the British pound had been losing value in foreign exchange markets. The British government can draw on its SDR account at the IMF to pay for the purchase of French francs from France's central bank, and use these francs to purchase British pounds in foreign exchange markets, increasing the demand for and therefore the value of British pounds in foreign exchange markets. The British government will not receive a sufficient allocation of SDRS to reverse a long-term downward trend in the value of the British pound, but the allocation will help smooth out short-term fluctuations. A government, perhaps of a less developed country, might choose to purchase goods and services with SDR-purchased foreign exchange. Daily fluctuations in the value of the individual currencies that make up SDRS automatically generate daily fluctuations in SDRS. Daily values of SDRS can be read in the *Wall Street Journal*'s foreign exchange tables. The IMF keeps its accounts in SDRS rather than in units of a national currency, and its financial reports are made with SDRS as the monetary unit of account. A few governments base the value of domestic currencies on SDRS. SDRS may evolve into a replacement for gold and US dollars as the principal assets held as international monetary reserves.

On 3 May 1998 leaders of the European Union finalized plans to form the European Monetary Union (EMU), and to introduce on 1 January 1999 a new all-European currency, the Euro, that will eventually replace the national currencies of Europe.[4] Current plans provide that by 1 July 2002 the Euro will replace national currencies and the European Central Bank will begin issuing Euro paper notes and coins, creating a new monetary zone called 'Euroland'. Greece is expected to adopt the Euro by 2001, but Britain, Sweden and Denmark remain hesitant to give up their own national currencies. In a referendum Danish voters turned down a proposal to join 'Euroland', and in Britain the adoption or not of the Euro is a highly charged issue. Members of the EMU own gold reserves five times the value of gold reserves held by the United States, and the EMU represents an economic bloc with a larger population than the United States, giving European leaders hope the Euro will soon rival the US dollar as the leading currency in the global financial system.

SEVEN

The Road to Flexible Exchange Rates

Noisy foreign exchange markets bring together busy buyers and sellers of national currencies, making it possible for US households and businesses to purchase British pounds, and British households and businesses to purchase Deutschmarks, US dollars, French francs, Japanese yen, etc. A handful of global financial centres, New York, Frankfurt, London, Tokyo, top the list of centres for trading in currencies, now part of a highly integrated global foreign exchange market that brings fluttering exchange rates into synchronization at different trading sites. During the business week foreign exchange is tirelessly traded around the clock, the large commercial banks with foreign branches accounting for most of the foreign exchange transactions in amounts of $1 million or more.

Prices of foreign currency, called exchange rates, fix the rate at which one currency can be converted into another. Major financial newspapers such as the *Wall Street Journal* report every day a mid-range or closing exchange rate for the previous day. On 26 March 1999, a British pound cost $1.62 cents in US dollars, which made US $1 equal to 0.616 British pounds. By convention most exchange rates show US dollar equivalents, facilitating the comparison of value between different currencies. Again on 26 March, a Deutschmark sold for $0.55 cents in US dollars, from which one could compute the exchange rate between British pounds and Deutschmarks. Exchange rates fluctuate throughout a trading day and instantaneous reports of exchange rates are available on financial websites.

Foreign exchange rates of major currencies such as the US dollar, Japanese yen, British pound, Deutschmark and others are traded either for delivery within two business days, within 30 days, 60 days or 90 days. The foreign exchange rate for delivery within two business days is called the spot rate, and the rates for delivery after a fixed period of time, such as 90 days, are called forward rates. Forward exchange rates afford some protection to importers and exporters who could suffer from unexpected shifts in rates, substantially changing the cost of imported goods in domestic markets, or the cost of exported goods in foreign markets. An importer might make an agreement to pay a price for imported goods when they arrive, and purchase foreign exchange in the forward market to lock in a given exchange rate for the time when payment for the goods is made. Likewise, an exporter needs to know what payment in foreign exchange will translate into as domestic currency when payment for exported goods is received, and a forward exchange rate allows the exporter to lock in a given exchange rate. Forward rates vary from spot rates by discounts or premiums up to 20 per cent, depending upon stability of the currencies involved. Currencies with forward rate discounts above 20 per cent are not traded in forward foreign exchange markets.

The effects of changes in foreign exchange rates are directly felt in national economies. A market appreciation of the value of the US dollar in foreign exchange markets, reducing the number of dollars needed to purchase Japanese yen, leaves Japanese goods less expensive in the US market, tipping the balance in favour of Japanese-produced goods over domestically produced goods and encouraging importation of Japanese goods. On the other hand, a market depreciation of the US dollar in foreign exchange markets, increasing the number of dollars needed to purchase Japanese yen, raises the costs of Japanese goods in the American market, tipping the balance in favour of domestically produced goods over Japanese and reducing the importation of Japanese goods into the United States. As a generalization for any national economy, the depreciation of domestic currency in foreign exchange markets raises the demand for domestically produced goods over foreign-produced goods, and appreciation of a domestic currency lowers the demand for domestically produced goods relative to foreign-produced.

The forces governing the market conditions for a particular currency can be gleaned from the balance of payments for the country represented by the currency. All international transactions that prompt either an inflow or outflow of money are summarized in a balance of payments account, which breaks down into a current account, a capital account and an official reserves transactions account. When a net inflow or outflow of funds results from the combined balance of current and capital accounts, central banks make a settlement, which shows up in the official reserves account.

The debit column in the balance of payments registers those transactions that lead to an outflow of money, bearing a negative sign in the balance of payments. The credit column registers transactions that lead to an inflow of money, bearing a positive sign in the balance of payments. A balance of payments deficit occurs when the combined current and capital accounts show a net outflow of money, and a balance of payments surplus occurs when the combined current and capital accounts show a net inflow of money.

A major source of money outflows on the current account is imports of foreign goods, and a major source of inflows is export of domestically produced goods. Exports minus imports is the balance of trade, which may also show a surplus or deficit, leading to a net money inflow on the trade account in the case of a surplus, and a net outflow in the case of a deficit. The current account is based upon the balance of trade adjusted for the effects of income earned from foreign investments and money transferred between different countries.

The capital account shows the effect on net money flows of capital movements between countries. Money flows out when domestic investors purchase financial or non-financial assets in foreign countries, and these transactions are reported in the negative column in the capital account. A US citizen purchasing either stock on the Tokyo Stock Exchange or a Toyota is causing dollars to flow out of the United States. Money flows in when foreign investors purchase financial or non-financial investments in the domestic economy, and these transactions are reported in the plus column of the capital account. Japanese investors purchasing US government bonds cause an inflow of dollars to the United States (and a yen outflow from Japan).

Net money flows on the capital account often offset net money flows on the current account, a situation readily seen in the bilateral relationship between the United States and Japan. US imports from Japan far exceed exports to Japan, creating a net dollar outflow on the US current account as far as trade with Japan goes. Japan takes the dollars earned selling goods to the United States and purchases US government bonds and real estate and builds factories in the United States, creating a net dollar inflow on the US capital account as far as Japan is concerned. A net inflow on the capital account can offset a net outflow on the current account.

A deficit or surplus on combined current and capital accounts requires that central banks settle accounts by compensating adjustments in holdings of gold, foreign exchange or other reserve assets. A deficit on current and capital accounts diminishes the reserves of the domestic central bank, while a surplus adds reserves to the domestic central bank. A deficit leaves foreign economies with a claim on domestic resources, and a surplus gives the domestic economy a claim on foreign resources.

A domestic currency will lose value in foreign exchange markets when persistent deficits flood foreign exchange markets with supplies of domestic currency. Currency depreciation increases the cost of imports and decreases the cost of exports, creating forces that balance the money flows and end currency depreciation. A domestic currency will gain value in foreign exchange markets when persistent surpluses on the combined current and capital accounts starve foreign exchange markets of supplies of domestic currency. Currency appreciation decreases the cost of imports and increases the cost of exports, creating forces that close the gap between money inflows and outflows and end the currency appreciation.

The history of foreign exchange markets dates back almost to the beginning of coinage itself, around 700 BC. In the ancient world a religious temple was often the site of a foreign exchange market. The sacredness of the grounds offered an added safeguard for the treasuries of coin often coveted by robbers and even hard-pressed governments. Precious metal coinage was a favourite religious offering at most temples, some of which even minted their own coins.

In the Middle Ages moneychangers worked from a 'bench', which evolved into the modern term 'bank'. Foreign exchange markets received a powerful stimulus from developments in bills of exchange during the Middle Ages. A bill of exchange is a written order to pay a certain sum of money to the individual named on the bill or to that person's account. In the thirteenth century Italian merchants, bankers and foreign exchange dealers turned the bill of exchange into a powerful financial instrument, which could remove the necessity for transporting bulky precious metals, and could serve as a credit instrument as well as an instrument for buying or selling foreign exchange.

Bills of exchange entered into foreign exchange transactions as follows: a Florentine merchant, purchasing goods from a merchant in Flanders, paid for the goods by giving the Flanders merchant a bill of exchange, promising to pay the Florentine agent of the Flanders merchant a certain amount of Florentine currency at a specified date. The Flanders merchant might sell the bill of exchange to a Flanders foreign exchange dealer for the currency of his choice, and the Flanders foreign exchange dealer would sell the bill of exchange to a Flanders merchant planning to buy goods in Florence at the time the bill of exchange was due to be paid. This bill of exchange transaction allowed two-way trade between Florence and Flanders to take place without the movement of bulky precious metals. It also allowed the Florentine merchant to purchase goods from Flanders on credit, sell the goods for a profit, and pay the bill of exchange in Florentine currency when it was due, after the goods were liquidated.

Bill of exchange transactions hid interest charges in fees and adjustments to foreign exchange rates. (Directly charging interest violated Church doctrine against usury and was prohibited.) In the example above the Florentine merchant is obviously purchasing goods on credit, but never overtly pays interest. Italian bankers developed a variant of bills of exchange, called dry bills of exchange, which served solely as instrument of credit, unconnected to the purchase or sale of merchandise. A dry bill of exchange constituted a credit transaction as in the following example: a Florentine banker advanced a sum of money to an Italian merchant, accepting in turn a bill of exchange payable at a future date to the banker's agent in another, perhaps distant, financial centre. On the day the bill of exchange came due, the banker's agent in the foreign market drew another bill of exchange on the Italian merchant, payable at a future date in Florence to the Florentine banker who advanced the sum to the Italian merchant. The Florentine banker essentially advanced financing to the Italian merchant over the time it took for these transactions to be completed, embedding interest charges in fees charged for the two bills of exchange. Dry bills of exchange were a none too subtle means of evading usury laws and periodically the Church pressured Italian governments to ban them. As governments, particularly Protestant governments, loosened usury laws, legalizing interest charges, bills of exchange evolved into means for converting short-term credit into long-term credit. These bills of exchange openly charged interest, but the practice of drawing bills and redrawing bills, adding interest charges at each step, postponed the date when payment had to be made. In whatever form, bills of exchange circulated as substitutes for money, and economized on the need to transport precious metal.

David Hume (1711–1776), one of the most famous philosophers in Western civilization, is credited for setting forth the forces that govern the inflow and outflow of precious metals from a particular country in a system of trading countries, and the adjusting mechanisms that tend to balance the inflow with the outflow.[1] Under the metallic monetary systems, a country's money stock expanded and contracted with the country's domestic holdings of gold and silver bullion and specie. Even the supply of paper money, as long as it was convertible into gold and silver, was directly proportional to domestic holdings of gold and silver. The import of goods from abroad led to an outflow of gold and silver as payments were made to outsiders, acting to reduce the domestic money stock. The export of goods to foreign markets led to an inflow of gold and silver as payment was received from outsiders, acting to expand the domestic money stock. Inflows and outflows of foreign investment worked similarly. An inflow of foreign investment brought an inflow of gold and silver, an outflow of domestic capital to foreign countries brought an outflow of gold and silver.

Economic forces acted to maintain a balance between the inflows of gold and silver arising from exports and investment attracted from foreign countries, and outflows of gold and silver arising from imports and investments made in foreign countries. An excess of gold and silver inflow over outflow raised domestic prices relative to foreign prices, increasing imports relative to exports and closing the gap between gold and silver inflows and outflows. An excess of gold and silver outflow over inflow depressed domestic prices relative to foreign prices, increasing exports relative to imports, again closing the gap between gold and silver inflows and outflows.

Mercantilism, the prevailing economic philosophy until late in the eighteenth century, argued that nations should strive for a favourable balance of trade, an excess of exports over imports bringing a net inflow of precious metals into a realm. Governments raised barriers to the import of foreign goods and to the export of raw materials needed by domestic manufacturing. The logic of mercantilism led to the conclusion that the wealth of a nation lay in its stock of precious metals rather that the productivity of its economy, a view that looked increasingly ridiculous as the history of Spain unfolded. (Adam Smith laid bare how the influx of New World precious metals sapped the vitality of the Spanish economy.) Probably a positive trade balance (an excess of exports over imports) and the attendant inflow of precious metals, did make it easier for monarchs to float loans and collect taxes, and for businesses to raise investment funds.

As long as governments officially defined currencies in terms of fixed weights in precious metals and maintained the metallic content of coinage accordingly, the exchange rate fluctuations remained within bounds set by the precious metals embodied in each currency. If the British pound sterling represented twice as much gold as the Swiss franc, then one pound sterling traded for two Swiss francs on foreign exchange markets. Market prices for gold purchased with silver or silver purchased with gold fluctuated freely, and if a gold standard country traded with a silver standard country, the exchange rates between the two currencies fluctuated with the prices of gold and silver. When a government debased its currency (reduced precious metal content relative to face value), as England did during the first half of the sixteenth century, its currency depreciated in foreign exchange markets, making its exports cheaper and imports more expensive. England experienced an economic expansion in the first half of the sixteenth century and a depression in the second half, each of which can be explained by a rise and fall in the value of the pound in foreign exchange markets. Elizabeth I restored the precious metal content of the currency in 1551. During the seventeenth century Spain radically debased its silver coinage and by 1680 the price of silver, purchased in Spanish coinage, rose to a 275 per cent premium over what it would have cost if the coinage had maintained its silver content. The Spanish economy entered into a prolonged economic slump largely owing to Spain's alternating reform and debasement of its currency.

The spread of paper money in the eighteenth century added a new element to foreign exchange markets since it raised the question of the paper money's convertibility into precious metal at an official rate. As long as banks and governments maintained a credible commitment to convert banknotes or government notes into precious metal or specie, then exchange rates functioned as if the foreign exchange value of a government's monetary unit, i.e. pound sterling, depended on the precious metal content of its coinage. When governments such as the Swedish government and American colonial governments during the eighteenth century, the French government during the French Revolution or the British government during the Napoleonic Wars, under the fiscal pressure of wars or financial chaos at home, turned to the printing press as a substitute for levying taxes, inflated currencies lost value in foreign exchange markets. Roughly, if prices increase domestically 10 per cent because of paper currency inflation, then the domestic currency will lose 10 per cent of its value in foreign exchange markets because it purchases 10 per cent less. This currency depreciation could be avoided if the government maintained the convertibility of its currency into precious metal at official rates, but that is usually not the case, since the same pressures that forced a government to excessive issuance of paper money also created a shortage of gold and silver reserves. The depreciation can be minimized if the government keeps the supply of inconvertible paper money in line with the demand. After the British government suspended the convertibility of the pound in 1797, it maintained its value in foreign exchange markets until 1809, because merchants and businesses outside Britain still needed to buy sterling in order to buy British goods. As long as the supply of pounds sterling was not excessive relative to the demand, sterling maintained its value. The outflow of sterling in subsidies to allies and military expenditure finally swamped the demand for it in the Hamburg foreign exchange market, and the pound depreciated significantly relative to other currencies.

The nineteenth century was a century of stability in foreign exchange markets. Even Spain's inconvertible paper standard in the heyday of the gold standard only saw one brief interlude of depreciation in foreign exchange markets, during the Spanish-American War. London and Paris were rivals as the premier world financial markets, although London edged Paris out in the 1870s, after the Bank of France suspended the convertibility of the franc into gold during the Franco-Prussian War (1870–71). The value of the British pound remained equal to $4.86 in US dollars, and $1 equalled 5.17 French francs. France suspended convertibility during the 1848 uprising and again in 1870, but otherwise the metallic equivalents and exchange rates of these currencies remained constant for 100 years.

The twentieth century after 1918 saw substantial turmoil in foreign exchange markets. The belligerent powers had substantially increased domestic money stocks to assist in financing the war effort, and domestic inflation was the unavoidable consequences. Both Britain and France emerged from war with currencies overvalued in foreign exchange markets. Britain put itself through a deflationary economic policy in a desperate effort to return to the pre-war parity of £1 to $4.86, which it finally achieved in 1925.

Speculators repeatedly sold francs in expectation of devaluation, forcing the depreciation of the franc, and causing large holdings of foreign currencies inside France at the expense of French francs. In 1926 the French government stabilized the franc at $1 to 25.51 francs, reducing the franc to one-fifth of its pre-war value, at which point it was substantially undervalued. Holders of foreign currency inside France began selling it in exchange for francs, and the Bank of France, insisting on holding gold instead of foreign currencies, began to experience an inflow of gold, helping France remain on the gold standard until 1936.

In February 1933, one month before the United States abandoned the gold standard, the pound sterling depreciated to £1 = $3.36. After March 1933 the pound and the franc rose with respect to dollars in foreign exchange markets, soon pushing the pound above its pre-war parity with the dollar. Strengthening US gold reserves and wartime economic policies in Europe tended to reduce the value of European currencies relative to the US dollar. Before a major devaluation in 1949 a British pound was equal to $4.03 dollars.

In 1949 several European governments officially devalued their currencies relative to the US dollar. It was an official devaluation because the international trading system then was based upon a system of fixed exchange rates, a system that would last until 1971. The Bretton Woods System (discussed in Chapter 3) created a system of fixed, but not unadjustable, exchange rates between currencies, setting fixed rates at which one currency could be converted into another. A change in the par value or official value of a currency of more than 10 per cent required the approval only of the International Monetary Fund, an international banking institution developed to help manage the Bretton Woods System.

As the world economy flourished following World War II, world gold reserves failed to keep pace with the need for monetary reserves, and members of the Bretton Woods System began to peg the value of their currencies in terms of dollars instead of gold, treating US dollars as comparable to gold. The vast gold stock of the United States seemed to justify this practice, and US dollars began to supplement gold as part of the world monetary reserves. The rest of the world was hungry for money stocks, and the United States stood in the enviable position of being able to run balance of payments deficits, causing more dollars to flow out from international transactions than was flowing in, finding the rest of the world willing to absorb vast amounts of dollars without redeeming them in gold.

According to the Bretton Woods System, a country consistently running balance of payments deficits had to devalue its currency, increasing the amount of its currency needed to purchase an ounce of gold or a foreign currency unit such as a US dollar. The devaluation of currency immediately increased the costs of imported goods and made exported goods cheaper, these forces acting together to close the gap between the outflow and the inflow of currency. Failure to devalue left the country facing a currency outflow exceeding inflow, creating an excess supply of domestic currency in the hands of foreigners. As foreigners presented these excess currency holdings to the home country for redemption in gold or dollars, the home country saw its reserves of gold and dollars depleted. If its gold and dollar reserves dropped to zero and its outflow of currency continued to exceed its inflow, its currency became worthless.

One of the defects of the Bretton Woods System was that countries running balance of payments surpluses felt no pressure to appreciate the value of their currency to ease the imbalance, even though their own domestic policies might be contributing to their balance of payments surplus, which may have translated as a balance of payments deficit to another country. Countries with balance of payments surpluses had an excess inflow of currency relative to outflow, an imbalance that could be addressed by pegging its exchange rate at a higher level, decreasing the costs of imports and raising the costs of exports.

Countries that faced balance of payments deficits and devalued their currency to avoid a depletion of gold and foreign currency reserves found the process politically painful and embarrassing. Speculators aggravated the process of devaluation by selling currencies they saw as weak and good candidates for devaluation, knowing these currencies could be purchased at a windfall gain after devaluation. For example, if prior to a devaluation of the British pound, £1 equalled $1 and after devaluation £2 equalled $1, holders of pounds would purchase dollars prior to the devaluation, and purchase twice as many pounds after devaluation, doubling their money in British pounds. Speculators, by selling British pounds in anticipation of devaluation, increased the pressure on the British government to devalue its currency. A currency crisis along these lines nearly forced Britain to devalue the pound during the Suez Crisis of 1956.

Under the Bretton Woods System France devalued the franc

in 1957, 1958 and again in 1969. Germany revalued the Deutschmark upwards in 1961 and 1969. The Netherlands revalued its currency upwards in 1961. Britain and a number of countries with currencies tied to the pound sterling devalued their currencies in 1967. Britain devalued the pound sterling so that the value of £1 dropped from $2.80 to $2.38.

The Bretton Woods System remained workable as long as the US dollar was as good as gold, convertible into gold at a fixed rate. The dollar was the currency linchpin in the system because other countries held it as monetary reserves, like gold. As United States involvement in Vietnam deepened after the mid 1960s, coupled with foreign spending connected with the Cold War and heavy private investment abroad, US balance of payments deficits widened, increasing the outflow of dollars relative to the inflow. Awareness spread in the rest of the world that the US gold stock was insufficient to redeem all dollars held outside the United States. Foreign governments steadily increased the rate of redemption of dollars into gold, draining the United States gold stock to a level of $12 billion by the early 1970s, substantially down from the $25 billion dollar gold stock held in 1949. Concern about the dollar rose to crisis proportions in August 1971, and by June 1973 the Bretton Woods System had been scuttled.

With the demise of the Bretton Woods System, the world's trading partners turned to a system of floating exchange rates, subject to management for smoothing out short-term fluctuations. Under the floating or managed-float exchange rate system, gold stocks remained an important component of world monetary reserves. Strong gold standard advocates pinned the blame for the burst of inflation that engulfed the world economy during the 1970s on the lack of monetary discipline that had formerly been provided by the gold standard. Under the Bretton Woods System, the exchange rates between currencies in Europe remained fixed, a constant conversion ratio existing between one national currency and another. The system of fixed exchange rates provided a modest measure of monetary unification in Europe that was lost with the introduction of a system of floating exchange rates, nudging Europe to make further steps towards monetary unification.

In the early 1970s, before the complete break up of the fixed exchange rate regime, the International Monetary Fund allowed the exchange rates of individual currencies to fluctuate within a range of 2.25 per cent of parity with the US dollar, plus or minus, allowing fluctuations within a 4.5 per cent band width centred around the dollar. Under that system members of the European Community (EC), now the European Union (EU), agreed to restrict variations between European currencies to 2.25 per cent, plus or minus, and to manage the variation of the aggregate of European currencies, keeping the variation of the aggregate to within the 4.5 per cent band of parity with the US dollar.

This agreement, restricting exchange rate fluctuations between European currencies, caused European currencies to fluctuate in step with each other, earning the collective European currencies the title of the 'snake in the tunnel'.[2] When members of the Belgium-Luxembourg monetary union further narrowed fluctuations of their own subset of European currencies, a 'worm in the snake' formed inside the 'snake in the tunnel'.

When the world trading system reverted to a floating exchange system in 1973, members of the EC continued to manage fluctuations between European currencies, creating was called the 'snake in the lake'. Under the European Monetary System, established in 1979, a measure of exchange rate divergence of one currency from other European currencies was used as a sign or signal, called the 'rattlesnake'. The 'rattlesnake' signalled that intervention might be necessary. The snake was an important transition step on the road to European monetary integration, a goal much closer to realization after the introduction in January 1999 of the Euro.

As the world's large trading partners turned to flexible exchange rates, many developing countries began the practice of pegging domestic currencies to the US dollar. These countries often maintained different exchange rates for those engaged in foreign trade and those engaged in investment. The decade of the 1990s, emphasizing financial liberalization, saw even these countries adopt more flexible exchange rate regimes.[3]

EIGHT

The Evolution of International Banking

Globalization becomes unthinkable without the intelligent aggressiveness of international bankers. The relationship between debtor and creditor, more subtle and delicate than the relationship between mere buyer and seller, requires confidence and trust between people with different cultures and religions, different technologies and goals. In the nineteenth century irrepressible international bankers acted as the advance agents for those covert forces of economic law that drew the different economies of the world into one trading system.

The Italian Renaissance marks the natural starting point for a study of the evolution of modern international banking. Italian banks dominated European banking during the fifteenth century and one bank, the Medici Bank, rose to become the premier financial institution of that era. With headquarters in Florence, the Medici operated branches in the major cities of Italy and in the European cities of London, Lyons, Geneva, Bruges and Avignon. It also acted as the principle bank of the Curia.

The official founding of the Medici Bank occurred in the year 1397, but members of the Medici family had been involved in Florentine banking before then. What became the Medici Bank had originally been a branch in Rome of another Florentine bank, also belonging to a Medici. The founder of the Medici Bank, Giovanni di Bicci de' Medici, acquired ownership of the Rome branch and moved it to Florence. Funds flowed into Rome because of the Church, but Florence afforded more ample investment opportunities, creating opportunities for Florentine banks to raise capital in Rome and invest that capital in Florence. As early as 1402 Venice, another city rich with investment opportunities, became the seat of a Medici branch bank. That same year the Florentine headquarters of the Medici

Bank employed seventeen people, five of whom were clerks. The year 1402 also saw a Medici family partnership open a shop for the production of woollen cloth, a venture made possible by a 3,000 florin loan from the Medici Bank, providing one-third of the project's capital. In addition to banking, the Medici conducted international trade in an impressive list of commodities, including wool, cloth, alum, spices, olive oil, silk stuffs, brocades, jewellery, silver plate and citrus fruit. Such diverse investments may have been a means of spreading risk.

In 1435 the bank opened a branch in Geneva, its first beyond the Alps. Bruges became the seat of a Medici branch in 1439, and the year 1446 saw branches open in London and Avignon. The Milan branch opened in 1452 or 1453, and in 1464 the Geneva branch moved to Lyons. The Medici system of branch banks enabled each bank to become an independent entity by rearranging accounts, protecting the main bank from the bankruptcy of individual branches. The main bank, headquartered in Florence, acted as a modern holding company. The Medici family owned a controlling interest in the main bank, which in turn held controlling interests in the branch banks. Predating the rise of the modern corporation with its concept of limited liability, these banks were organized as partnerships. At a time when most large banks emphasized handling fund transfers arising from international trade, the Medici Bank was a lending institution, and raised capital from time deposits far in excess of its own capital. The bank circumvented legal prohibitions against charging interest by hiding interest charges in bills of exchange. These bills of exchange provided for the purchase of foreign currency for future delivery, and profits could vary with fluctuations in exchange rates between foreign currencies.

The Medici Bank reached the apex of its development under the leadership of Cosimo de' Medici, the eldest son of the bank's founder Giovanni de' Medici, who died in 1429. Under Cosimo the Medici Bank became the largest banking house of its time. Cosimo died in 1464 and management of the bank passed into the hands of an invalid son, Piero de' Medici, who may have instigated a financial crisis by calling in loans. With the death of Piero, responsibility for the bank fell into the hands of his son, Lorenzo the Magnificent, famous for

Renaissance statesmanship, but not interested in the management of the bank. He turned over the bank's management to professional managers, and the bank gradually lost ground. When Lorenzo died in 1492, his son, Piero de' Medici, assumed the leadership of the family's political interest. In 1494 the Florentines ousted the Medici. The bank, already standing at the edge of bankruptcy, was confiscated, and failed under the management of its new owners.

The Medici Bank as a lending institution was something of an exception in the ranks of the major international banks of that era, most of which belonged in a class of banks that Adam Smith described as banks of deposit in a famous digression in the *Wealth of Nations*.[1] Smith specifically put the banks of Venice, Genoa, Amsterdam, Hamburg and Nuremberg in the category of banks of deposit. These banks evolved to meet the unique needs of small states, usually city-states, whose circulating coinage, mainly consisting of coinage pouring in from neighbouring states, was often worn and clipped, trading at various discounts in foreign exchange markets. With no direct recourse for reforming domestic coinage that was mostly foreign, these small states, concerned that coinage disorder hindered commercial activity, established banks of deposits as a substitute for coinage reform.

Unlike the Medici Bank, which accepted and held deposits to finance loans, banks of deposits accepted deposits of domestic and foreign currencies only to hold as reserves to back up bank deposits. A bank of deposit kept a ledger book maintaining a record of each merchant's deposits, and shifting funds for one merchant's account to another merchant's account was simply a matter of accounting entries, not requiring the removal of coinage from the bank. These deposits, called bank money, replaced coinage as the medium of exchange in commercial transactions.

Regardless of whether coinage was worn, clipped or new, banks of deposit accepted all coinage for deposit on equal terms, charging a discount on all deposits in the 5 per cent range as compensation for coinage wear and tear. These banks were public banks, operating with the support of a state government that guaranteed the value of bank deposits. The bank money represented uniform money that spared merchants conducting transactions in coinages with inconsistent values owing to wear and clipping. This explains why bank money usually traded at a premium over metallic coinage. According to Adam Smith the bank money of the Bank of Hamburg traded at a 14 per cent premium over the clipped and worn coinage of neighbouring states that circulated in Hamburg.

At first banks of deposit only transferred money from one account to another if both parties, payer and payee, were present to approve the transfer of funds. Later a practice developed of allowing payer and payee to conduct the transfer anywhere as long as a notary was present. Luca Pacioli, who wrote the first published account of double-entry bookkeeping, published in 1494, uses the example of a bank of deposit transferring funds from one account to another. Adam Smith cited in *Wealth of Nations* several advantages of bank money over metallic coinage, accounting for the premium paid for bank money.[2] His list of advantages included security from fire, robbery and other accidents, the state's responsibility for its integrity, and the ability to make payments by a simple transfer without incurring the trouble of counting coins, or risking the transportation of precious metals.

Perhaps the most famous and successful if not the oldest bank of deposit in Italy, the House of St George, has already featured our discussion of central banks (Chapter 5). A public bank in Genoa, it flourished between the sixteenth and seventeenth centuries when Genoa briefly became the financial hub of Europe on the strength of a thriving banking industry. Bankruptcies of the French and Spanish crowns may have played a role in bringing down Genoa as the financial headquarters of Europe, making way for Amsterdam, and later London, to become the financial centre of Europe.

Between 1557 and 1647 the Spanish crown defaulted on its debt a total of six times. Repeated bankruptcies of the Spanish crown would ruin the most powerful banking family in Europe in the sixteenth century, a family as important to European banking in the sixteenth century as the Medici had been in the fifteenth. The Fuggers usually financed Spain in the wars between Spain and France and the Genoese usually financed the French. Both countries stopped fighting when bankruptcy forced them to the peace table.

The founder of the Fugger family was Johannes Fugger, a weaver's son, twice marrying guild masters' daughters, rising to become a prominent textile merchant before leaving a modest fortune at his death in 1469. Andreas and Jakob I, Johannes' sons, continued the family business, but also took up the goldsmith's trade. Following his father's example, Jakob I married the daughter of the mint master, and died the seventh wealthiest citizen of Augsburg. He left three sons, Ulrich, Georg and Jakob II, to run the family business, which grew to become international in scope. Feudal princes in Germany, Austria and Hungary turned to the Fuggers for loans.

Jakob II was the financial genius of the family, adopting the most advanced techniques of business management, even double-entry bookkeeping, relatively new at the time. He organized competing firms for the purpose of fixing prices, and with his brothers cooperated with Augsburg merchants to corner the market for Venetian copper in 1498. The Fuggers' talent for strategic marriages made them party to a cartel for mining silver and copper deposits in Hungary. By 1501 the Fuggers, in addition to a family business based upon imported and manufactured textiles, presided over a mining empire with mines in Germany, Austria, Hungary, Bohemia and Spain. Silk, velvet, furs, spices, citrus fruits, jewellery and munitions belong on the list of goods traded by the Fuggers.

The beginning of the end for the Fugger banking dynasty came when Jakob II became financier for Charles I, King of Spain, extending loans to Charles to finance his ascendance to Emperor of the Holy Roman Empire, making him Charles V. Later Jakob II wrote letters to Charles V reminding him that he might not have become emperor without Jakob's financial support, and that he wanted Charles V to repay his loans.³ These loans were usually granted upon the security of revenue from mining operations. By 1540 the Antwerp bourse was furnishing capital to the Fuggers, which they in turn loaned to Spain. In 1557 the Spanish crown, then headed by Philip II, son of Charles, defaulted in the first of a series of bankruptcies spread over nearly a century. Philip forced the Fuggers to refinance his debts in the form of a long-term loan at 12 per cent interest. Tax receipts from the Netherlands secured the loan. The third Spanish bankruptcy, occurring in 1596, finished the Fuggers as European bankers.

The next banking institution to achieve international stature was the Bank of Amsterdam, founded in 1609 and lasting until 1820. If the banks of the small Italian city states of Venice and Genoa supplied the model for banks of deposit, the Bank of Amsterdam put the model into practice on a grand scale, rarely making loans, except to Dutch municipalities and the Dutch East India Company, exceptions that proved the rule. Before 1609 Amsterdam faced a currency problem similar to the problems of the small Italian city-states, its circulating coinage consisting partially of its own coinage and partially of the coinage of neighbouring states. Clipped and worn coinage poured in from surrounding states, and merchants could not count on the value for foreign bills of exchange paid in this coinage. Because of this coinage in Amsterdam depreciated 9 per cent below the value of coinage fresh from the mint, and Amsterdam merchants could hardly find good money to pay bills of exchange. Like the Italian city-states, Amsterdam sought a solution to this problem in a government secured bank of deposit, the Bank of Amsterdam.

The bank accepted at face value worn, clipped and diminished currency, domestic or foreign, on the same terms as good currency. The bank's depositors paid a small re-coinage and management fee out of each deposit, and the balance of each deposit was credited to the depositor's account. These deposits were a money of account, called bank money, that changed ownership without coinage leaving the bank, never suffering wear, clipping or government initiated debasement, always equivalent to coinage fresh from the mint. The government of Amsterdam enacted a law requiring payment in bank money on all foreign bills of exchange drawn on Amsterdam if the bills were for 600 guilders or more. Merchants accepted bank money at a premium over coinage, and the bank supplemented its income by selling bank money at a price above the prevailing price for equivalent coinage, allowing the bank to purchase coinage at one price and sell bank money at a higher price.

Not a lending institution, the Bank of Amsterdam maintained possession of the stores of coinage and bullion that bank
customers left on deposit, holding it for the day it was needed
to redeem withdrawals of outstanding bank money. In return
for deposits of bullion, the bank gave the depositor a receipt for
a stated amount of bullion valued in bank money, and credited
the depositor's bank money account for the value of the bullion. More convenient to handle than bullion, bank money
originating from bullion deposits enjoyed the same advantages
as bank money originating from coinage deposits. The receipt
bore the price in bank money at which the bank would resell
the bullion deposit back to the depositor. The bank charged a
modest storage fee for acting as the custodian of bullion left by
depositors, and ownership of bullion reverted to the bank if the
depositor defaulted on the fees. Bullion acquired from such
defaults added to the bank's profits. Vast deposits of coin and
bullion put the Bank of Amsterdam in possession of a considerable portion of European monetary reserves, giving the bank
substantial regulatory power over the European monetary
system. In the 1780s the Bank of Amsterdam, under pressure of
wartime difficulties, underwrote loans to merchants, a departure from its usual practice. Reserves of coinage and bullion fell
markedly below bank money deposits owed to the public, and
the public lost confidence. In 1795 a French invasion sparked a
panic, forcing the bank to close. With the assistance of a forced
loan the bank reopened in 1802, and wobbled along until it was
liquidated in 1820.

The prestigious private banking houses of Europe, called
merchant bankers, began to appear in the 1700s. The House of
Rothschild, the Morgan banking dynasty, and Baring Brothers
are among the names prominent in the history of merchant
bankers. According to Walter Bagehot they went back to generations of merchant princes in Venice and Genoa, a class of
people who combined the insight and verve of businessmen
with an inheritance of wealth, power and culture.[4] The merchant bankers were not deposit banks in the modern sense, at
best only holding large deposits for regular customers. They
often served as middlemen, floating loans and stocks for railways, canals and other vast undertakings, buying commodities

for wholesalers and manufacturers, sometimes floating loans for kings to finance wars or transferring funds to armies fighting in foreign lands. Merchant bankers also bought and sold financial securities and commodities on their own account.

An impressive aura of integrity, trust, and loyalty surrounded the merchant bankers, based upon a code of behaviour far superior to the practices brought to light in recent insider-trading scandals. To access capital, a merchant banker developed long-term relationships with customers who learned to count on the banker to stand by his word, and to engage in fair dealing. The London market for bills of exchange owed part of its growth and development to the impeccable reputation of merchant bankers whose endorsement on any bill of exchange made it possible to discount the bill at a lower interest rate. Having established themselves in the confidence of their customers, merchant bankers marshalled Europe's capital to finance railways and other projects in remote lands, and their interest rates were reasonable.

The Rothschilds may be the most famous of the European merchant banking houses to wield vast political and financial power during the nineteenth century. The most powerful of the merchant banking houses during the first half of the nineteenth century, Rothschild banks have remained prominent in financial circles, enjoying a prestige that lasted into the post-World War II era. The Rothschild banking dynasty traces its ancestry to Mayer Amschel Rothschild, born in Frankfurt am Main in 1743. From a poor Jewish family, he achieved success advancing loans to the nobility and managing the finances of German states. Frankfurt was headquarters for the House of Rothschild until 1820. Of his five sons the eldest, also called Mayer Amschel, stayed in Frankfurt, the other four, Nathan, James, Solomon and Karl, established Rothschild branches in the major European capitals, Nathan in London, James in Paris, Solomon in Vienna and Karl in Naples. In principle the branches were separate organizations, but in practice the brothers consulted on large ventures and undertook cooperative initiatives.

Even within the ranks of the Rothschild family, Nathan stands out as a financial genius. During the Napoleonic Wars, his branch of the House of Rothschild arranged credit for the allied governments in the order of £100 million. He arranged the transfer of British subsidies to Prussian and Austrian allies, and delivered money in the right mix of currencies to battlefield armies. The Paris branch of the Rothschilds, perhaps stifled during the Napoleonic era, rose to prominence after Nathan in 1817 decided to turn it into a full-fledged banking institution, laying the groundwork for the Paris branch to become the flagship branch by 1820, displacing Frankfurt.

Even the Rothschilds failed to recognize the importance of seminal technological advances that marked the Industrial Revolution, but they learned from their mistakes. Refusing to help finance the first railway construction boom in Britain, they threw themselves wholeheartedly into financing railway construction on the continent, helping Nathan to earn the title of railway king of Europe. Governments building railways also arranged financing through the Rothschilds. In the course of the Industrial Revolution the Rothschilds became what are still called investment bankers, buying large blocks of stock offerings for newly formed companies, often in cooperation with other banking houses. Once these companies began to report profits, the Rothschilds stood to earn handsome profits selling these shares to the public, accumulating a vast fortune in the process. The Rothschilds continued to keep a hand in the market for public securities. The French government floated a loan through the Rothschilds to pay a war indemnity after losing the Franco-Prussian War. In 1875 the Rothschilds raised the £4 million that enabled the British government to become the principle stockholder in the Suez Canal Company.

Credit for being the oldest merchant bank in London and the oldest banking dynasty in Britain belongs to Baring Brothers, a family of bankers whose history began even earlier than the Rothschilds'. Cardinal Richelieu is said to have observed that there were six great powers in Europe, England, France, Russia, Prussia and the Baring Brothers.[5] Johann Baring, founder of the Baring family in England, first visited England in 1717 as a wool merchant from north Germany. Deciding to stay, he married well and two of his sons opened John and Francis Baring & Company in London, an export and import business that grew into a merchant banking business. Political connections were part of the ingredient of success, William Pitt the Younger figured among Francis Baring's circle of friends. After John Baring's retirement in 1800, the business became Francis Baring & Company before becoming Baring Brothers & Company in 1806. Barings placed a loan of 315 million francs for the French government in the aftermath of the Napoleonic Wars.

America became a focus of interest of the Barings after Francis Baring in 1783 opened a business in Philadelphia and sent his son, Alexander, over to investigate a land deal in Maine. Following his grandfather's example, Alexander married into a wealthy American family, and Barings became the largest banking house in the pre-Civil War United States, handling the financing on major deals for the US government. On his roster of friends Alexander Baring included such notables as John Quincy Adams and Daniel Webster.

Baring Brothers invested heavily in Argentina, helping it to absorb nearly half of Britain's foreign investment by 1890, the year the Water Supply and Drainage Company of Argentina failed to meet a contract agreement. Argentina was soon embroiled in a political revolution, leaving Barings in possession of unmarketable Argentine financial assets. The Baring Crisis of 1890 threatened to develop into a major financial crisis, which London was only able to dodge by marshalling the financial resources of the city to support Barings. The banks of London, including the Bank of England and other merchant banks, shared in the effort. After the crisis, Barings reconsituted itself as a limited company, limiting the potential losses of its owners to the amount of their investment in the company in the event the business failed. Barings remained a London banking institution, dealing in acceptance credit, new security issues, conventional banking services and investment advisement services, until 1995 when speculative positions taken by a 27-year-old Singapore manager cost it millions of dollars, forcing it into bankruptcy.

The power and prestige of the private international bankers reached its apogee in the two decades prior to World War I. During that time one banking dynasty in the United States rivalled the Rothschilds and Barings in power if not in family history or the number of generations of the family that had carried on the family business. John Pierpont Morgan, the most powerful banker in American history, got his start from his father, Junius S. Morgan, an American citizen who moved to London and became a successful investment banker, beginning as a junior partner with George Peabody and Company in 1854. Handling American railroad stock for British investors accounted for most of his business, but the firm also handled stock and bond transactions for some American clients. After Peabody withdrew in 1864, the firm became J. S. Morgan and Company, an up and coming firm that placed a bond issue for the French government during the Franco-Prussian War, a task that more established institutions shirked at the time.

In 1861 the son, John Pierpont Morgan, opened a firm in New York, J. P. Morgan and Company, and the firm prospered with the help of his father's contacts and the Civil War. In 1871 Morgan joined a partnership, Drexel, Morgan, & Company, and the new firm had partnerships in New York, Philadelphia, London and Paris. The US government turned to this firm for most of its financing, and foreign governments floated loans through this firm. It also dealt widely in railroad securities. The deaths of Junius S. Morgan in 1890 and Tony Drexel in 1893 lifted J. P. Morgan to senior partner in London and the United States. By 1895 these partnerships became J. P. Morgan and Company. The two decades leading up to World War I saw J. P. Morgan granting loans to governments and railways worldwide, sometimes refusing foreign loans at the request of the US or British governments.

Morgan came to symbolize the so-called money trust, an informal conspiracy among bankers, international in scope, which ran the economy for the benefit of bankers. At least that was the public's fear at the time, sufficiently strong to induce Morgan to testify before a Congressional Committee in 1912, trying to quell resentment against perceived Wall Street domination. The money trust was a reference to bankers that sought to destroy competition among clients as a means of protecting banks, which were often left holding the defaulted loans of failed businesses. Morgan placed his associates on a corporation's board of directors as part of the price for securing a loan, increasing his power to protect his interest as a lender. By placing the same person on multiple boards, Morgan created a system of interlocking directorates that placed vast power in his hands. He consolidated railroads and manufacturing firms. The United States Steel Corporation, which at its formation became the world's largest corporation, owes its existence to the consolidation efforts of Morgan. Morgan took a transatlantic voyage, perhaps to escape the criticism that was bearing down on him at home, and died in Rome on 31 March 1913. One purpose of the banking and antitrust legislation that Congress passed in the first term of Woodrow Wilson's administration was to make it difficult or impossible for another J. P. Morgan to arise.

As the merchant bankers lost ground in the twentieth century, an important world banking centre emerged that enjoyed as much notoriety as the nineteenth-century merchant bankers, but for entirely different reasons. Switzerland had been a bit of a latecomer to European banking. Geneva was the first Swiss city to develop a banking industry, home of a dozen bankers who left their mark on Swiss financial history. Louis XIV financed his wars by floating loans in Geneva, and France continued to turn to Geneva to finance its public debt until the end of the nineteenth century.

As early as the sixteenth century Zurich showed signs of financial activity. In 1679 the city council issued an injunction against cutting interest rates from 5 to 4 per cent. Around the mid eighteenth century merchant bankers began accepting deposits for investment in securities. In 1786 Zurich saw its first full-fledged bank, and the Zurich official register for 1805 reported two banks exclusively devoted to banking. Basle was slower than Zurich in developing a banking industry, showing little evidence of it until the nineteenth century. Twenty banks appear in the Basle Register of 1862, nine exclusively devoted to banking. By the first decade of the twentieth century Switzerland belonged in the first rank of international financial centres. Swiss banking developed a centralized system that put a nationwide system of branch banks under the control of six large banks, Swiss Credit Bank, Swiss Bank Corporation, Union Bank of Switzerland, Trade Bank of Basle, Federal Bank and Swiss People's Bank. European governments and US railroad and industrial companies borrowed capital from these banks.

After World War I serious inflation erupted in several former belligerent countries, and capital, seeking the safety of Switzerland's sound currency, flowed to Swiss banks. In the 1930s Swiss banks won an added attraction when the Swiss government enacted laws shielding depositors in Swiss banks with anonymity, allowing Swiss banks to issue the so-called 'numbered accounts' severely limiting the number of bank employees knowing a depositor's name. The Swiss government also gave up its own access to private bank accounts for the purpose of collecting information either on Swiss citizens or citizens of foreign governments. The numbered accounts protected depositors living in countries whose citizens faced criminal penalties for holding deposits in foreign banks. Foreign citizens, not knowing when they would be expelled from their own country for political or racial reasons, kept deposits in Swiss banks. Three of the six major Swiss banks survived into the post-World War II era, the Swiss Credit Bank, Swiss Bank Corporation and Union Bank of Switzerland. Large numbers of smaller banks and rural loan associations, and branches of foreign banks dotted the economic landscape, giving Switzerland one bank office for every 1,400 individuals by 1968. Foreign governments gradually protested louder to the Swiss government about the anonymity afforded depositors in Swiss banks. The Swiss government has become more cooperative in providing deposit information in cases of criminal activity or tax evasion.

Long regarded as a neutral country, Switzerland actually served as a banking centre for Nazi Germany during World War II, according to information that came to light in 1997. Nazi Germany's central bank had deposited three times as much gold in Swiss banks as originally thought. Since Swiss banks were laundering much of the gold confiscated from Holocaust victims, Jewish groups brought legal action against the banks, and on 12 August 1998 Swiss banks and representatives of Holocaust survivors announced a settlement that awarded $1.25 billion to Holocaust survivors and their heirs.[6]

The post-World War II era saw a new type of institution, much more public in character, enter the field of international banking. The Bretton Woods Conference of 1944 provided for the organization of two major world financial institutions, the International Monetary Fund and the World Bank, sometimes called the Bretton Woods twins. The World Bank opened its headquarters in Washington, DC on 25 June 1946. The purpose of the World Bank, officially the International Bank for Reconstruction and Development, lay in the need to finance the reconstruction of war-torn Europe and Japan, and to meet the financing needs of the developing world. Designed to function as an arm of the United Nations, the World Bank marshalled capital by selling subscriptions to member countries and selling bonds in private financial markets. The bank can raise money in private financial markets at low interest rates because member governments guarantee bonds issued by the World Bank, reducing the interest rate these bonds must pay to attract buyers. The bank has become a clearinghouse of ideas for promoting economic development, and publishes statistical data and research on world economic conditions. The *World Development Report*, first issued by the World Bank in 1978, publishes articles on current development issues and important economic statistics for individual countries.

Investments in basic economic infrastructure drew much of the bank's attention during the first quarter-century of its operation. Approximately 77 per cent of the bank's lending went to finance electric power and transportation projects for fiscal years 1961 to 1965. Developed countries figured prominently upon the lists of the bank's major borrowers until Robert MacNamara assumed the helm in 1968. Under MacNamara's leadership the bank began to focus on the importance of directly lifting people out of poverty in the developing part of the world. Agricultural and rural development projects, which accounted for 18.1 per cent of the bank's lending in 1968, rose in importance, accounting for 31 per cent of the loans by 1981. In 1960 the World Bank organized the International Development ment Association (IDA), a division devoted to granting soft loans and interest-free loans to the poorest countries. The conservative philosophy of the World Bank prohibited it from extending loans to very low-income countries where risks are necessarily high.

The International Financial Corporation, another organization affiliated with the World Bank, came into existence in 1956. Its mission lay in marshalling capital from the private sector to finance private enterprise ventures, structuring loans on commercial principles and ranging maturities from seven to twelve years.

At first the World Bank restricted itself to financing public ventures, as opposed to private ventures, but in the 1980s the bank began to look much more favourably upon private sector ventures, recognizing the importance of a strong private sector in financing economic development, even financing the privatization of public enterprises.

The IMF, the World Bank's sister institution, began as a lending institution designed to meet the needs of countries experiencing balance of payments difficulties, a common problem under the Bretton Woods System of fixed exchange rates. Under the fixed exchange rate regime, a country facing a balance of payments deficit could either devalue its currency, or pay for continuing deficits out of its own foreign exchange reserves, or borrow foreign currency from the IMF to pay for the deficit. The IMF specialized in providing short-term loans to countries suffering balance of payments deficits.

The IMF raised its lending capital from member country subscriptions, each country contributing a sum of its own currency according to its national income and foreign trade. It was out of these funds that countries could borrow the foreign currency needed to purchase excess amounts of their own currency in foreign exchange markets, putting up an amount of its own currency as collateral. As growth in the world economy put a squeeze on international gold reserves, the IMF responded by the creation of Special Drawing Rights (SDRS), a form of fiat international monetary reserves. In 1969 member countries of the IMF ratified an agreement to distribute SDRS to each member country proportional to each country's subscription quota to the IMF. Sometimes referred to as paper gold, SDRS could be traded for foreign exchange on the same terms as gold reserves.

The fixed exchange rate regime that lasted from 1946 to 1971 gave the IMF a clearly defined mission. The floating exchange regime that displaced it provided for the resolution of balance of payments deficits or surpluses through fluctuations in currency values in foreign exchange markets, removing the immediate necessity for an institution such as the IMF. After 1972 the IMF found a new role for itself when mounting oil prices put pressure on less developed countries dependant upon imported oil, forcing these countries to incur vast amounts of foreign debt. As interest rates escalated, particularly in the early 1980s, less developed countries founded it increasingly difficult to service their foreign debt. A recession in the United States complicated the situation since export to the United States was an important means of earning dollars needed to pay interest on foreign loans.

Facing these two problems, many governments of less developed countries initiated inflationary policies, directly threatening the interest of holders of the foreign debt in these countries. The IMF inadvertently became the regulating force in this environment by insisting on responsible monetary and fiscal policies as a prerequisite for receiving IMF credit. By obtaining a loan from the IMF a less developed country could avoid currency depreciation from a balance of payment deficit, maintaining the purchasing power of the currency for the purchase of plant and equipment from the developed countries. The IMF began to make soft loans to the poorest countries of the world for similar reasons. IMF loans became a means of financing economic development, increasing a country's ability to import capital.

The IMF invariably prescribed a policy of high interest rates, depreciated currencies and less deficit spending, policies that were unpopular partly because they required reductions in social spending. Countries failing to meet the IMF's conditions usually lost access to private credit, substantially increasing the IMF's power as an international regulatory force. While developed countries had little need of the IMF as a lending institution under the floating exchange rate regime, they were happy to have an international agency helping to protect the interest of foreign investors in less developed countries.

International banking, practised by incorporated private sector banks, saw rapid growth and continued evolution post World War II. After the war large banks in world financial centres, particularly New York and London, and later Tokyo, conducted most international banking. Expanding overseas operations of US banks helped spur the growth of international banking in the 1950s and 1960s. The sudden wealth of the OPEC countries after crude oil prices quadrupled in 1973 substantially expanded the need for international banking services. International banking surged ahead trying to recycle OPEC's wealth to less developed countries. During the 1980s Japan's surplus of capital made Tokyo a major banking centre. Japanese banks opened offices in Africa, Asia, Europe, Middle East, South America, Mexico and even the United States. In the worldwide slow down of the 1980s a number of developing countries, beginning with Mexico in 1982, failed to meet debt obligations, and renegotiating and rescheduling these loans took up the remainder of the 1980s.

Towards the end of the twentieth century a trend became evident in the evolution of international banking that made a significant contribution to globalization.[7] Many countries had raised barriers limiting the ability of foreign banks to set up branches that competed with domestic banks, but in the 1980s and 1990s these barriers began to come down, opening up further opportunities for growth in international banking. Another development levelling the playing field between foreign and domestic banks was the international standardization of capital requirements established by the Bank for International Settlements in 1989. By 1998 thirty-five nations required banks to maintain capital ratios according the rules set forth by the Bank for International Settlements. These regulatory changes made it much easier for foreign banks to enter a domestic market, compete with domestic banks and gain market share. In London, between 1967 and 1996, branches of foreign banks grew from 88 to 428. In 1997 the ten largest Asian economies were host to 107 banks headquartered in non-Asian countries and many of the banks operated multiple branches. At the close of 1996 the 300 largest US banks operated 681 foreign branch offices.[8]

In addition to megabanks opening foreign offices, technological advances had enabled smaller regional banks to enter the field of international banking without opening foreign offices. During the economic slowdown of the 1980s many regional economies sought to expand exports to foreign countries as a means of promoting economic development. As regional industries made foreign contacts and expanded involvement in international trade, regional banks, aided by advances in electronic communication, have followed regional clients into foreign countries, financing exports to foreign countries, extending loans to foreign buyers of regional exports, handling foreign currency exchanges and assessing risks in foreign markets. The infusion of smaller banks into the international banking field increased competition in the world financial system, helping to lower interest rates in parts of the world where banking had been monopolized by a few large banks.

The close of the twentieth century saw New York, London and Tokyo holding their positions as the premier world financial centres. Six of the world's ten largest banks were located in Japan, one in Switzerland, one in Germany, one in the Netherlands and one in Britain.

NINE

The Paths of Foreign Investment

In 1487 Bartholomeu Dias, a Portuguese mariner, rounded the southern tip of Africa, and summed up his experience by naming it the Cape of Storms, his mind perhaps overly focused on the difficulty of the passage. King John of Portugal, free to think of future possibilities rather than the difficulty of past accomplishments, renamed it the Cape of Good Hope, symbolizing the confident hopes that inspired Europe to explore the globe. After colonizing the world, Europe saw its foreign investment arrangement, based upon colonies controlled by parent countries, graduate into a global market system, passing from imperialism to expropriation, and from nationalization to privatization.

Perhaps it was the vast profits that Venice earned monopolizing the spice and pepper trade between Europe and the Muslim world that inspired Portugal to seek an all-water route to India, and by 1540 open up trade with China and Japan. European capital would follow in the wake of European mariners, and competition in the search for foreign investment opportunities became a powerful force in European politics, lasting until the beginning of World War I. Portugal did not encounter the same opportunities for foreign investment that would occur later, as European economic and technological development raced ahead of development in other parts of the world. Portuguese foreign trade was organized along the lines of monarchial capitalism, the king supplying the capital, and the king's ships carrying the merchandise. Portuguese royal capitalism succeeded without substantial foreign investment because Portugal was establishing commercial contact with highly developed trading centres, areas with a longer history of involvement in world trade than Portugal itself, and was simply using its military and naval power to divert this trade through Portugal.

Spain faced an entirely different challenge after Columbus's discovery opened for Spain's exploitation vast amounts of undeveloped land in the New World. Spain began trading with the New World along the lines of the Portuguese model of monarchial capitalism, but found the Portuguese model unable to marshal the amounts of capital and labour necessary to exploit the resources of the New World. The Spanish crown soon contented itself with the requirement that all ships en route to or from the New World travel in fleets guarded by royal ships. After an initial period of virtually unlimited freedom for Castilian subjects to travel to America for exploration and settlement, the Spanish crown established the Casa de Contratación (House of Trade), an elaborate customs house that became the primary instrument for enforcing a highly restricted trade policy with Spanish colonies. Spain's trade policy emphasized detailed regulation, enriching the crown, and granting monopoly privileges, all at the expense of economic development in the Spanish colonies. One rule required that all colonial trade be conducted by Spaniards, and begin and end in the Port of Seville, conferring upon the Seville merchants a monopoly on trade with the New World.

The discovery of precious metals claimed an inordinate amount of attention from the Spanish crown, which owned all the mines in the New World until 1584. The crown claimed a share of the output from each mine, a share that eventually dropped to one-fifth, and a royal smelter stamped and taxed all gold before shipment to Spain. The feudalistic societies of Portugal and Spain, unprepared to unleash the brute force of private initiative, could not fully take advantage of the boundless resources of the New World. Nevertheless a military spirit drove these two countries to open up trade with the East Indies and the New World, discovering opportunities for foreign investment and colonial exploitation on a scale unmatched in history. The price of spices in Europe soared as Portugal took full advantage of its monopoly on the supply of spices from the East Indies, inspiring the Dutch on a quest to wrestle the spice trade out of the hands of Portugal. The Dutch reached the East Indies by 1597, opened trade with Japan in 1610, with Siam in 1613, and assumed monopoly control on East Indian spices in

European markets by the mid seventeenth century.

The latter part of the sixteenth century saw the rise of joint-stock companies in England and Holland, precursors of the modern multinational corporations. Among the most famous were the English East India Company and the Dutch East India Company. These companies were suited to marshal vast amounts of private capital in Europe for the purpose of organizing foreign trade and production, often with areas less developed than Europe, where land and perhaps people were in abundant supply but capital was scarce and embodied in ancient technology. In areas were people were not abundant, European governments tolerated slavery, indentured servitude and other forms of forced labour, further adding to the returns to capital.

In addition to abundant supplies of natural and human resources that enhanced returns to capital exported to a colony, European governments also imposed colonial policies that forced exported capital into complementary rather than competitive relationships with capital in the parent country. Colonies were usually forbidden to import goods from any country besides the mother country, and to export goods to any country besides the mother country. These policies enabled Holland to monopolize the spice trade between its East Indian colonies and Europe. In the American colonies the Boston Tea Party occurred after the British Parliament granted the East India Company a monopoly on the colonial tea trade. Britain used its colonies to feed raw materials to its industry, forbidding them from exporting to any country besides Britain goods such as tobacco, sugar, cotton, dyewoods, indigo, rice molasses and naval stores.

The governments of mother countries acted to inhibit the colonial development of industries that competed with domestic industries. In 1750 the British Parliament enacted legislation that banned the construction and operation of various iron works in the American colonies.[1] The colonies were free to export pig iron and bar iron to Britain, but could not manufacture iron or steel products, such as pots, pans, guns, etc. Britain also forbade the colonial manufacture of woollen goods and fur hats. Mother countries not only monopolized trade with colonies but forbade that colonial trade arrive indirectly through a foreign port, or be carried on a ship not built and owned by citizens of the mother country. These restrictions came under navigation acts promulgated by both the British and French governments.

Colonial policies acting to hinder industrialization in less developed areas moderated the opportunities for foreign investment until the nineteenth century, when the Industrial Revolution spread beyond Britain, transforming methods of production and transportation around the world, often substituting capital for labour. While manufacturing industries remained concentrated in Europe, countries supplying food and raw materials, including the newly independent United States, needed canals and railways to transport goods to coastal ports for shipment to Europe.

During the nineteenth century British merchant bankers arranged much of the financing required for the construction of canals and railways around the world, including most such construction in the United States. The Erie Canal received most of its financing from Britain. Between 1870 and 1872 British capital helped finance the construction of the first railway in Japan. In 1875 the Rothschilds enabled the British government to become the principal stockholder of the Suez Canal Company. Governments around the world, including individual states in the United States, relied on European merchant bankers to float loans for the construction of internal improvements, i.e. roads and bridges. British investors financed railway construction in China, India, South America and Canada.

The Suez Canal and the Baghdad Railway rank among the major capital improvement projects financed with European capital during the nineteenth century. In 1859 the company building the Suez Canal issued 400,000 shares of stock, over half of which were sold in France. Originally British investors showed little interest. The Egyptian government had to buy 85,000 shares itself to get the project started. In 1875 the Egyptian government, heavily in debt, sold its shares to the British government, which purchased them with financing arranged by Lionel Rothschild, making the British government the largest stockholder.

The project leading to the construction of the Baghdad

Railway began in 1888, an initiative of the Deutsche Bank of Germany, which received a concession from the Turkish government to construct a major railway. The British were not interested, but promoted the project for the Germans because they were already wary of too much French influence in the Ottoman Empire. After the importance of the Persian Gulf as an oil-producing area became apparent, Britain changed its attitude, and by the eve of World War I the Baghdad Railway had become an international project, including investors from Britain, France and Russia. Argentina became a favourite home of British capital, absorbing nearly half of British foreign investment by 1890. The concentration of British foreign capital in one country left Britain precariously dependent upon stability and prosperity in a small part of the world, a point felt intensely in 1890 during the Baring Crisis, discussed in Chapter 8.

Foreign investment grew into an instrument of imperialism towards the end of the nineteenth century. Governments in countries receiving European capital were often eager to have railways pass through certain cities, giving European financiers leverage over those governments that could be used to extract concessions. European financiers, having the natural tendency of creditors to impose conditions on debtors, used their power to impose conditions favourable to European governments and industries.

A page from the financial history of the Young Turks demonstrates how strings were attached to foreign investment to further the interest of the capital exporting country.[2] The Young Turks established a new government, constitutional monarchy, in Turkey between 1908 and 1909. In 1910 David Bey, Minister of Finance, travelled to France at the behest of his government to negotiate a loan for them. At first his proposals received a chilly reception from French financiers, but the Crédit Mobilier of Paris acceded to his proposal. Before the loan could be quoted on the Paris Bourse the French government had to approve it according to an executive decree in 1880 that gave the French Minister of Finance the final say in the negotiation of foreign loans. As conditions for approving the loan to the Young Turks, the French government wanted more guarantees for the security of the loan, fiscal reforms to end recurring budget deficits, a guarantee that French industry receive a share of that part loaned to purchase foreign goods and services and the resolution of a long-standing political dispute between France and Turkey. To satisfy the French government that the Turkish government was implementing fiscal reform, the French government wanted two French citizens placed in the Turkish Finance Ministry. The Young Turks rejected these terms, and the loan was never finalized, but the episode demonstrates how European governments exploited access to European capital for political leverage.

The British government took an active role in the establishment of banks in areas it wanted to bring under British influence.[3] These banks became loyal supporters of British foreign policy. The National Bank of Turkey was founded with the strong encouragement of the British government, which helped to secure the support of British financiers. The Imperial Bank of Persia owed its formation to the facilitation of the British government, again a major factor in the attraction of British financiers. Both the Turkish bank and the Persian bank were heavily involved in financing their respective governments.

While the British government was not involved in the formation of the Hong Kong and Shanghai Banking Corporation, a bank engaged in financing the central government of China, it did form a special working relationship with that bank. Through this bank the British government controlled China's access to European capital, and it used this control to exert influence over China's internal affairs.

Critics of capitalism saw the late-nineteenth-century surge of imperialism as symptomatic of a maturing capitalistic system that favoured the accumulation of capital by concentrating income in a small percentage of privileged families. Internal investment opportunities dwindled as the capitalist economic system matured, just at a time when saving was at a peak, forcing these capitalist countries to search for an outlet for surplus capital. European governments sought control over foreign governments as a means of protecting European capital invested abroad.

Criticism of capitalism helped fuel the resentment in host countries against foreign investment, and against foreign influence in home governments designed to protect foreign capital. In 1897 Russia adopted the gold standard as a move to make Russia a safer haven for foreign capital. The gold standard gave foreign investors assurances that foreign investments and interest payments on foreign investments could be redeemed into something besides a paper money that had no value outside the country that issued it. Russia needed foreign capital to finance the Siberian railway and other railways and internal improvements. Nevertheless, the Russian government faced strong opposition to the adoption of the gold standard, critics charging that Russia was becoming a colony of Europe. In 1905 Russia saw a major working-class uprising against the government, a harbinger of things to come.

The winds and clouds of wars and depressions ruled out significant accomplishments in the foreign investment area during the first half of the twentieth century. After 1918 world leadership in financial and monetary affairs began to pass from Britain to the United States. During the 1930s many countries tried to insulate themselves from depression by imposing tariffs, import controls, barter agreements, exchange rate controls and currency depreciation. Every year between 1931 and 1937 saw debtor countries suffering from capital outflows as capital sought the security of safe havens, particularly the United States. From 1933 to 1938 the net capital inflow to the United States exceeded the net capital outflow between 1921 and 1934, helping to explain why the United States' share of world gold stocks increased from 38 per cent in 1929 to 71 per cent in 1939.

During the nineteenth century major European powers, while rivals within Europe, felt a common interest in maintaining political stability in non-European countries receiving foreign investment, which helped protect the interest of foreign investors in debtor countries. The twentieth century saw a sometimes secret, sometimes open war between communism and capitalism, in which the main antagonists often launched major efforts to foment unrest in areas needing foreign investment. This political rivalry led to a wave of foreign property expropriation in less developed countries. The ideology of Karl Marx and Vladimir Lenin absolved less developed countries of any scruples they might have felt for the confiscation of foreign investments. Governments in less developed countries began to see foreign investment as an impoverishing instrument of exploitation rather than a contribution to economic development, easing concern that confiscation of foreign owned property might discourage future foreign investment.

The political climate in Latin America particularly favoured expropriation of foreign investment. Between 1936 and 1938 the Mexican government launched a programme of expropriation that would infect the rest of Latin America, confiscating plantations, ranches and the property of Sinclair Oil Group and Standard Oil of New Jersey. Between 1959 and 1960 Cuba confiscated vast amounts of property held by US citizens as part of a revolution that would make that country a communist state. In Brazil, between 1959 and 1962, the holdings of American and Foreign Power Company and International Telephone and Telegraph fell victim to a government policy of expropriation. In 1963 eleven oil companies, including Standard Oil of New Jersey, lost their Argentine holdings at the hands of an expropriating government. In 1969 and 1971 the government of Bolivia swept up the properties of Gulf Oil and United States Steel. In Peru a sugar plantation belonging to W. R. Grace and other agricultural estates, and mining and smelting industries suffered expropriation between 1969 and 1974. Foreign investment from nine countries was affected by the expropriation. Between 1971 and 1973 the government of Chile took over Chilean holdings of International Telephone and Telegraph and US copper companies. In some cases the governments compensated the companies for the expropriated property, but not on terms that satisfied the companies.

The spurt of expropriation ended in the 1970s, a casualty of the disillusioned hopes held out by socialist reformers and the renewed vigour of capitalism. Trading blocs replaced expropriation and socialist policies as the best instrument for raising economic standards in less developed countries. To take full advantage of the growth in international trade opportunities, countries needed to have cooperative relationships with large trading partners such as the United States, and they needed to attract foreign investment, none of which was possible when holdings of multinational corporations headquartered in large trading partners faced the threat of expropriation. Besides inflicting substantial damage on a country as a potential host for foreign investment, expropriation had often put production facilities under the management of inexperienced government workers, leading to a substantial reduction in efficiency. Where compensation was involved, expropriation only attracted capital away from other projects, cancelling out much of the benefit for economic development.

After ending the practice of expropriation, countries remained wary of foreign investment, often imposing restrictions such as Mexico's long-held requirement that foreign capital could not account for more that 50 per cent of business ventures. Countries in the western hemisphere were particularly concerned about the intrusion of US capital, which they saw as a vehicle for enforcing the economic, political and cultural dominance of the United States.

During the nineteenth century Britain was the major exporter of capital to less developed areas, and the United States, because of its wealth and political hegemony, could have been expected to play a similar role in the twentieth century, but it never happened. In the 1950s the United States would have had to increase its export of capital ten-fold, to match on a per capita basis Britain's export of capital during the nineteenth century. By the mid 1980s the United States, which had been a net capital exporter since the end of World War I, had become a capital importer, drawing capital from countries such as Japan and preventing these countries from supplying capital to developing areas.

In a relative sense capital outflow from the United States during the post-World War II era was a trickle compared to the flood of capital flowing from Britain in the nineteenth century. Nevertheless, the United States launched major foreign aid initiatives intended to promote economic growth in poorer countries. In absolute amounts the United States supplied by far the most, but Britain, France, West Germany, Netherlands, Australia, Japan, Italy, Norway and Canada furnished foreign aid in significant amounts when expressed as a percentage of each country's gross domestic product. In 1961 France spent 1.5 per cent of its GDP in foreign aid, the United States 0.67 per cent, and Canada 0.17 per cent. As a percentage of GDP France spent the largest share, and Canada the smallest, with other developed countries somewhere in between, the United States among the highest. While foreign aid initiatives did not change the overall picture of subdued capital outflows from wealthy countries, they did bring to light the moral obligation many wealthy countries felt to finance economic development in poorer countries. The Eastern bloc countries also sent aid to developing countries.

Britain and France sent most of their foreign aid to former colonies. The United States, eager to show that capitalistic countries can generate faster growth than communist countries, tended to channel aid to those areas in the world geographically adjacent to communist regimes. The United States, fearful that poverty was a breeding ground for communism, also sent foreign aid to combat poverty in areas of strategic advantage to it. While the Eastern bloc countries did not send foreign aid to any country openly allied with the West, the United States did send some aid to Poland and Yugoslavia when those countries were in the Eastern bloc. Egypt was a major beneficiary of aid from the Eastern bloc.

The last decade of the twentieth century saw a major upsurge in private capital flows. At the beginning of the last decade private capital flowing to developing countries approximately equalled the capital supplied to developing countries from official sources, foreign governments and official institutions such as the World Bank. In the course of the decade direct foreign investment to developing countries increased over seven-fold, and even after a major international financial crisis, private portfolio investment had doubled between 1990 and 1998. By the end of the century private capital flows dwarfed official capital flows, the largest increase in the former since the late nineteenth century.[4] Unlike the capital flows of the nineteenth century, which largely went to financing infrastructure such as railways, the capital flows of the late twentieth century entered foreign countries through the channels of multinational enterprises financing their own ventures in host countries.

While US multinational enterprises furnished a significant share of direct foreign investment, foreign capital flowed into the United States faster than US capital flowed out, leaving the United States a net debtor country. By the end of the twentieth century Japan had emerged as a major source of private capital to the rest of the world, accounting for 24 per cent of direct foreign investment in the United States.

TEN

The Struggle for Free Trade

If corporations, international banking, world currencies, financial and currency markets quietly nourished the development of a unified global financial system beyond regional economies, a thorny maze of trade restrictions acted as the point of resistance, a hampering shell that the global financial system had to crack before manifesting itself. The existence of a global financial system presupposes a flow of goods and resources across national boundaries, a flow that historically received varying measures of encouragement from governments and other public entities. International trade can expose domestically owned resources to brutal competition from other countries where these resources may exist in larger quantities or meet higher standards of quality. Workers and worker organizations in a country such as the United States, historically a labour-short country, often stand against the importation of goods from countries where labour is in abundant supply and wages are low. Likewise, farmers in industrialized countries are reluctant to remain quiet while agricultural commodities are imported from less developed parts of the world where land is abundant and less expensive. As producers, voters and politically powerful groups invariably favour some trade barriers that protect the threatened resources and skills. As consumers, voters and politically powerful groups will benefit from international trade, which tends to draw goods and services from the least expensive producers worldwide. Since consumption is the ultimate purpose of economic activity, and production resembles a necessary evil, it is surprising that governments have often protected the producers and owners of resources at the expense of consumers by restricting international trade. Just as workers, however, focus more attention on individual wages rather than on the prices of individual goods or services they purchase, governments often enforce policies that protect incomes of specific groups of resource owners, rather than policies that focus on low prices for all consumers.

During the nineteenth and twentieth centuries advanced economic thinking and doctrines have come down on the side of free trade, while during the seventeenth and eighteenth centuries mercantilism dominated economic thinking in Europe. Mercantilism was an all-inclusive school of thought that called for detailed government regulation of all phases of economic activity, the polar opposite of nineteenth-century *laissez-faire* economics. Unlike current government regulation, which emphasizes protecting consumers, workers and the environment from business, mercantilism emphasized economic development, nurturing and protecting business activity. One of the most famous advocates of mercantilism was Jean Baptiste Colbert, finance minister under Louis XIV. Colbert once compared the art of taxation to plucking a goose so as to obtain the largest possible amount of feathers while provoking the smallest possible amount of hissing.

With economic development as the prime objective, the cold logic of mercantilism led to the conclusion that ambitious governments should emphasize the promotion of exports over imports, creating a favourable trade balance that produced an influx of precious metals. (Exporters received payment in precious metal coinage, adding to the domestic supplies of precious metals. Importers paid foreign suppliers in precious metal coinage, detracting from domestic supplies of precious metals.) A favourable balance of trade (an excess of exports over imports) supplied and replenished a reservoir of capital that paved the way for the growth of capital markets. Capital markets marshalled capital for financing manufacturing development and governments turned to these capital markets to finance wars when necessary. In present times Japan has consciously or unconsciously pursued a similar policy, explaining why Japan is home to most of the world's largest banks.

To restrain imports governments imposed taxes, quotas or complete bans on the importation of foreign goods, particularly foreign goods competing with domestically produced goods. Exceptions were made for goods imported for the purpose of re-exportation. To encourage exports, governments subsidized the costs of producing goods with an export market, imposed quality standards on domestic manufactures, negotiated advantageous commercial treaties and financed expeditions for the establishment of colonies. The colonies supplied raw materials for domestic manufactures and purchased the finished products of domestic manufactures. Governments usually exempted essential raw materials from import restrictions. Likewise, governments imposed export restrictions on or banned exports of domestic raw materials needed by domestic manufactures.

A longer-term trend towards freer trade made itself felt even during the mercantilist era. Governments following mercantilist policies swept away internal tariffs and tolls that restricted trade between government entities within national borders, and built roads and canals to facilitate internal transportation. Shipbuilding industries were also a favourite for government subsidies as a means of promoting foreign trade.

Even in its heyday mercantilism had its notorious failures. Between 1614 and 1617 the English government, acting at the instigation of a cloth merchant, Alderman Cockayne, launched a plan to convert England from an exporter of unfinished white cloth to an exporter of finished, dyed cloth. In 1614 England exported unfinished white cloth to Germany and the Low Countries where it was dyed and turned into finished textiles. English merchants envied the finished textile industry on the continent, seeing it as rightly belonging to England, source of the raw material. The finished, dyed cloth sold for approximately twice the value of the unfinished white cloth exported from England, which seemed strategically located in the production chain to become a major player in the market for finished, dyed textiles.

In July 1614 the English government banned the export of unfinished white cloth, gambling that the finished, dyed cloth industry would move to England if it was denied access to English unfinished white cloth abroad. Simultaneously the government chartered a regulated company, the King's Merchant Adventurers, with a royally sanctioned monopoly on the export of finished, dyed cloth from England. Another regulated company, the Merchant Adventurers, lost its monopoly on the export of unfinished white cloth, but not before warning the government that English dyed textiles were significantly inferior to those manufactured in Germany and the Low Countries, and that English output of finished textiles could not meet a substantially increased demand. Germany and the Low Countries found other sources of unfinished white cloth, and the Dutch went so far as to ban the importation of finished dyed cloth from England. By 1616 the English textile industry was in complete disarray, idling one-third to one-half of the looms in some districts. White cloth prices plummeted and unemployment spread. The government saw customs revenue fall, as white cloth was no longer eligible for export. Admitting failure in its effort to convert England from an exporter of unfinished to finished cloth, in December 1616 the English government lifted the ban on the export of white cloth.

It is an open question whether mercantilism was valid in ideal circumstances where trading partners were assumed not to retaliate with trade restrictions of their own. When countries retaliated, banning or restricting imports from other countries, the net effect of mercantilism was that no country could export, depriving every country of that export engine that drove economic development according to mercantilist doctrine. Mercantilism therefore reduced to an absurdity except for one escape hatch, and that was the acquisition of colonies. The possession of colonies enabled governments not only to determine their own trade policies but also those of their colonial trading partners.

Therefore it was in colonial policies that the full force of mercantilism manifested itself as an exploiting relationship between parent countries and colonies. Not only did exports of parent countries have open access to colonial markets but parent countries restricted the ability of colonies to import goods from any country besides the parent. The most famous of these restrictions, the Tea Act of 1773, gave the East India Company a monopoly sanctioned by the British government on the sale of tea in the American colonies, inspiring the Boston Tea Party. With the Molasses Act of 1773 Parliament laid a heavy import tax on molasses imported into the American colonies from the West Indies. Occasionally colonies imported goods from another country, often on condition that the goods were carried on ships of the parent country or were rerouted through ports of the parent country.

Parent countries also imposed restrictions on the freedom of colonies to export goods to any country besides the parent. Spain monopolized the precious metal trade of its colonies in the New World, and Holland monopolized the spice trade with the Dutch colonies in the South Pacific. The British Navigation Acts banned the export to any country besides England of numerous colonial goods including tobacco, sugar, cotton, dyewoods, indigo, rice, molasses and other naval stores. Colonies were also frequently prevented from exporting goods to the parent country via foreign ports of other countries, particularly if these ports were competing with ports of the parent country.

Adam Smith vigorously challenged the logic of the mercantilist system of thought.[1] He emphasized that per capita output was the determining factor in measuring a nation's wealth and economic welfare, and not stores of precious metals. Access to vast treasures of precious metals in the New World had failed to stimulate industrial and commercial development in Spain, a country that lagged behind Britain and France in economic development during Smith's time. The Spanish experience seemed to prove that the accumulation of precious metal treasures was neither a good indicator of the economic well-being of Spanish citizens nor an indicator of potential for future growth. Smith advanced the position that free trade, by forcing countries to specialize in the production of goods and services that made the best use of resources, encouraged the maximum output per unit of resource, maximizing the output per person. The higher the output per person, the more goods were available and the higher the standard of living enjoyed by the citizens.

While Adam Smith was advocating free trade in Britain, disciples of a new school of economics, the Physiocrats, had risen to positions of influence in the French government. The Physiocrats, who left a marked influence on Smith's thinking, wholeheartedly embraced the concept of free trade, trade between nations unfettered by taxes, quotas and other restrictions. The first step toward abandoning mercantilist doctrine, and liberalizing trade, came with the Anglo-French Commercial Treaty of

1786. (By the end of the War of Independence between Britain and the American colonies, trade between Britain and France had slowed to a trickle, a victim of trade restrictions, retaliations against trade policies and periodic wars.) By mutual agreement Britain and France agreed to scale down trade restrictions. It was an experiment with freer trade, hesitant and cautious, cut short by the French Revolution, but marking the beginning of a trend that manifests itself with increasing strength to the present day.

Under the treaty of 1786, France removed its ban on the import of British goods. The provisions of this treaty allowed trade between France and Britain to be carried on French ships, a practice that had not been allowed under the British Navigation Acts. The price each country paid for linens could not exceed what the Dutch paid for the same commodity, and a modest 12 per cent ad valorem tax fell on imports of cotton, hardware, chinaware, pottery and glassware. The low taxes imposed on manufactured imports favoured Britain, which had developed industrially to a greater extent than France. French silks, the one manufactured good France could export to Britain at a profit, remained banned, but French agricultural interests received concessions on exported wines, brandies and olive oil. The favouring of British manufacturing interest and French agricultural interest may have been a fatal flaw. French manufacturing entered into a deep depression as British exports of manufactured goods to France rose from 13 million livres in 1784 to 58.5 million in 1787. France suffered one of the deepest depressions of the eighteenth century on the eve of the Revolution.

As the forces of depression in France gathered strength, many textile districts saw a 50 per cent reduction in the number of working looms, and more than half of the textile workers lost their jobs. Bankruptcies mounted, and the depressed state of the economy cost the government much needed revenue, forcing the king of France to call the Estates General, a necessary step for the approval of new taxes. The Estates General first met on 4 May 1789, and by the end of June had remade itself into a revolutionary congress, beginning the French Revolution. The deputies of the Estates General complained bitterly about the Anglo-French Commercial Treaty, which even a government agency, the Bureau of Commerce, blamed for the industrial depression ravaging France.

A succession of revolutionary congresses assumed political power in France, the National Assembly, the Legislative Assembly, and on 21 September 1792 the Convention. On 1 February 1793 the Convention declared war on Britain and annulled the Anglo-French Commercial Treaty. Within a few months the Convention banned the import of numerous British-manufactured goods, returning France to a highly protectionist trade policy which lasted through most of the nineteenth century. On 21 September 1793 the Convention enacted the first French Navigation Act, patterned after the British Navigation Acts. Navigation Acts conferred a virtual monopoly upon domestic shipping at the expense of foreign shipping in the conduct of foreign trade. These Acts were one of the few trade restrictions that Adam Smith extolled, arguing that protecting the shipping industry was necessary for national defence.[2] The English Parliament had enacted Navigation Acts in 1651, 1660, 1662 and 1663. Dutch shipping transported the bulk of world trade when tension between the Dutch and English reached fever pitch in 1651, erupting into war in 1652. The Dutch experience suggested that shipping was a strategic industry, stimulating growth in shipbuilding, marine insurance, warehousing and industries related to processing goods. Dutch ships transported one-half of England's sea commerce when England enacted its first Navigation Act. By 1791 foreign ships transported only one-fourteenth of Britain's sea trade.

The British Navigation Acts provided that only British ships, with three-quarters of the crews British subjects, could carry trade along the coast of Britain, or between Britain and British colonies. The acts also created an enumerated list of bulky goods. Imports of enumerated goods from another country could not be carried by third country ships, but could be brought in on ships from the country of origin, defined by the same criteria used to define British ships. Neither British ships nor foreign ships could bring in enumerated goods from a port outside of the country where the goods originated. This provision was directly aimed at trading centres such as Amsterdam that had a large entrepôt (transshipment) trade. British authorities confiscated ships and cargo found in violation of the Navigation Acts.

At the time of the enactment of the French Navigation Act of 1793, British ships transported two-fifths of French sea trade and, of the 16,255 ships carrying French sea commerce, only 3,373 ships belonged to the French. Under the act of 1793, all French export trade had to be carried on French ships, and French import trade had to be carried either on French ships or the ships of the country where the imported goods originated. Trade along the coast of France, and between France and French colonies had to travel in French ships. The foreign ships carrying goods to France paid a surtax for the privilege. The French government hoped the French Navigation Act would strike the same blow against British shipping as the British Navigation Acts struck against Dutch shipping.

Governments of the French Revolution suspended the Navigation Acts for a while but, beginning in 1814 and lasting until 1869, these Acts formed the basis of French shipping regulation. In 1816 the government relaxed the restriction against foreign ships bringing into France goods from third countries, that is, countries other than the ones from where the goods originated. It also allowed foreign ships to bring non-European goods into France from other European countries, but only by paying a special tax. This tax encouraged direct importation of non-European goods into France, sidetracking other European trading centres.

France began relaxing its Navigation Acts in 1845, removing the provision requiring entirely French ownership and the construction in France of ships defined as French ships. After 1845 French ships were defined as ships in which Frenchmen owned no less than a 50 per cent share. The Anglo-French Treaty of 1860 ended the requirement that only ships built in France could fly the French flag. This treaty allowed British-built ships to become French ships by paying a special levy. By 1866 ships of any nation could become French ships by paying an insignificant fee. By 1869 France had abolished all vestiges of the Navigation Acts, an action in step with a brief flirtation with free trade during the reign of Louis Napoleon III.

The sentiment for free trade struck deeper roots in Britain, where Parliament began to relax the Navigation Acts during the early nineteenth century. After 1783 Parliament began to ease restrictions as they applied to the United States. In 1822 Parliament exempted goods imported into Britain for the purposes of re-exportation, an action that stimulated Britain's entrepôt trade. In the same year Parliament also dropped the requirement that only ships from countries where imported goods originated could bring the goods into English ports. Foreign ships were then free to bring goods in from any country. In 1849 Parliament repealed all Navigation Acts except the monopoly of British ships on British coastal trade.

The French Navigation Acts claimed a relatively small place in the aggressive trade warfare that France waged against Britain during the Napoleonic era. On 21 November 1806 Napoleon launched the Continental System in the Decree of Berlin, essentially ostracizing Britain from the European economic system.[3] This system closed all French or French ally ports to ships arriving from Great Britain or her colonies, and subjected British subjects to imprisonment if found in France or areas occupied by French troops, which included most of continental Europe at the time. Britain retaliated by trying to force all ships trading with continental Europe to stop at British ports first. Goods coming into Britain were allowed to come duty free if they were destined for re-export. On 17 December 1807 Napoleon extended the Continental System in the Decree of Milan, which subjected to confiscation ships sailing from British ports or ports occupied by British troops. When his effort to completely ban goods from British ports failed, Napoleon levied a 50 per cent tariff on all goods imported to the continent, and authorized searches for British goods. In October 1810 the residents of Bayonne, Nantes, Antwerp, Zurich, Civita Vecchia, Ratisbon, Leipzig, Königsberg and Memel put a match to bonfires of British goods.

The Continental System failed utterly, partly because it went too far in trying to suppress economic realities. Britain, buffeted by food riots, unemployment, wage reductions and bankruptcies, formed an alliance with Spain in defiance of Napoleon, gaining access to raw materials and consumers in Spanish colonies. Invigorated by the development of the steam engine, British manufacturing expanded trade with the New World.

Napoleon waged wars in Spain and Russia, trying to pressure these countries into honouring the Continental System. The System collapsed in 1815 with the end of Napoleon's empire, but France remained a highly protectionist country where ideas of free trade found little acceptance.

The protectionism of France may have been the driving force behind the formation of a customs union that eventually evolved into the German nation. A customs union allows free trade between its members, and raises a common tariff wall against goods and services imported from areas outside. During the first years of the nineteenth century Germany was the name applied to a medley of independent states, dukedoms and municipalities, the last remnants of the Holy Roman Empire. Each of these independent political entities erected its own trade barriers, which acted to constrict trade within Germany itself as much as protecting German producers from other European competition. Approximately 1,800 local tariff barriers hindered trade between German localities, and Prussia boasted 67 different internal tariffs. Each internal tariff, protecting only a small market, could not effectively retaliate against protectionist trade policies of major economic powers such as France. After the defeat of France in 1818, Prussia abolished all internal trade barriers, and raised an external tariff wall that levied an average of 10 per cent on imported manufactured goods. This new tariff was only mildly protectionist, reflecting the influence of Adam Smith's free trade ideas in Germany, and agricultural products were completely exempt from import duties.

The smaller German states organized their own customs union in 1828, the South German Union. The same year Prussia and Hesse combined in the Northern Customs Union. The year 1834 saw these two unions merge into one customs union called the *Zollverein*. By the 1840s the *Zollverein* was a force to be dealt with on the international stage, and into the 1850s German states continued to come into the union. Adam Smith's free trade ideas remained an influential force shaping tariff policy in the *Zollverein*, and Germany shared in the trend towards trade liberalization that spread through Europe during the 1860s. After the Franco-Prussian War (1870–71) Germany began to move towards protectionism and in 1879 the protectionist policies of the *Zollverein* ushered in a new burst of European protectionism. By uniting economically, Germany was able to retaliate against the trade barriers of France and other European powers. Only after Germany took up protectionism did the trend towards European trade liberalization come to an end.

The next important victory for the principles of free trade came in Britain. In 1838 a Manchester group formed the Anti-Corn Law League, what might now be called a political action group devoted to the repeal of the Corn Laws. The Corn Laws regulated the taxation of grain importation and exportation. The first Corn Law, enacted in 1670, taxed the importation of grain according to an inverse scale based upon the domestic grain price. When domestic markets were flush with grain, pushing grain prices below the lowest legal threshold, imported grain automatically paid the highest tax rates. When domestic markets for grain were tight, sending grain prices above the highest legal threshold, imported grain automatically came in at the lowest tax rate. The Corn Law provided for three tiers of thresholds. In 1689 Parliament supplemented the inverse tax system with an export subsidy that kicked in whenever the domestic grain price dropped below a certain threshold. This export subsidy encouraged the export of grain, draining the domestic markets, which tended to raise domestic grain prices. The purpose of the law lay in the need to smooth out fluctuations in domestic grain prices, and maintain grain prices in a range fair to consumers and farmers, keeping both reasonably content until the second half of the eighteenth century.

Around 1750 British population growth began to outpace agricultural productivity, putting pressure on domestic grain supplies, virtually ending the payment of export subsidies and often allowing grain to enter untaxed. In 1773 Parliament changed the thresholds and banned exports when prices rose above the highest threshold. Pressure on domestic grain supplies continued to increase, often pushing prices above the highest threshold. Towards the close of the eighteenth century British landowners began arguing that low domestic prices were discouraging grain production and that threshold prices should be raised.

In 1815 Parliament adopted a revised Corn Law along lines favourable to landowners. This new law established a new threshold price below which it became illegal to import grain, protecting domestic grain producers from foreign competition when prices dropped below a certain level. When domestic grain prices exceeded the threshold level, foreign grain came in tax-free. The Anti-Corn Law League voiced the concern of industrialists who felt that Corn Laws protected agriculture from foreign competition at a time when a more logical policy would protect manufacturing. In 1846 Parliament abolished the Corn Laws, beginning a policy of free trade that lasted until the Depression of the 1930s.

The next significant step towards freer trade in Europe occurred with the negotiation of the Anglo-French Commercial Treaty of 1860. Britain gradually liberalized trade during the first half of the nineteenth century, approaching a free-trade posture by mid century, but France stood staunchly protectionist. French tariffs on imported manufactured goods varied between 50 and 100 per cent, and outright bans forbade the importation of selected goods, such as iron and castings. The tariff on imported steam engines and locomotives stood at 50 per cent, and unbleached cotton yarn paid an import tariff in the 300 to 400 per cent range.

France took tentative steps toward the liberalization of trade in 1853, but the Anglo-French Commercial Treaty of 1860 marked a sharp break with the philosophy of protectionism. This treaty allowed France five years to slash all tariff rates to a maximum of 25 per cent. Britain lifted remaining import duties on French goods, with a few exceptions, one of the most notable being duties on wine and spirits, which were only scaled down. Britain, already at the forefront of the free trade movement, had fewer concessions to make.

The treaty provided that France and Britain give 'most favoured nation status' to each other's goods, and authorized both countries to grant most favoured nation status to other nations. France immediately set to work negotiating similar treaties with other European trading partners, signing a treaty with Belgium in 1861, Prussia in 1862, Italy in 1863, Switzerland in 1864, Sweden, Norway, the Grand Duchy of

Mecklenburg, Spain and the Netherlands in 1865, Austria in 1866 and Portugal and the Papal States in 1867. In 1864 the Zollverein, the trading block of German states, received the same trade status as Prussia. By virtue of French leadership in trade policy continental Europe flirted for a while with free trade, beginning an era of moderately protectionist trade policies that lasted until the 1880s.

Fears the treaty would trigger an economic depression in France comparable to the economic crisis that followed the treaty of 1786 proved illusory. Industrial production remained strong, and benefited from the stimulus of foreign competition. Between 1860 and 1864 the number of operating steam engines grew from 178 to 242 while the number of operating hand-looms fell significantly. Competition from imports eased upward pressure on domestic prices. The Anglo-French Commercial Treaty remained in effect until 1881, when the tide in continental Europe again turned in favour of protectionism. The United States had remained protectionist during this European experiment with trade liberalization, and Britain remained committed to a policy of free trade until the Depression of the 1930s.

After suffering a severe commercial crisis in 1873, Germany became the first European country to turn away from the experiment with trade liberalization that followed the Anglo-French Commercial Treaty. Watching its iron industry undersold by British iron manufactures, and its agriculture facing competition with grain shipped in by railway from Russia, or by railway and boat from the heartland of the United States, Germany turned a deaf ear to the proponents of free trade. Historically manufacturing interest had favoured protectionist trade policies and agricultural interest had supported free trade. Rapid and sudden improvements in transportation after the mid nineteenth century increased the threat of foreign competition to agriculture, causing agricultural interest and manufacturing interest to make common cause in favour of protectionism.

Another factor putting Germany squarely on the road to protectionism lay in the need to reform finances and find new sources of revenue. The imperial government of Germany exacted contributions from individual German states to finance its operations, but this practice was incurring resistance and becoming a source of discontent, partly because the contributions were increasing in size. Taxing imported goods seemed a more acceptable way for the central government to raise revenue from its citizens. The Emperor proposed a revised tariff law in February 1879, and the Reichstag enacted it into law in July 1879. The law was based upon the principle that all domestic industries deserved protection from foreign competition, trying to sidestep the criticism that tariffs were special interest legislation protecting selected industries.

The revised tariff law seemed to help the German economy rise out of the economic doldrums, maintaining stable prices while wages rose and exports steadily climbed to new levels. Between 1879 and 1884 the iron industry saw employment grow 35 per cent. Low prices continued to plague agriculture, prompting the Reichstag to enact another tariff in 1885, specifically directed at protecting domestic agricultural production. Germany proudly rose to become one of the economic miracles of the nineteenth century, a factor that may have added credibility to protectionist trade policies.

While most European powers were reducing trade barriers by mutual agreement, the United States and European colonial powers forced Japan to open its market to Western goods with minimal taxes on imported goods. In 1853 the US government sent Matthew Perry, commanding a squadron of four ships, on a mission to end Japan's self-imposed isolation, and pry open Japanese markets. The provisioning of US ships, the treatment of US sailors and the establishment of official relations led the list of issues on which Perry sought an agreement. He returned in the following spring for an answer, this time with nine ships, and struck an agreement that addressed these issues but not trade issues, except for the provision to exchange consuls in the future. Britain and Russia signed similar agreements with Japan.

In 1856 Townsend Harris, the first US consul to Japan, arrived in Tokyo, and began urging the Japanese to open up commercial relations. In 1858 the United States and Japan signed a commercial treaty and several western powers negotiated similar treaties soon afterwards. These treaties with Japan were called the 'Unequal Treaties', referring to the lack of reciprocity in their provisions. Western traders could not be held accountable under Japanese law, even in cases involving Japanese. Court cases involving Japanese citizens and Western traders were heard in courts with the consul of the offending party presiding as the judge. Japanese citizens in Western countries were not given the same immunity from domestic law. The treaties also provided that Western traders live in prescribed foreign settlements. Later Japan agreed to accept a maximum of a 5 per cent tariff on goods imported into Japan, and a 'most favoured trade' clause that extended to all Western powers any trade concession granted to a specific nation.

In 1871 Japan sent a diplomatic delegation to the United States and Europe hoping to renegotiate the treaty on better terms for Japan. The delegation failed in its primary purpose, but returned home awestruck with Western technology. Its findings helped launch Japan on a programme of accelerated industrialization. Only in 1911 did Japan finally regain control over its tariff policy. As a result of the Unequal Treaties, Japan exported raw silk, tea, coal and other raw materials to Western nations, who found in Japan a market for manufactured goods. The absence of tariff protection for its infant manufacturing industries may have forced Japan to develop its economy on a foundation of low wages and government support for industry. While the Unequal Treaties were restrictive, they were not as harsh as the treaties imposed upon China.

The United States, while playing a leading role in forcing upon Japan a commercial agreement that allowed Western goods to enter Japan with few trade restrictions, was not a leader in the nineteenth century movement towards trade liberalization. Quite the contrary, the McKinley Tariff of 1890 led the world into an era of pronounced protectionism that lasted until World War I. The United States had remained protectionist throughout the nineteenth century. Alexander Hamilton, the first Secretary of Treasury, had proposed a tariff as a primary source of revenue for the federal government and as an instrument for encouraging the development of manufacturing.[4] Congress enacted the first tariff in 1789, and tariffs generated 80 per cent of government revenue in the pre-Civil War era.

In addition to tariffs, the US government forbade all trade to

Britain and Europe between 1807 and 1809. That was while Napoleon defiantly enforced the Continental Blockade, and Britain tried to force all trade between the European continent and the New World through British ports. Britain determined what cargo neutral ships could carry to the continent, and assumed the right to board and seize neutral ships, ignoring the rights of neutrals amid war. France conferred upon itself the right to seize neutral ships complying with England's control of shipping. Rather than trying to enforce the rights of neutrals with military action, President Thomas Jefferson chose to impose an embargo on all trade with Europe and Britain. The embargo failed in its first objective, pressuring Britain to recognize neutrals' rights, but succeeded in stimulating the development of US manufacturing industries. Up to that point, the United States had mainly exported raw materials to and imported manufacturing goods from Europe. The number of incorporated factory businesses grew from seven in 1808 to 26 in 1809.[5]

The spirit of free trade expressed in the Anglo-French Commercial Treaty of 1860 left the United States untouched, largely because the Civil War placed heavy demands on sources of public revenue. Following the Civil War strains on the federal budget remained a factor hindering the liberalization of trade barriers. The tariff had also been a major battleground of the political struggles that divided North and South. The North wanted tariffs to protect its manufacturing interests and the South wanted free trade, hoping to keep American markets open to British manufactured goods, and British markets open to the South's exports, such as cotton. The outcome of the Civil War gave the pro-tariff forces the upper hand.

During the post-Civil War period the tariff revenue was equivalent to about 45 per cent of the value on imported goods subject to import duties. While Republicans made no apologies for high tariffs, Democrats agitated for lower tariffs, and eventually pressured Congress into appointing a Tariff Commission in 1882 to study the tariff and make recommendations for reform. The Commission recommended tariff reduction in the range of 20 to 25 per cent, but Congress in the Tariff Act of 1883 approved a 4 per cent reduction, more a symbolic concession than a serious effort at tariff reform. In 1884 Grover Cleveland, a Democrat, urged tariff reform, but Congress was unmoved, and in 1888 the Republicans unashamedly ran on a pro-protectionist platform, blaming the whisky trust and foreign manufacturers for inciting free trade agitation. The Republicans won the election and set to work enacting the most restrictive trade policies that had ever existed in the United States.

President William McKinley, serving as chairman of the House Ways and Means Committee when the tariff bill passed Congress, lent his name to the law. The Republicans aggressively supported the tariff as a permanent policy, eschewing the idea of tariffs as temporary measures protecting start-up or infant industries. The McKinley Tariff pushed duties on some fabrics over the 100 per cent mark, and for the first time individuals bringing goods home from foreign travel had to pay duties. Congress had added a sweetener for farmers, subjecting agricultural products to import duties, a meaningless gesture since the United States exported agricultural products. Imported farm machinery, however, continued to pay high tariffs. The most promising feature of the Tariff authorized the executive branch, without Senate approval, to negotiate reciprocal agreements mutually reducing tariffs on an individual country basis. In 1894 Congress repealed this provision, but the concept would reappear in legislation enacted in 1934. Congress revised the rates upward again in 1897 before reforming the tariff structure during the first term of the Woodrow Wilson presidency.

Russia became the next country to hoist higher the banner of protectionism, establishing higher tariffs in 1891 that virtually stopped imports in some industries, exceeding anything in the way of tariffs that had been seen before in Europe. Like Germany and the United States, Russia turned to the tariff as a major source of tax revenue. After sharing in the trend towards trade liberalization that had spread through Europe in the 1850s and 1860s, the Russian government began inching towards protectionism in 1877, requiring the payment of tariff duties in gold. At the time the Russian government was probably more interested in accumulating gold reserves than in protecting domestic industry from foreign competition. Officially Russia had been on a silver standard since 1839, but the financial stress of the Crimean War (1853–6) forced the government to suspend the convertibility of Russian roubles into silver, putting Russia on an inconvertible paper standard. Following the Crimean War the silver rouble remained a weak currency in foreign exchange markets, experiencing wide fluctuations in value. The rouble owed part of its weakness to the spread of the gold standard, which was rapidly becoming the premier monetary standard among the world's trading partners. Russia stood in need of foreign investment, but foreign investors hesitated at investing in a country on the silver standard, where capital, interest and profits could only be withdrawn in the form of a silver rouble that fluctuated in value. To win the confidence of foreign investors Russia had to adopt the gold standard.

Tariffs bolstered Russia's gold reserves for two reasons. First, payment of tariffs brought gold into Russia. Second, tariffs restricted imports, reducing the outflow of gold. The Russian government raised tariffs in 1881 and again in 1885, before increasing them in 1891 to levels that surpassed all precedent. This relatively modern application of mercantilism seemed to achieve its objective, creating an excess of exports over imports that brought an inflow of gold into Russia. By 1897 Russia had sufficient gold reserves to establish the gold standard, and soon foreign capital flowed into Russia. The tariff revenue also helped the government finance public works and economic development projects.

One year after the enactment of the Russian tariff, France substantially strengthened its protectionist stance with the enactment of the Meline Tariff of 1892, named after Felix Jules Meline, secretary general of a tariff commission in France. Meline was a strong proponent of protectionism, arguing that it benefited not only the owners of capital but also the working class. The enactment of the Tariff added momentum to the worldwide trend towards protectionism that began with the tariff policies of the German *Zollverein*. The rise of Germany as a major manufacturing producer probably pushed France towards protectionism.

On average the Meline Tariff raised import duties 80 per cent above the old rates. Unlike previous French tariffs, the Meline Tariff awarded significant protection to agriculture, albeit that the rates agricultural products paid were lower than the rates manufacturing goods paid. Improvements in railway and shipping transportation had substantially increased the threat of competition from agricultural products from the United States and Russia, increasing support for protectionist trade policies within the agricultural community, traditionally a stronghold of free-trade sentiment. The new tariff levied a minimum rate on imports from countries that negotiated commercial treaties with France entitling them to a most favoured nation status. Imports from other countries paid a maximum tariff. The French government gave itself the privilege to adjust these rates without renegotiating commercial treaties with individual countries. The wisdom of the Meline Tariff seemed vindicated by the strong prosperity that followed its enactment, but it also touched off a round of tariff wars that plunged Europe into a period of pronounced protectionism.

Britain resisted the temptation to follow the example of its other Western trading partners and raise tariff rates towards the end of the century, remaining faithful to the principles of free trade that governed its trade policy. After World War I Britain made a few token concessions to the advocates of protectionist trade polices, but remained a free-trade country. The United States revised downwards its tariff rates on the eve of World War I, and the world was spared further escalation of trade barriers until the Smoot-Hawley Tariff of 1930, the most protectionist tariff ever enacted by the US government.

By the 1930s the educated world had largely accepted the doctrine of free trade and had come to see trade barriers as a shortsighted hindrance to productivity. Herbert Hoover, President of the United States (1928–32), normally sympathized with liberal trade polices, and when the Smoot-Hawley legislation came before Congress, a thousand members of the American Economics Association signed a statement denouncing it. Hoover, looking towards restoration of business confidence in the aftermath of the stock market crash of 1929, had decided an aggressive tariff would pave the path for economic recovery in the United States.[6] It turned out to be one of the most mistaken judgements in the history of economic policy.

The first pressure for stiffer tariff barriers to protect domestic producers had come from agriculture, an industry that had not recovered from the economic depression following World War I. The Smoot-Hawley Tariff took its name from two strongly protectionist legislators, Senator Reed Smoot of Utah and Congressman Willis C. Hawley of Oregon, who introduced a bill aimed at protecting domestically produced agricultural products. As the bill passed through Congress, its list of goods receiving added protection grew, expanding into manufactured goods, and the degree of protection rose. The version that became law raised tariffs on Cuban sugar, cattle, mutton and lamb, corn, milk, lemons, hides, flax, hemp cotton, wool, clothing, lumber, boots and shoes, silk and woollen goods, hydraulic cement and bricks. It lifted US tariff rates from an average of 25.9 per cent to 50.02 per cent. On 17 June 1930 Herbert Hoover signed the bill with six gold pens. At first the Tariff showed signs of fulfilling its supporters' expectations. In 1930 prices fell in the United States, but at a slower rate than experienced in other countries, and the US balance of payments turned from a deficit to a surplus, which among other things added to the gold stock.

The new policy met with retaliation from the outset, leaving success shortlived. In 1931 Britain, Canada, Cuba, Mexico, France, Italy, Spain and numerous smaller countries retaliated with higher import duties. Another round of retaliation erupted the following year. Some countries imposed quantitative restrictions and quotas more inflexible than import duties that simply made imports less profitable. World trade slowed precipitously, falling to about one-third of its 1929 level. As the rest of the world raised trade barriers against US products, the United States saw its exports descend into a downward spiral, falling from $842 million in 1929 to $225 million in 1933, falling faster than imports, despite the higher tariffs.

Even Britain buckled under the pressure of worldwide depression, abandoning its nearly century-old commitment to free trade. With the enactment of the Import Duties Act of 1932, Parliament effectively shifted Britain from a free trade country to a protectionist one. While exempting many food and raw material items, this Act levied a general ad valorem tax of 10 per cent on remaining imported goods and services. It also provided for the formation of an Import Duties Advisory Committee charged with identifying specific industries that needed additional protection and making recommendations accordingly. The Exchequer made the final decision on these recommendations. Individual industries turned to this Committee for additional protection. Britain's pig iron producers and lace and lace net producers persuaded the committee to recommend tariffs in the order of 33 per cent and 30 per cent respectively. After 1933 the Exchequer could grant concessions to individual countries, allowing the Exchequer to negotiate mutually advantageous concessions.

During the 1920s the forces of protectionism began to build as British exports fell relative to imports, a natural result of an overvalued pound artificially pegged at its pre-war level. The eminent economist John Maynard Keynes, an avowed free trader, created a sensation when he advocated tariffs and export bounties as desirable policies in the face of Britain's ailing economy.[7] With the Depression of the 1930s the British government faced declining government revenues while expenditure on unemployment insurance increased. The Depression hit British industries such as iron and steel, already sick in the 1920s. With the United States' enactment of the infamous Smoot-Hawley Tariff, the forces of protectionism stole the upper hand, and Britain abandoned its long time free-trade stance.

While Britain, historically the world's most consistent and faithful defender of free trade, appeared in the 1930s to be won over to protectionism, history was on the side of trade liberalization. After World War II, the world's trading partners opened up multilateral negotiations to lower trade barriers. Remembrance of the destructive trade barriers raised during the Depression remained a vital force during the years following World War II, spurring interest in multilateral tariff reduction.

The year 1947 saw the formation of GATT (General Agreement on Tariffs and Trade), an international organization, originally consisting of 29 countries committed to the reduction of trade barriers through multilateral negotiation. In the same year the first round of negotiations was held in Geneva. Negotiations were fruitful, succeeding in the multilateral reduction of trade barriers on a significant scale. Annecy,

France, hosted the second round of negotiations, in 1949, and in 1951 a third round of negotiations was conducted in Torquay, England. In 1956 Geneva was again the seat of multilateral negotiations to reduce barriers. These subsequent negotiations failed to live up to the expectations created by the first.

The formation of the European Economic Community (EEC) in 1958 brought added urgency to these negotiations from the perspective of the US. The EEC was a common market that liberalized trade policies among its members while erecting a common tariff wall against goods imported from outside the EEC. In 1962 the US Congress enacted the Trade Expansion Act of 1962, conferring upon the President authorization to negotiate tariff reductions in the order of 50 per cent. By granting authorization to treat broad categories of goods as a single item, this empowered the President to negotiate reductions across the board, rather than item by item. The Act also provided financial assistance to workers losing jobs to foreign competition, including extended unemployment compensation, and help for retooling. The Trade Expansion Act reinvigorated multilateral trade negotiations. Between 1962 and 1967 a new round of negotiations, known as the Kennedy Round after President Kennedy, brought in 70 countries, and succeeded in reducing tariffs by an average of 35 per cent on manufactured goods. The reductions were spread across a wide variety of goods, touching 64 per cent of manufactured goods.

Success in the reduction of tariff rates brought to light other, non-tariff, trade barriers that seemed to turn up in larger numbers as tariff rates fell. In 1973 Tokyo was the seat of a preliminary meeting that organized another round of trade negotiations. The actual negotiations were held in Geneva between 1974 and 1979, but became known as the Tokyo Round. Again the US President received authorization from Congress to substantially reduce trade barriers. The Tokyo Round succeeded in slashing tariff rates on manufactured goods by 33 per cent, phased in over eight years, leaving the average tariff rates on manufactured goods for major trading partners ranging from as low as 2.9 per cent in the case of Japan, to 6.3 per cent for West Germany, the lowest tariff levels in the history of the industrialized world. One innovation in the Tokyo Round of trade negotiations lay in the exemption from reciprocity in tariff reductions granted to developing countries that felt that infant manufacturing industries still needed tariff protection.

Punta del Este, Uruguay, was the seat of the last round of GATT trade negotiations, known as the Uruguay Round and lasting from 1986 to 1990. Tariff reductions for agricultural products and reductions of non-tariff barriers topped the agenda. Despite its ambitious agenda this round failed to produce important agreements liberalizing trade. The United States was disappointed at the failure to agree upon more worldwide protection for patents and copyrights.

The GATT negotiations represent the most serious and sustained commitment to freer trade since Adam Smith wrote *The Wealth of Nations*, his classic work, which attacked trade barriers along with other forms of government regulation. Free trade seemed the wave of the future except for one disturbing trend, the growth of free trade areas, customs unions and common markets. These trading blocs raised the spectre of another era of protectionism as they raised tariff barriers against outside trade.

Europe became the seat of the first of these post-World War II trading blocs, themselves a peculiar manifestation of the trend towards free trade, blazing a new trail with the organization of the EEC, which officially came into existence on 1 January 1958. It created what was called the Common Market, a form of trade zone that involves a higher degree of economic integration than either a free-trade area or a customs union. A free-trade area allows goods and services to move between its members without trade restrictions. A customs union takes integration a step further by raising trade restrictions (identical for all members of the union) against goods imported from outside the union. A common market eliminates legal barriers against the flow of capital and labour between its members, allowing workers to work in other member countries.

The European Common Market superseded the European Coal and Steel Community, an organization of six countries (Belgium, France, West Germany, Italy, Luxembourg and the Netherlands), established by the Treaty of Paris in 1951, that coordinated production and distribution of coal and steel among themselves. In 1957 the Treaty of Rome, signed by the same six countries, pushed Europe further down the road of economic integration with the establishment of the EEC, forerunner of the European Union. In the same year another Treaty of Rome established the European Atomic Energy Commission, an organization devoted to the coordination and development of atomic energy in Europe. The EEC owed its constitution to the principles set forth in these treaties and the earlier Treaty of Paris. The mission of this new organization was the development of an integrated market in Europe, one that allowed the free movement of goods, services, capital and people. In 1967 the EEC changed its name to the European Community (EC). Membership expanded beyond the original six countries, Denmark, Ireland and Britain joining in 1973, Greece in 1981, and Portugal and Spain in 1986.

By 1968 trade between members of the EC was no longer obstructed by tariffs, and a common external tariff protected industries within the EC from external competition. Either because of or in spite of the trade policies of the EC, member countries saw trade rapidly expand throughout the 1960s, but the worldwide stagflation of the 1970s struck hard at the European economies, prompting a re-examination of trade policies. A policy paper of the EC called attention to numerous restrictive, non-tariff trade policies that continued to hamper trade among EC countries. Member country governments demonstrated favouritism toward domestic suppliers at the expense of suppliers from other EC countries, and trade was often held up at customs by delays, administrative burdens and differences in technical jargon. Differences of production costs between member countries emerged hardly intelligible after the distortions of various value added tax (VAT) rates. Out of this policy paper came 282 proposals for lifting restrictions hampering trade between EC members. The proposals were endorsed by the EC, but some national governments have been slow to embrace them, putting implementation of the proposals in the category of an ongoing process.

The Treaty of Maastricht, drawn up in December 1991 by the leaders of the EC, changed the name from EC to European Union (EU), and laid the foundation for the establishment of a European monetary union, which became a reality in January

1999. This treaty had received the approval of all members by 1993. The year 1995 saw Austria, Finland and Sweden join the EU, and European members of the former Soviet bloc are expected to join. The governance of the EU bears the marks of a political organization. Each member country elects representatives to a European Parliament. The population of each country determines the number of representatives it can seat in the Parliament. Proposals advanced by the European Parliament come before a European Commission, an executive body also responsible for the implementation of the treaties. A Council of Ministers, consisting of political leaders from member countries, act as the decision-making body on community-wide matters. Disputes are heard by a European Community Court of Justice, which is also responsible for interpreting the EU constitution.

The organization of the EU may have been the driving force behind the North American Free Trade Agreement (NAFTA), an agreement between Canada, Mexico and the United States establishing a free-trade area in North America. A free-trade area is a rather cautious step towards economic integration, abolishing tariffs and quotas between member trading partners, but allowing each member to set its own tariffs on goods imported from outside the area, and its own rules governing the migration of resources such as labour. The enactment of NAFTA in 1993 put an end to many tariffs and quotas restricting trade between Canada, Mexico and the United States, and in some cases provided for the progressive removal of tariffs and quotas over a period of five to ten years. Goods produced within these countries were considered North American goods, and could be transported across borders subject to the provisions of NAFTA. Goods partially produced outside North America required special treatment. Automotive goods can be traded under the provisions of NAFTA if the North American content meets a set percentage, varying between 60 and 62.5. NAFTA also lifted barriers that restricted foreign investment between its members, such as occurs when General Motors builds an assembly plant in Mexico, and established procedures for resolving disputes between foreign investors and host countries within NAFTA. Measured in numbers of consumers and combined GDP, NAFTA rivals the EU as one of the world's largest markets.

The trend towards large trading blocs may not only plunge the world into another period of protectionism, but may also inflect damage on small economies, such as Hong Kong, that do not fit into a trading bloc. Presently the trends towards large trading blocs and free trade appear on a collision course.

ELEVEN

The Vicissitudes of Capitalism

Globalization has brought the synchronization of business cycles between countries, creating new issues in economics involving global recession and global growth, global inflation and global deflation, global confidence and global panic. Business cycles influence the evolution of the global financial system through the operation of inflation and deflation. Deflation invariably encourages clever sellers to find ways of propping up prices, either through government-fixed prices or price-fixing schemes with competitors. Deflationary periods produce a maze of government regulations that discourage price competition and downward price flexibility. Late-six-teenth-century England, late-nineteenth-century Germany and the United States of the 1930s furnish examples of govern-ments faced with deflation, favouring policies that dampen price flexibility and involve more regulation. Inflationary peri-ods, by helping debtors at the expense of creditors, often redis-tribute wealth in favour of risk-taking households and businesses that proudly credit free enterprise for their new found wealth when they are often beneficiaries of hidden specu-lative opportunities afforded by inflation. As the voice of this new wealth is heard in the corridors of government, govern-ments switch to *laissez-faire* policies again. Inflation, making it easier for businesses to sell goods for more than they paid for them, gives birth to a desire to let markets work. The 1970s saw the global economy engulfed in a wave of inflation, and the 1980s saw governments turn sharply away from regulated economies, instead promoting privatization, free markets, freer exchange rates, unrestricted flows of capital and lower taxes. Now East Asian countries, after suffering a severe financial crisis in 1997, are quietly re-evaluating policies of financial and trade liberalization, fearing these policies may have been enacted too quickly and without proper sequence, hoping that government regulations can avoid a recurrence of crisis.

Sketchy information on business cycles stretches at least as far back as the Italian Renaissance. According to Machiavelli, Piero de' Medici, invalid son of Cosimo de' Medici, upon assuming management of the Medici Bank after Cosimo's death, sternly began calling in loans, causing a contraction in credit and a wave of bankruptcies.[1] The muffled mountain ranges of boom and depression can be dimly gleaned from the history of England during the sixteenth century. The first half of the century saw a hurried boom in cloth production, lifting cloth exports by 50 per cent from 1500 to 1550. After reaching a peak in 1550, cloth production entered rough seas, floundering at least 20 per cent below the mid-century peak for the last half of the century. In addition the second half of the century suffered two sharp contractions in which cloth exports fell to 50 per cent of their mid-century peak. The impetus for expansion during the first half of the century received added momentum from a depreciation of the pound sterling in foreign exchange, reducing the cost of English exports to foreign buyers. The expansion turned to contraction when the value of the pound in foreign exchange turned upwards in 1550, increasing the cost of English exports to foreign buyers and thus reducing the demand for English goods. The appreciation of the pound also made foreign goods cheaper in England, to the extent that mercantilist policies allowed imports.

To meet the challenge of economic depression, the English Parliament enacted legislation that restricted production and alleviated the sufferings of the poor. The deteriorating economic conditions at home were perhaps what prompted the English to send a ship to Morocco in 1551 and others to Guinea in 1553, searching for new markets. During this time the English also commenced trade with Russia and re-established direct trade with the Levant.

Both Britain and France suffered jolting financial debacles around 1720, followed by long periods of economic sluggishness, probably caused by contractions in investment spending, which often happens when confidence is threatened. Towards the end of the eighteenth century, business cycle information appears to be more abundant. According to T. S. Ashton, the British economy experienced depressions during the years 1762, 1765–9, 1773–4, 1778–81, 1784 and 1788.[2] The last three decades of the eighteenth century in England were marked by a climate of economic depression, punctuated with mild recoveries that climaxed in financial crises erupting in the years 1763, 1772–3, 1778, 1783–4 and 1788. France had a similar experience, but the timing of the French cycle seemed to lag the British cycle by about a decade. One of the most severe economic contractions France suffered during the eighteenth century occurred between 1787 and 1789, which contributed to the outbreak of the French Revolution in 1789. The colonies of Britain and France shared in the economic travails of their mother countries.

The economic depression of the late eighteenth century seems to owe its origins to the ebb and flow of gold production from the New World, an explanation made more plausible by the credibility currently given to monetary theories of business cycles. Brazilian gold production began a steady climb at the dawn of the eighteenth century, rising from an annual rate of 1,000 kg to peak at 15,000 kg for the years between 1740 and 1760. Between 1760 and 1780 Brazilian gold production fell off markedly, averaging 10,000 kg per year between 1760 and 1780, and for the remainder of the century averaging 5,000 kg per year. Measured in pounds sterling, Brazilian exports of gold fell from 2.5 million to 1 million pounds between 1760 and 1780, and gold production worldwide shared the same trend, dropping from an average annual rate of 781,000 ounces between 1741 and 1760, to an average annual rate of 665,000 ounces between 1761 and 1780. Declining worldwide gold production continued into the nineteenth century. Worldwide silver production doubled to fill the monetary gap left by gold, rising from an annual rate of 14 million ounces for the years 1721–40, to 28 million ounces for 1781–1810. Paper money experiments also flourished in the New World and the Old World as gold production sagged, a response to pressures created by shortages of precious metals.

While data on the late-eighteenth-century depression is sparse by modern criteria the general outline of development is seen in the ideas of Nikolai Dmitrievich Kontratieff, famous Russian theorist of economic cycles.[3] Kontratieff is best known for his theory of 50-year waves, now called Kontratieff Cycles, suggesting a degree of precise periodicity in business cycles that subsequent research has not validated. Nevertheless many of his observations are perceptive, roving spotlights identifying areas that deserve further study.

Born in 1892, founder and director of the Moscow Business Conditions Institute, Kontratieff thought he had discovered evidence of long waves of business-cycle-type fluctuations in capitalistic systems, based upon time-series studies of production and prices. Since his theories left no room for an ultimate economic crisis of a fatal dimension, destroying the capitalistic system, Kontratieff's theories fell outside the pale of Marxian orthodoxy, in 1928 costing him his position as director of the Moscow Business Conditions Institute, held since 1919. He never recovered from his fall from grace, being deported to Siberia in 1930 where he was detained for the remainder of his life.

According to Kontratieff's evidence for a 50-year wave, European economies experienced the start of an upswing in the 1780s, followed by a sustained expansion reaching a crescendo during the 1810–17 time period, which marked the beginning of a downswing that lasted until the 1844–51 period. The end of the first wave marked the beginning of a second wave, starting with a sustained expansion that topped out during the 1870–75 period, followed by a downswing that bottomed out during the 1890–96 period. Since Kontratieff's data ended around 1920, he could not identify a third complete cycle, but he claimed the 1914–20 period was the peak of an expansion begun during 1890–96. These waves were international in scope, identified by synchronized peaks and troughs in individual countries.

Professional economists remain sceptical at best towards Kontratieff's theories, finding no theoretical reason to expect an economic cycle of exactly 50 years in duration. As procedures for analysing time-series data have grown in sophistication, new studies of the Kontratieff cycle have been performed, but without significant results for verification of 50-year cycles. While his findings have not passed modern empirical test, his thought-provoking speculations about the character of cycles yielded important insights. Kontratieff found that agriculture suffers acutely in downswings while innovations appear to receive a stimulus. The following upswing owes its strength partly to a cluster of innovations originating in the downswing and applied in the upswing. The downswing wears out capital goods such as factories, warehouses and transportation facilities, which are replenished in the upswing, providing the driving force that distinguishes the upswing. The long expansions are also fertile ground for wars and revolutions.

Kontratieff's theories are still cited, particularly in the popular press, for possible explanations and prognostications.[4] If the downswing that began in the 1914–20 period reached its grand finale in the 1930s, the next downswing should have bottomed out in the 1980s, a time that encompassed a severe recession, but also the beginning of a long expansion that, with only one interruption, lasted until the end of the century. The long expansion of the 1990s has received much of its momentum from the application of innovations developed in the 1970s and 1980s.

The first financial crisis to spread internationally along clearly delineated lines was that of 1857, a crisis that began in the United States but spread to global dimensions. By 1857 railroad stocks and bonds had advanced to the forefront of instruments for financial speculation on Wall Street, replacing the government securities and bank stocks that had dominated financial speculation when Wall Street experienced its first financial crisis in 1837. As a boom in railroad construction ran its course, the profits from railroads, particularly from older lines, fell, a trend exacerbated by slower immigration from eastern to western United States. Western land prices began falling and in mid 1857 the prices of railroad securities peaked and began to slide downward.

A crisis began to take shape in August 1857 after the Ohio Life Insurance and Trust Company, whose New York office had invested heavily in railroad securities, declared bankruptcy. The New York office had concentrated one-quarter of its investments in a single railroad company that was failing. The list of railroads that failed in this crisis included the Illinois Central, the Fort Wayne and Chicago, the Erie and the Pittsburgh, and the Reading lines. The bankruptcy of the Ohio Life Insurance and Trust Company seems to have sparked a run on New York banks, which were known for financing stock market speculation. Stockbrokers, unable to renew loans on financed stock, sold off securities, creating panic conditions on Wall Street. Stocks held as collateral for loans suddenly lost value, leaving New York banks holding loans without sufficient collateral, threatening the solvency of the banks themselves. During the period 10–14 October, New York banks lost half their specie reserves, and a scramble for specie forced numerous banks to suspend specie payments, leaving banknotes and bank deposits no longer redeemable in specie.

Since the United States bought one-fifth of Britain's exports, and British investors owned large holdings of American securities, economic tremors in the United States were directly felt in Britain. The Borough Bank of Liverpool and at least two large Scottish mercantile houses had closed their doors by 27 October, and banks throughout Scotland suspended payments and sometimes failed. After the British Parliament suspended the Bank Charter Act of 1844, freeing up gold reserves, the Bank of England, acting as a lender of last resort, sent gold to Scotland in support of Scottish banks. Under the Bank Charter Act of 1844, the Bank of England held reserves in gold bullion for all Bank of England banknotes in circulation above a legal maximum. The Bank of England also advanced assistance to George Peabody and Company, an American banking and mercantile company.

Scandinavia and Hamburg felt shock waves from the financial crisis, and Germany saw the decimation of its banking industry just after going through a period of rapid proliferation of banks. The stock market in France crashed after the Bank of France lifted interest rates to ease a drain on gold reserves.

The origin of the first shock that sent the world into a contraction, propagated through the financial system, may be found in the close of the Crimean War in 1856. The end of that war decreased the demand for US wheat, sending American wheat prices tumbling, putting a liquidity squeeze on western wheat farmers, and ending land speculation in the west. Western banks began withdrawing funds on deposit with eastern banks, draining the reserves of those banks, and forcing a contraction of loans in the east. These depressing economic currents, coupled with overspeculation in railroad shares, may have created a condition ripe for financial crisis, and the psychological shock from the bankruptcy of the Ohio Life Insurance and Trust Company supplied the spark. It was a short-lived crisis, most American banks resuming specie payments in 1858, and the American Civil War pulling the world out of an economic slump that followed.

In 1873 a financial panic spread to most European trading partners and the United States, marking the beginning of a long deflationary trend lasting until 1896, an era sometimes called the 'Great Depression' before the experience of the 1930s eclipsed it. It began in May with a stock market crash in Vienna, spreading to the United States because American railroad issues had been popular with German and Austrian investors. The US stock market closed for ten days when the unloading of stocks overburdened a system of selling by certified cheque, and one of the major financial institutions in the United States, Jay Cooke & Company, failed. After a speculative frenzy in 1872 German stock markets crashed in 1873. Britain dodged the financial crisis but later struggled against economic depression.

Economic depression, lasting a quarter of a century, followed the debacle of 1873, but it was a depression with a silver lining. Prices fell and workers saw wages fall, but retail prices fell faster than wages, increasing their real purchasing power. Industrial output also grew, but at a slower rate, and mild upswings were followed by sharper downswings. The prevailing economic outlook was pessimistic, but some historians argue that the Great Depression was a myth because output continued to expand.

Beneath the depression lurked a marked reduction in investment spending, particularly in railway construction, which was the real underlying cause of the prolonged depression. The decade leading up to 1873 saw a boom in railway construction, doubling railway mileage in the United States, nearly trebling railway mileage in Austria, and between 1868 and 1873 adding 12,000 miles of railway in Russia. Railway construction and faster steam transportation over water substantially increased European access to food supplies produced in the hinterlands of the United States and Russia, starting a downward trend in agricultural prices that lasted until the end of the century. Overexpansion of railways into sparsely populated areas reduced railway profits, forcing them to default on bank loans, causing bank failures.

One last contraction, chronic and deep, signalled the end of the prolonged depression, lasting from 1890 until 1895 in Britain and Germany, and from 1893 until 1897 in the United States. This last contraction was preceded by a mild expansion in the late 1880s. In the United States the Panic of 1893, in addition to a stock market crash, saw bank failures and suspensions surpass all past records, putting one-quarter of US railroad mileage in receivership by mid 1894. Prices fell so sharply in the United States between 1893 and 1896 that the cost of living remained below its 1890 level to the end of the century. The deflationary forces encouraged the growth of cartels in Germany, and trusts and interlocking directorates in the United States evolved as a means of fixing prices among competitors and avoiding price competition that often broke into vicious price wars in a deflationary environment. As a reaction to the deflation, the United States, France, Russia and Germany strengthened trade barriers to protect domestic producers from foreign competition.

In 1896 the discovery of gold in Alaska, Australia and South Africa gave the world economy a respite from deflation and depression, lifting prices in the United States by 35 per cent between 1896 and 1910. In Germany the growth in industrial output returned to the levels that existed between 1849 and 1873.

The decade following World War I was remarkable mainly for sluggish economic growth, the United States being perhaps an exception. England kept the pound sterling overvalued in foreign exchange markets, making exports too expensive and imports too cheap. France kept the franc overvalued until 1926. The first signs of what would become the economic debacle of the century surfaced in the summer of 1929 when the Federal Reserve System in the United States reported that its index of industrial production had declined 5 per cent. US investment spending had been subsiding since a peak in 1926. To tame excessive speculation in the stock market, the Federal Reserve System began tightening the monetary reins in 1928, selling bonds in the open market and raising the discount rate on three different occasions, which caused the money supply to fall at an annual rate of over 1 per cent for the period between April 1928 and November 1929.

Stock prices crested on 7 September 1929, and lost about 10 per cent of value before beginning to fall off rapidly in mid October. On 24 October, 'Black Thursday', softness in the stock market turned to panic, and almost thirteen million shares changed hands, overburdening exchange technology and leaving sellers without knowing the prices they received for their stock until late in the evening. The sell off continued and by mid November stocks had lost 40 per cent of their value. Panic on Wall Street hit foreign stock markets like a thunderclap, triggering a crash in London that spread to Berlin, Paris and Tokyo.

The crash of 1929 led the world into a prolonged period of subdued output and high unemployment. More than one-third of US banks in existence at the close of 1929 had failed by 1933. The United States' real output of goods and services shrank by 29 per cent between 1929 and 1933, a substantial decrease when considering that the US long-term growth rate is 3 per cent. The United States waited until 1937 before seeing output return to 1929 levels. Gross investment spending in the United States, which historically had accounted for the production of about 15 per cent of real output, fell to 1 per cent of real output between 1932 and 1933. Commodity wholesale prices fell 23 per cent between 1929 and 1933. Unemployment rates, which had dropped as low as 3.2 per cent over the last decade, rose to 25 per cent by 1933, increasing the number of unemployed Americans from 1.5 million to 12 million. By the end of the 1930s the unemployment rate had dropped into the teens but remained unusually high.

Given weak economic conditions in Europe the Depression would have spread under any circumstances but the United States gave substantial impetus to the international propagation of the Depression by the passage of the Smoot-Hawley Tariff of 1930, plunging the world into a retaliatory trade war that reduced world trade by 20 per cent. By the end of 1932 unemployment in Western Europe stood at 15 million, up from 3.5 million unemployed during the mid 1920s. Unemployment in Germany climbed to 43 per cent by 1932.

The 1930s became the most influential decade of the twentieth century when judged in light of the future development of economic policy and institutions. People questioned whether capitalistic systems were consistent with steady long-term growth in wealth and income, free from terrifying bouts of economic crisis and insecurity, and most governments eagerly embraced reforms that increased the less cyclical public sector and provided more economic security. At the same time that governments distanced themselves from capitalistic models at home, they remembered the costly trade wars of the 1930s and promoted an international trade regime shaped by the principles of free trade.

World War II put an end to the Depression but many observers expected another depression or severe recession at the end of World War II, a common phenomenon following wars. Perhaps the need to replace the devastated industrial capital of Europe, combined with the Cold War, continuing arms race, and war in Korea and later in Vietnam, helped keep the post-war economy expanding. Rapid growth in West Germany and Japan raised those countries to the status of economic miracles. Between 1948 and 1972 Japan saw output per person grow at an average annual rate of 8.2 per cent, and Germany for the same period saw output per person grow at average annual rate of 5.7 per cent. Output per person grew at an average annual rate of 2.2 per cent for the United States over the same period.

The pace of growth slowed significantly in the 1970s when shortages of commodities, particularly crude oil, became the driving force behind a worldwide wave of inflation. The price of crude oil began the decade at $3 per barrel, and finished in excess of $30 a barrel, thanks partly to wars and revolution in the Middle East. Increases in productivity slowed as industry found laboursaving machinery more expensive to operate, and therefore less profitable. A condition called 'stagflation' developed in the industrialized countries, characterized by slow or no productivity growth, high inflation and high unemployment.

In looking for causes of stagflation, the finger of suspicion was pointed at the redirection economic policies had received from the Depression, growth in the public sector, economic regulation at the expense of free markets, and the expansion of social welfare programmes that protected people from economic insecurity. The economic paradigm that justified many of these policies, Keynesian economics, which emphasized the maintenance of a high level of demand as the linchpin of prosperity, lost much of its credibility during this era in favour of policies that emphasized increasing incentives to produce by cutting taxes, rather than reinforcing demand with heavy government spending.

Renewed interest in free-market policies paved the way for a modest renaissance of capitalism in the 1980s. Strong anti-inflation policies, mainly in the form of restricted growth in money stocks, brought down inflation rates worldwide, precipitating a crash in crude oil prices by 1986. The early 1980s saw unusually high unemployment rates, in the double-digit range in the United States, a by-product of the anti-inflation policies. By the mid 1980s a recovery was underway in the United States, which, with one interruption triggered by a stock market crash in 1987 and a rash of thrift institution failures, lasted until the end of the century. About one-third of the savings and loan institutions in the United States failed between 1988 and 1991.

While the US economy led the global economy into an era of enduring and sustained growth in the 1990s, the growth was not robust and not all the world's major trading partners shared in significant growth. The average growth rate for the United States between 1990 and 1998 was 2.9 per cent; worldwide average annual growth averaged 2.4 per cent. In 1990 Japan slid into a decade of economic doldrums, prompted by a crash in the Tokyo stock market. The crash may have been caused by an overly lax monetary policy, intended to strengthen the dollar by weakening the yen.[5] Before crashing, the Nikkei index, at 12,000 in 1986, rose to the dizzy height of 39,000 in 1989. By the end of the century the Nikkei was still fluctuating under 20,000. Real estate prices plummeted, leaving many of Japan's banks and insurance companies standing on the edge of a financial abyss, a situation that had shown only modest improvement by 2000. Between 1990 and 1998 Japan reported an average annual growth rate of 1.3 per cent.

Germany is another country that ranked in the forefront of economic success from 1948 to 1972, but has since fallen behind, perhaps because of difficulties merging the two Germanys, coupled with some of the difficulties all of Europe is experiencing because of economic unification, and stern monetary policies in the aftermath of the inflationary 1970s. Between 1990 and 1998 Germany experienced an average annual growth rate of 1.6 per cent.

Europe generally suffered from sluggish economic growth in the decade of the 1990s. Between 1990 and 1998, France averaged growth of 1.5 per cent, Britain 2.2 per cent, Italy 1.2 per cent, Switzerland 0.04 per cent, Netherlands 2.6 per cent and Spain 1.9 per cent. Ireland, however, reported 7.5 per cent annual growth for the period, comparing favourably with Malaysia, Singapore and Thailand, usually ranked among the fastest growing countries between 1990 and 1998. Europe may owe its slow growth to the trend towards economic unification that is bringing each European economy, individually subject to high levels of government regulation, into closer competition with each other. Europe is known for extensive government regulation, particularly in the area of employment practices, which may account for high levels of European unemployment. European governments may have aggravated the unemployment problem by imposing excessively tight monetary policies as the best insurance against a recurrence of inflation.

The last fifteen years of the twentieth century saw a complete economic and financial cycle from boom to bust in East Asia where a new group of 'economic miracles' had surfaced.[6] Between 1989 and 1994 Indonesia experienced an average annual real GDP growth rate of 6.9 per cent, which accelerated to over 8 per cent annually for 1995 and 1996. In Thailand real GDP growth rates exceeded 8 per cent for every year between 1992 and 1995. South Korea reported real GDP growth rates in excess of 8 per cent for the years 1994 and 1995, and growth in Malaysia exceeded 9 per cent for the same years. In 1994 real GDP in Singapore grew at 11.4 per cent, and over the next three years growth ranged between 7.5 and 8.4 per cent. Real GDP growth in Hong Kong fell within more normal bounds, varying between 3.9 per cent and 5.4 per cent for the years 1994 to 1997. For a while, however, it seemed as if the virus of financial euphoria had passed from Japan to Hong Kong. The Hang Seng Index of the

Hong Kong stock market was in the range of 2,200 in 1988, and steadily climbed, reaching a jittery height in excess of 16,000 in 1997. Hong Kong also experienced a boom in real estate prices that mirrored its stock market boom. The secret to these high growth rates lay with strong export demand. These countries tended to keep their currencies tied to the value of the US dollar, which fell in value during the first half of the 1990s, making it possible for these countries to export products at lower prices when measured in other countries' money. In the case of Singapore, exports grew by 25 per cent in 1994 alone, and even Hong Kong saw exports grow 14 per cent in 1995.

In 1997 a financial crisis erupted in East Asia that nearly graduated into global financial meltdown, and may have put an end to the East Asian economic miracle.[7] In 1996 and 1997 the value of the dollar turned upwards, hurting exports from these countries, which had to turn to tighter monetary policies to keep the value of their currencies in line with the value of the dollar. Exports suffered, stock markets reacted negatively, and tighter monetary policies encouraged an inflow of foreign loans. Corporations in East Asia were already highly dependent upon debt financing, as opposed to equity (stocks) financing, rendering them vulnerable to bankruptcy in an economic downturn. (Stockholders cannot sue corporations for falling stock prices, but lenders can sue corporations for failure to make interest payments.) As falling exports hurt profits, foreign capital, much of which was negotiated on a short-term basis, stopped flowing in. Without an inflow of foreign capital countries could not maintain the value of their currencies relative to the dollar. Thailand was the first East Asian country to devalue its currency, followed by devaluations throughout East Asia. Financial markets crashed throughout the region and foreign capital began leaving these countries.

After going through a phase of negative growth, the East Asian countries seem to have entered a sustained recovery, entering the twenty-first century with stock markets that have returned to pre-crash levels, and subdued but clearly positive economic growth. The long-term effects of the financial crisis remain a question mark, but the crisis may have put an end to the supernormal growth rates in East Asia.

TWELVE

The Age of Financial Integration Begins

The rate, complexity and variety of change in the global financial system is now without precedent, itself perhaps taking on the character of revolutionary change. As global financial institutions and systems develop and evolve, old customs and practices crumble, affecting the relation of debtors and creditors, labour and capital, rich and poor, skilled and unskilled, and of developing with developed countries. The integration of the global financial system has spawned conditions where the economic and financial environment changes too rapidly to form sound instincts and habits, forcing individuals to marshal all available knowledge for intelligent adaptation to new stimuli. Financial systems have always been integrated to an extent, depending upon the technology of transportation and communication, and the degree to which cultural and legal environments permit capital and goods to move freely between legal entities. A near microcosm of the integrated global financial system can be found in the fragmented city-states of Renaissance Italy. The Medici Bank, headquartered in Florence, not only maintained branches in Milan, Rome and Venice, but also had branches in London, Lyons, Geneva, Bruges and Avignon. Europe adopted the Italian model on a larger scale, nation states replacing city-states, but again revealing the outlines of an international financial system against the backdrop of autonomous political entities connected by systems of communication and transportation. The Rothschild merchant bankers had branches in Germany, London and Paris, and a branch of the famous Barings banking house of London was the largest banking house in the United States before the Civil War.

The nineteenth century saw a net of European financial interest spread worldwide, much as European culture itself took over the world during that era, drawing the economic landscape into a world financial system headquartered in London and a handful of other European financial capitals. In the late 1840s the telegraph began to link stock markets, increasing the correlation of closing prices at different regional markets. It remained only for the twentieth century to furnish the advances in technology that, as far as financial transactions are concerned, would abolish the barriers of time and distance. As European countries ran out of new lands to explore and colonize, continued technological advances accelerated the process of bringing into a tighter network of communication the leading world financial centres dotting a planet of known and fixed dimensions. The disappearance of metallic coinage as an exchange medium in international transactions, and the gold standard's demise, removed whatever role transportation costs played as a resistance to the integration of the global financial system. With the rise of electronic bookkeeping, digital cash and electronic transfer of funds, only legal and cultural barriers hinder complete integration of the global financial system.

As early as 1857 the tendency for financial crises to become international in scope became evident after a stock market crash in the United States spread to stock markets in Britain, France, Germany and Scandinavia. In 1873 a crash in Vienna spread throughout Europe and to the United States, again showing that disturbances in one financial system were quickly felt in other financial systems. In the Baring Crisis of 1890, London banks narrowly avoided financial crisis after an Argentine company failed to meet obligations to the Baring banking house of London. By 1929 the merciless logic of a world financial system, without the aid of the worldwide web, could amplify the financial shock of a US stock market crash into worldwide financial debacle, plunging the world into depression.

Towards the end of the twentieth century the trend towards global financial integration received added strength from the technology of electronic communication. Presently, the smallest bank in a rural community can electronically transfer funds to any financial institution on earth. Just as the invention of gunpowder left high-walled castles obsolete, global computer and telecommunication systems perform a similar function in

liberalization of financial markets, allowing capital to move freely between politically autonomous economies, involved a few more twists and turns, but began on a note of liberalization in the nineteenth century, a time of peace, security and technical innovation in Europe.

Throughout the nineteenth century, leading up to World War I, London served as headquarters for a world financial system that needed to move capital from Europe to colonies. Britain, a relatively small country geographically, was the seat of the Industrial Revolution, and it managed to meet the hungry demands of its industry for resources and markets by acquiring a worldwide colonial empire, and promoting a system of free trade. Britain, controlling vast amounts of capital and colonies well-endowed with resources needed by British and European industry, served as the advance agent in Europe for the development of a colonial system that gave an outlet for surplus European capital, provided European industry with sources of raw materials and opened markets for European industry. Other European powers, particularly France and Germany, became important players in a system of financial imperialism that made use of access to European capital as a tool for controlling foreign governments in less developed areas of the world. International cooperation on financial matters flourished, and establishment of a virtually worldwide gold standard helped guarantee investors in foreign countries that their investments could always be redeemed. Countries such as the United States, Russia and Japan adopted the gold standard to become safer havens for European capital, and European governments found that a gold standard helped them float bonds in international markets.

The nineteenth century was a time of peace and security, without major wars in Europe, a time when international cooperation, the need to move capital to raw material sources, and adoption of the gold standard encouraged the movement of capital relatively unhindered across political borders. Stock exchanges grew up in far away areas such as Tokyo (1858) and Hong Kong (1891) where stocks could be purchased by European investors. By the time (the early twentieth century) New York had become a world class financial centre, 90 per cent of all international capital movements represented portfolio investment, composed of the ownership of stocks in corporations controlled by a management separate from the owners.

Following World War I, Europe was in dire need of capital, and the United States became a net exporter of capital. Countries devoted to raw material production remained capital importers during this period. Legal restrictions on capital flows between politically autonomous economic systems began to assert themselves during the Depression of the 1930s when countries abandoned precious metal monetary standards (the gold and, to a lesser extent, the silver standard), equity prices plummeted, and countries defaulted on foreign debt. Countries felt that sudden capital outflows contributed to the severity of the crisis. After the crisis phase of the Depression was over, what mobile capital existed in international markets tended to flow to the relatively safe United States, a trend resented in the less wealthy parts of the globe. The overall effect of the Depression was to weaken the credibility of free markets as socially responsible instruments for allocating resources.

The legacy of the Depression and lack of confidence in free market solutions continued for the three decades following World War II. Many countries had imposed exchange rate controls during the 1930s, and countries in less developed areas clung to these controls into the 1970s and 1980s. Controls either established multiple exchange rates between domestic currency and foreign currencies, the rate depending upon the reason foreign exchange was bought or sold, or forbade the purchase of foreign exchange for certain purposes, such as the acquisition of luxuries. Normally a low exchange rate makes exports cheap and imports expensive, while a high exchange rate does the opposite. A less developed country wanting to industrialize might want a low exchange rate for the purpose of exporting the products of a fledgling industry, but a high exchange rate for the export of a traditional cash crop such as sugar. Such a country might also want a high exchange rate for the import of necessary raw materials and capital for its new industry, but a low exchange rate for the import of consumer goods. To impose systems of multi-tiered exchange rates, countries required that all foreign exchange transactions go through

lion in 1994, and has since fallen off to closer to $40 billion. Mexico's debt crisis of 1994 and the East Asian financial crisis of 1997–8 reminded the international investing community of the risk attached to financial assets in developing countries, accounting for the yearly decrease in portfolio investment directed towards them.

The East Asian crisis of 1997–8 brought to light the vulnerability of economies highly dependent upon short-term inflows of foreign capital. The sentiment of international investors can shift suddenly, triggering an outflow of capital and depreciation of domestic currencies and substantially increasing the burden of debt contracted in foreign currencies. Indonesian companies by 1997 had accumulated $56 billion dollars in foreign debt, mostly contracted (denominated) in US dollars. After the rupiah declined 40 per cent against the US dollar, these companies faced a debt burden increased to unbearable levels when measured in rupiahs. Unable to generate the rupiahs needed to service the foreign debt, the companies had no choice but default and bankruptcy.

Financial crises such as the East Asian one can become contagious because when one country experiences a financial crisis, its currency depreciates, making its exports cheaper in foreign markets. The currency depreciation of one country creates a fear that others will depreciate their own currencies in an effort to protect themselves from cheap foreign imports. Foreign investors in countries where depreciation is possible or expected have an incentive to convert foreign investments into their own domestic currencies as soon as possible, causing a capital outflow for at-risk countries, increasing the chance that an at-risk country will have a financial crisis. Thus a financial crisis in one country triggers a financial crisis in another, creating the potential for a global financial crisis wave that could engulf the global economy.

An exacerbating factor arises because investors in the developed countries find information about companies in emerging markets costly to collect. This circumstance does not prevent investors from investing in emerging markets, but does make them skittish, willing to dump stocks at the slightest indication that other investors are selling, leading to herd behaviour among investors in foreign stocks. If one investor sells a large amount of stock in an emerging market, other market participants tend to assume the selling investor is acting on news that is not yet fully dispersed, and precipitately sell their own stock.

The fallout from the East Asian crisis will bring additional reform of the global financial system.[6] To discourage sudden outflows of capital governments may insist on more long-term borrowing than short-term borrowing, and prevent foreign investors from investing in riskier stocks. Banks may be required to hold larger amounts of foreign exchange reserves, and all financial institutions and markets in emerging markets will face more regulation aimed at corruption and fraudulent practices. The trend towards financial market liberalization may be slowed slightly, but shows no signs of retrograding in a direction that significantly interferes with the global allocation of capital.

THIRTEEN

In the Shadow of the Global Financial System

convert pesos into dollars, while the exchange rate deteriorated hourly, in a few days changing from 500 000 to 900 000 pesos per dollar. Hairdressers, lawyers, accountants, manicurists huddled in corners counting wads of pesos, while their patrons lay neglected. Whenever someone made their selections, a watch dealer set a price, took their dollars into pesos, returned to the street and converted the pesos back into dollars. The fishermen government required that pesos be the legal medium of exchange, but ignored the black market inflation.

legal depositions to satisfy legal proceedings in a foreign country.

The countries drawn to the financial secrecy business are mostly small and without a strong export base that can drive economic development. The practice is not new. There is extant a decree that Frederick the Great issued in 1765 requiring persons taking employment with a bank to swear a solemn oath, promising to take to the grave banking transactions that come to their attention in the course of their work. In the last half of the twentieth century Switzerland was perhaps the most famous country with banking secrecy laws, but other European countries, either currently or in the past, have protected the confidentiality of bank depositors, including Luxembourg, the Netherlands, Monaco and Gibraltar. In the Caribbean the Cayman Islands, Grenada, Bahamas, Bermuda and Panama belong on the list of countries that make good tax havens. Hong Kong, Singapore, Guam and many more serve a similar purpose in the Asian-Pacific area. After tourism, becoming a financial centre is often one of the few options these countries have to finance and stimulate economic development.

The effect of the global shadow economy is directly felt by the global financial system since it limits the ability of individual countries to isolate themselves from what is happening in the rest of the world. Consider the case of a country striving to maintain low domestic interest rates in the name of promoting economic growth. To aid in this purpose the said country might impose restrictions on the outflow of domestic capital, preventing its citizens from investing their savings in a part of the world where interest rates were higher, or where political and economic trends were less threatening. This country would also refuse to sell foreign currency to residents who wanted to import certain goods or purchase real estate or other investments in foreign countries. If such a country could successfully enforce these controls, then it could increase its money supply at a faster pace, helping to finance economic development projects, and keep its exchange rate elevated, reducing the cost of goods that could be legally imported. The flaw in the plan is that a black market in dollars and other major currencies springs up, and citizens convert their domestic currency into foreign currency, investing their savings in foreign countries and frustrating the government's efforts. Dual exchange rates, one official and one black market, also raise difficulties for multinational enterprises that must calculate the book value of foreign assets at official exchange rates but expect to remit profits to home countries at black market rates, usually less favourable.

While the global financial system owes some of its ills to black markets, the development of black markets has added momentum to the forces of global integration, stimulating forces that are creating a single global financial market to serve the needs of national economies.[4] By enhancing the mobility of capital across national borders, black markets contribute to a convergence of interest rates and credit availability in various parts of the world. Black markets may also contribute to global instability, allowing a rapid influx or exodus of capital from parts of the world suffering from political instability and uncertainty, perhaps in areas where investors have poor quality information even when political conditions are ideal.

Optimists who find some good in every circumstance interpret black markets as advance agents for irrepressible market forces that will eventually break through the crust of government regulation and give shape and form to officially sanctioned markets. Black markets force the hand of governments to enact market solutions to economic problems, which to advocates of capitalism is the pathway to robust economic development, enabling mankind to eventually finance the solutions to most of the world's ills. Even those fearful of market solutions to problems of resource allocation may find in black markets a force driving the countries of the globe towards greater cooperation, and maybe larger political entities. Black markets represent a failure of government policies, and one avenue to more effective government is more cooperation among governments, more uniformity in government policies, and perhaps bringing more regional governments under one political umbrella.

Market', *Economic History Review*, XXXVIII/1 (1985), p. 66.

7 R. C. Michie, 'The London and New York Stock Exchanges, 1850–1914', *Journal of Economic History*, XLVI/1 (1986), p. 174.
8 *Ibid.*, p. 175.
9 *Ibid.*, pp. 176–7.
10 *Ibid.*, p. 178.
11 *Ibid.*, p. 185.
12 Lloyd Wendt, *The Wall Street Journal* (New York, 1982), p. 68.

THREE · GOLD AND SILVER: ARISTOCRATS OF MONETARY STANDARDS

1 Paul Einzig, *Primitive Money in its Ethnological, Historical, and Economic Aspects* (London, 1966), pp. 166–7.
2 John M. Keynes, *A Treatise on Money: The Pure Theory of Money* (Cambridge, 1971), p. 11.
3 Curtis P. Nettels, *The Money Supply of the American Colonies before 1920* (New York, 1964), pp. 213–19.
4 W. T. K. Nugent, *Money and American Society: 1865–1880* (New York, 1968), p. 254.
5 Kia-Ngau Chang, *The Inflationary Spiral: The Experience in China, 1939–1950* (Cambridge, 1958), p. 5.

FOUR · THE TRIUMPH OF PAPER MONEY

1 Davis R. Dewey, *Financial History of the United States* (New York, 1968), pp. 38–9.
2 Georges Lefebvre, *The French Revolution from 1793–1799*, trans. J. H. Stewart and J. Frigugliette (London, 1964), p. 118.
3 *Julliard v. Greenman*, 110 U.S. 421 (1884).
4 Michael Mussa, 'Sticky Individual Prices and the Dynamics of the General Price Level', *Carnegie-Rochester Conference on Public Policy*, XV (1981), pp. 261–96.
5 Lester Chandler, *American Monetary Policy: 1928–1941* (New York, 1971), pp. 280–82.

FIVE · THE PASSAGE FROM FREE BANKING TO CENTRAL BANKING

1 Adam Smith, *An Inquiry into the Nature and Causes of the Wealth of Nations* [1776] (New York, 1937), pp. 280–98.
2 Hugh Rockhoff, 'The Free Banking Era: A Reexamination', *Journal of Money, Credit, and Banking*, VI/1 (1974), pp. 146–57.
3 'Banks and Banking', *Handbook of Texas* (Austin, 1996), p. 371.
4 Thomas B. Macaulay, *The History of England from the Accession of James II* [1849–61] (London, 1914), vol. 5, p. 2435.
5 John F. Chown, *A History of Money* (London, 1994), p. 237.
6 Alexander Hamilton, *Papers on Public Credit, Finance, and Commerce*, ed.

S. Mckee Jr (New York, 1957), pp. 51–95.

7 Peter Johnson, *The Government of Money: Monetarism in Germany and the United States* (London, 1998), pp. 176–90.

8 Jim Karouf, 'Start the Presses: Euro Set to Debut', *Futures*, XXVII/9 (1998), p. 30.

SIX · THE BIRTH OF WORLD CURRENCIES

1 Arnold Toynbee, *A Study of History*, vol. VII (London, 1955), p. 316.

2 Charles Kindleberger, *A Financial History of Western Europe* (London, 1984), p. 413.

3 Peter Johnson, *The Government of Money: Monetarism in Germany and the United States* (London, 1998), pp. 59–62.

4 'Economic Climate Looks Good for Launch of New Currency', *Wall Street Journal* (4 May 1998), pp. A17–18.

SEVEN · THE ROAD TO FLEXIBLE EXCHANGE RATES

1 David Hume, *Writings on Economics*, ed. Eugene Rotwein (Madison, WI, 1955), pp. 60–77.

2 Charles Kindleberger, *A Financial History of Western Europe* (London, 1984), pp. 457–8.

3 *Entering the 21st Century: World Development Report 1999/2000* (Washington, DC, 2000), p. 71.

EIGHT · THE EVOLUTION OF INTERNATIONAL BANKING

1 Adam Smith, *An Inquiry into the Nature and Causes of the Wealth of Nations* [1776] (New York, 1937), pp. 447–55.

2 *Ibid.*

3 I. Jacob, *Jacob Fugger* (New York, 1931), p. 153.

4 Joseph Wechsberg, *The Merchant Bankers* (Boston, 1966), p. 100.

5 *Ibid.*, p. 99.

6 'Settling Switzerland's Debts', *New York Times*, 16 August 1998, p. 1.

7 Serge Bellanger, 'Two Current Trends in International Banking', *Bankers Magazine*, CLXXVI/6 (1993), pp. 39–46.

8 Daniel Yohannes, 'U. S. Banking Moving Toward a Global Economy', *Denver Business Journal*, XLVIII/39 (1997), p. 26.

NINE · THE PATHS OF FOREIGN INVESTMENT

1 Douglas A. Fisher, *The Epic of Steel* (New York, 1963), p. 86.

2 Donald C. Blaisdell, *European Financial Control in the Ottoman Empire* (New York, 1966), pp. 215–17.

3 David McLean, 'Finance and "Informal Empire" before the First World War', *Economic History Review*, XXIX/2 (1976), pp. 291–305.

4 *Entering the 21st Century: World Development Report 1999/2000* (Washington, DC, 2000), p. 69.

3 GREECE: IN THE SHADOW OF THE GLOBAL
FINANCIAL SYSTEM

1 Young, *International Economics*, pp. 338, 357, 367.

2 UNCTAD, Porto-Alegre Brazil Intergovernmental Committee on Designing Countries' (the New Statesman, 9 August 1989), p. 1.

3 Financial and International Bulletin (27 August 1989), p. 10.

4 Robert Solomon, *Money on the Move: The Revolution in International Finance* (Princeton, N.J.: Princeton University Press, 1999), pp. 66–67.

Bibliography

Adams, W., ed., *The Structure of American Industry* (New York, 1990), p. 115

Alkhafaji, A. F., *Restructuring American Corporations: Causes, Effects, and Implications* (New York, 1990)

Appleyard, D. R., and A. J. Field Jr, *International Economics* (Homewood, IL, 1992)

Ashley, P., *Modern Tariff History: Germany, United States, and France* (New York, 1970)

Ashton, T., *Economic Fluctuations in England* (Oxford, 1959)

Atack, J., and P. Passel, *A New Economic View of American History from Colonial Times to 1940* (New York, 1994)

Ayling, D. E., *Internationalization of Stockmarkets* (Brookfield, VY, 1986)

Bagehot, W., *Lombard Street* [1873] (Homewood, IL, 1962)

Baklanoff, E. N., *Expropriation of U. S. Investments in Cuba, Mexico, and Chile* (New York, 1975)

'Banks and Banking', *Handbook of Texas* (Austin, 1996)

Barnes, D. G., *A History of the English Corn Laws* [1930] (New York, 1961)

Baskin, J. B., and P. J. Miranti, Jr, *A History of Corporate Finance* (Cambridge, 1997)

Bauer, H., *Swiss Banking: An Analytical History* (New York, 1998)

Baye, M. R., and D. W. Jansen, *Money, Banking, and Financial Markets: An Economics Approach* (Boston, 1995)

Bellanger, S., 'Two Current Trends in International Banking', *Bankers Magazine*, CLXXVI/6 (1993), pp. 39–46

Berry, B. J. L, E. C. Conkling and D. M. Ray, *The Global Economy: Resource Use, Locational Choice, and International Trade* (Englewood Cliffs, NJ, 1993)

Bezanson, A., *Prices and Inflation during the American Revolution, Pennsylvania, 1770–1790* (Philadelphia, 1951)

Blaisdell, D. C., *European Financial Control in the Ottoman Empire* (New York, 1966)

Bordo, M. D., 'The Classical Gold Standard: Some Lessons for Today', *Federal Reserve Bank of St. Louis, Monthly Review* (May 1981), pp. 2–17

Born, K. E., *International Banking in the Nineteenth and Twentieth Centuries*, trans. V. R. Berghahn (New York, 1983)

Braudel, F., *The Mediterranean and the Mediterranean World in the Age of Philip II*, vols I–II, trans. S. Reynolds (New York, 1972)

——, *Civilization of Capitalism: 15th–18th Century*, vols I–III, trans.

S. Reynolds (New York, 1979)

Brock, L. V., *The Currency of the American Colonies: 1700–1764* (New York, 1975)

Broz, J. L., *The International Origins of the Federal Reserve System* (Ithaca, NY, 1997)

Bruck, W. F., *Social and Economic History of Germany from Wilhelm II to Hitler: 1888–1938* [1938] (New York, 1962)

Calomiris, C. W., and L. Schweikart, 'The Panic of 1857: Origins, Transmission, and Containment', *Journal of Economic History*, LI/4 (1991), pp. 807–34

Calomiris, C. W., and C. M. Kahn, 'The Efficiency of Self-Regulated Payments Systems: Learning from the Suffolk System', *Journal of Money, Credit, and Banking*, XXVIII/4 (1996), pp. 766–97

Cameron, R. E. (in collaboration with O. Crisp, H. Patrick, R. Tilly), *Banking in the Early Stages of Industrialization* (London, 1967)

Carosso, V. P., *The Morgans: Private International Bankers, 1854–1913* (Cambridge, 1987)

Carswell, J., *The South Sea Bubble* (London, 1960)

Challis, C. E., ed., *A New History of the Royal Mint* (Cambridge, 1992)

Chandler, L., *American Monetary Policy: 1928–1941* (New York, 1971)

Chang, K-N., *The Inflationary Spiral: The Experience in China, 1939–1950* (Cambridge, 1958)

Checkland, S. G., *Scottish Banking History: 1695–1973* (Glasgow, 1975)

Chown, J., *A History of Money* (London, 1994)

Clapham, J. H., *The Economic Development of France and Germany* (London, 1955)

Coats, W. L., 'In Search of a Monetary Anchor: A New Monetary Standard', *International Monetary Fund Working Paper* no. 82 (1989)

Coghlan, R., 'The Wave Is Your Friend', *Barons*, LXXIII/23 (7 June 1993), pp. 18–19

Cope, R. C., 'The Stock Exchange Revisited: A New Look At the Market in Securities in the Eighteenth Century', *Economica*, XLV/177 (1978), pp. 8–10

Cowitt, P. P., *World Currency Yearbook* (New York, 1989)

Cowles, V., *The Rothschilds: A Family of Fortune* (New York, 1973)

Daniels, J. D., and L. H. Radebaugh, *International Business*, 8th edn (Reading, MA, 1998)

Daniels, J. P., and D. Vanhoose, *International Monetary and Financial Monetary Economics* (Cincinnati, 1999)

Daunton, M. J., *Progress and Poverty: An Economic and Social History of Britain, 1700–1850* (Oxford, 1995)

Davies, G., *A History of Money from Ancient Times to the Present Day* (Cardiff, 1994)

Davis, C. B., and K. E. Wilburn Jr, eds, *Railway Imperialism* (New York, 1991)

De Roover, R., *The Rise and Decline of the Medici Bank: 1397–1494* (New York, 1966)

De Vries, M. G., *Balance of Payments Adjustment, 1945 to 1986: The IMF Experience* (Washington, DC, 1987)

Kroszner, R., *Free Banking: The Scottish Experience as a Model for Emerging Economies*, World Bank Policy Research Dept, Finance and Private Sector Development Division and Financial Sector Development Dept. (Washington, DC, 1995)

Lamoreaux, N. R, *The Great Merger Movement in American Business, 1895–1904* (New York, 1986)

Lane, F. C., and R. C. Mueller, *Money and Banking in Medieval and Renaissance Venice*, vols I–II (Baltimore, 1997)

Laue, T. H. Von, *Sergei Witte and the Industrialization of Russia* (New York, 1963)

Laughlin, J. L., *A History of Bimetallism in the United States* [1896] (New York, 1968)

Lefebvre, G., *The French Revolution from 1793–1799*, trans. J. H. Stewart and J. Frigugliette (London, 1964)

Lester, R. A., *Monetary Experiments* [1939] (New York, 1970)

Louis, A., *The Anglo–French Commercial Treaty of 1860 and the Progress of the Industrial Revolution in France* [1930] (New York, 1971)

Lustig, N., B. B. Bosworth and R. Z. Lawrence, eds, *North American Free Trade* (Washington, DC, 1992)

Macaulay, T. B., *The History of England from the Accession of James II* [1849–61] (London, 1914)

Machiavelli, N., *History of Florence and the Affairs of Italy* [1532], trans. C. E. Detmold (New York, 1960)

Martin-Acena, P., 'The Spanish Money Supply, 1874-1935', *Journal of European Economic History*, XIX/1 (1990)

Marx, J., *The Magic of Gold* (Garden City, NY, 1978)

McAlister, L. N., *Spain and Portugal in the New World: 1492 – 1700* (Minneapolis, 1984)

McCallum, B. T., *Monetary Economics* (New York, 1989)

McCarthy, D. M. P., *International Business History: A Contextual and Case Approach* (Westport, CT, 1994)

McCord, N., *Free Trade* (New York, 1970)

McKinnon, R. I., *The Order of Liberalization* (Baltimore, 1991)

McLean, D., 'Finance and "Informal Empire" before the First World War', *Economic History Review*, 2nd ser., XXIX/2 (1976), pp. 291–305

Michie, R. C., 'The London Stock Exchange and the British Securities Market', *Economic History Review*, XXXVIII/1 (1985), p. 66

——, 'The London and New York Stock Exchanges, 1850–1914', *Journal of Economic History*, XLVI/1 (1986), p. 174

Montesquieu, *The Spirit of Laws* [1748], trans. T. Nugent (New York, 1900), vol. II, p. 473

Mussa, M., 'Sticky Individual Prices and the Dynamics of the General Price Level', *Carnegie-Rochester Conference on Public Policy*, XV (1981), pp. 261–96

National Resources Committee, *The Structure of the American Economy* (Washington, DC, 1939), pp. 306–17

Nettels, C. P., *The Money Supply of the American Colonies before 1720* [1934] (New York, 1964)

Nugent, W. T. K., *Money and American Society: 1865–1880* (New York,

1968), p. 254

Nussbaum, A., *A History of the Dollar* (New York, 1957)

Ohkawa, K., M. Shinohara and L. Meissner, eds, *Patterns of Japanese Economic Development: A Quantitative Appraisal* (New Haven, 1979)

Paarlberg, D., *An Analysis and History of Inflation* (Westport, CT, 1993)

Padoa-Schioppa, T., *The Road to Monetary Union in Europe* (Oxford, 1994)

'Precarious Peso – Amid Wild Inflation, Bolivians Concentrate on Swapping Currency', *Wall Street Journal*, 13 August 1985, p. 1

Prentice, A., *History of the Anti-Corn Law League*, vols I–II, 2nd edn [1853] (New York, 1968)

Reardon, J. J., *America and the Multinational Corporation: A History of a Troubled Partnership* (Westport, CT, 1992)

Reisen, H., and B. Fisher, eds, *Financial Opening: Policy Issues and Experiences in Developing Countries* (Paris, 1993)

Ritter, G., *Gold Bugs and Greenbacks: The Antimonopoly Tradition and the Politics of Finance in America* (Cambridge, 1997)

Roberts, R., ed., *The Bank of England: Money, Power, and Influence, 1694–1994* (Oxford, 1995)

Rockhoff, H., 'The Free Banking Era: A Reexamination', *Journal of Money, Credit, and Banking*, VI/1 (1974), pp. 146–57

Rose, H., 'The Continental System, 1809–1814', in *Cambridge Modern History*, IX (New York, 1934), pp. 361–89

Roy, W. G., *Socializing Capital: The Rise of the Large Industrial Corporation in America* (Princeton, 1996)

Sayers, R. S., *The Bank of England: 1891–1944* (Cambridge, 1976)

Schlesinger, A., *Crisis of the Old Order: 1919–1933* (Boston, 1957)

Schmitz, C. J., *The Growth of Big Business in the United States and Western Europe, 1850–1939* (Cambridge, 1993)

Schnitzer, M., *Contemporary Government and Business Relations* (Chicago, 1978), pp. 161–3

Schwartz, A. J., 'From Obscurity to Notoriety: A Biography of the Exchange Stabilization Fund', *Journal of Money, Credit, and Banking*, XXIX/2 (May 1997), pp. 135–53

Selgin, G. A., and L. H. White, 'Monetary Reform and the Redemption of National Bank Notes', *Business History Review*, LXVIII/20 (1994), pp. 205–43

'Settling Switzerland's Debts', *New York Times*, 16 August 1998, p. 1

Shannon, H. A., 'The Coming of General Limited Liability', in *Essays in Economic History*, vol. I, ed. E. M. Carus-Wilson (London, 1954), pp. 358–79

Smith, A., *An Inquiry into the Nature and Causes of the Wealth of Nations* [1776] (New York, 1937)

Sobel, R., *The Rise and Fall of the Conglomerate Kings* (New York, 1984)

Solomon, S., *The Confidence Game: How Unelected Central Bankers are Governing the Changed Global Economy* (New York, 1995)

Spiro, G. W., *The Legal Environment of Business: Principles and Cases* (Englewood Cliffs, NJ, 1993)

Stillman, R. J., *Dow Jones Industrial Average: History and Role in an Investment Strategy* (Homewood, IL, 1986)

shares 17, 21–2, 27–8, 30, 40, 70–71,
    105, 176; transferable 42, 44
Sherman Antitrust Act (1890)
    30–31, 33
shunters 61
Siam 174; *see also* Thailand
Silver Repurchase Act (1934) 85–6
silver 11, 72, 74, 77–8, 80, 84–6, 92,
    123, 126–8, 134, 147–9, 159,
    201, 212; standard 72, 74–6, 79,
    84–5, 100, 126, 138, 148, 200,
    227
Singapore 133, 164, 221–2, 234
slavery 175
Smith, Adam 18, 101, 148, 157–8,
    188, 190, 193, 206
Smoot–Hawley Tariff (1930) 14,
    202–4, 218
'snake, the' 154
Société Générale de Crédit
    Mobilier 25
South Africa 82, 217
South Korea 221
South Sea Bubble 21, 48–50
Soviet Union 132, 137
Spain 12, 18, 20–22, 26, 42–3, 51,
    73, 92–3, 124, 129, 148–50,
    158–9, 174, 188, 192–3, 196,
    203, 207, 221
Spanish-American War 93, 150
Special Drawing Rights System
    (SDRS), 140–41, 169
speculation 152, 210, 215
spices 19–20, 42, 156, 173–4, 188
spot rate 142–3
Standard Oil 30–31, 34, 180
stock exchanges 41, 46–7, 59–60,
    63–4, 67; Frankfurt 54–5, 63,
    69–70; Hong Kong 226; London
    48, 50, 55–6, 58–65, 69–70; New
    York 57, 63–5, 69–71; Tokyo
    70–71, 144, 220, 226
stock markets 15, 21, 40, 47–8, 52,
    222; crashes 66, 71, 92, 202,
    216–18, 220, 224
stockholders 9–10, 15, 19–20, 23–4,
    30, 33, 38, 65, 67–8, 105–6, 114,
    118–19, 176, 222
stockjobbers 47–8

Suez Canal Company 12, 163, 176
Suez Crisis 153
Suffolk System 120
suicides 62
Sweden 11, 74–5, 88, 100, 105–6,
    141, 195, 208
Swiss Bank Corporation 166–7
Swiss Credit Bank 166–7
Switzerland 12, 22, 26, 79, 83,
    134–6, 166–7, 172, 195, 221, 234
Sydney 130

Taiwan 84
takeovers 68
Tariff Act (1883) 199
taxes 56, 89–90, 93, 106, 108, 128,
    137, 148–9, 160, 167, 185,
    188–9, 194, 197, 200, 203, 207,
    210, 220, 228, 233
telegraph 58–60, 63, 224
telephone 60–61, 63
Texas 103
Thailand 221–2; *see also* Siam
ticker machine 59–60, 63
tobacco 10, 72, 175, 188
Tokyo 70–71, 125, 142, 144, 171–2,
    197, 205, 218, 220, 226
Tontine Coffee House 57
tontine loans 56
Toynbee, Arnold 126
Trade Expansion Act (1962) 205
Trichet, Jean-Claude 124
trusts 30–31
tulips 45–6
Turkey 45, 178; National Bank of
    178
TWA (Trans World Airlines) 68

Uganda 72
unemployment 95–6, 187, 192,
    218–21
Unequal Treaties 197–8
Union Bank of Switzerland 166–7
unions 38
United Fruit Company 34
United Kingdom 228; *see also*
    Britain; England
United Nations 168
United States of America 12–14, 22,